THE
MAGIC
BOOK

THE
MAGIC
BOOK

MASTER THE MYSTERIES OF OVER 150 MAGIC TRICKS

EDITED BY LYDIA DARBYSHIRE

CHARTWELL
BOOKS, INC.

A QUINTET BOOK

Published by Chartwell Books
A Division of Book Sales, Inc.
114 Northfield Avenue
Edison, New Jersey 08837

This edition produced for sale in the U.S.A., its territories and dependencies
only.

ISBN 0-7858-0791-8

This book was designed and produced by
Quintet Publishing Limited
6 Blundell Street
London N7 9BH

Creative Director: Richard Dewing
Art Director: Clare Reynolds
Designer: Pete Laws
Project Editor: Kathy Steer
Editor: Lydia Darbyshire
Photographer: Paul Forrester

Typeset in Great Britain by
Central Southern Typesetters, Eastbourne
Manufactured in China by Regent Publishing Services Ltd
Printed in China by Leefung-Asco Printers Ltd

Material in this book previously appeared in
The Ultimate Card Trick Book by Eve Devereux,
Start a Craft Magic Tricks by Peter Eldin,
100 Magic Tricks by Ian Adair

Publisher's Note
This book is not specifically aimed at children, and some of the tricks
described in it involve the use of lighted matches, burning cigarettes,
and ignited materials. Adult supervision is essential throughout
all such tricks. Care should always be taken to perform such effects
in a responsible manner.
The tricks described in this book can be performed equally well by left-
handed and right-handed people. For the purposes of this book, it has been
assumed that the person performing the tricks is right-handed.

CONTENTS

Welcome

TO THE WONDERFUL

WORLD OF MAGIC! WELCOME TO

MEETING MAGICIANS AND BEING ABLE

TO SHARE THEIR MAGICAL SECRETS AND WELCOME

TO THE PAGES OF THIS BOOK, WHICH WE HOPE WILL

put you firmly on the road to success, whether your interest in magic

and conjuring arises from a desire to take up an enjoyable and rewarding

hobby, or whether you are thinking about pursuing a career in this field.

Magic and conjuring offer color, excitement, and mystery, but the prime aim must always be to entertain those who are involved, either as spectators or as participants. Perfecting your techniques and putting them into practice is one thing, but it is quite another to go out and face an audience, knowing that they are waiting to be entertained and mystified. Pure bewilderment is not enough, however, and students of magic will soon realize that clever patter, rehearsed movements, and an ability to keep control of numbers are as important as a grasp of the secrets of the tricks they have to execute.

This book will show that in the world of magic there are many fascinating avenues to explore. There are magic dealers who specialize in selling professional properties; there are magic conventions, dinners, events, and social functions that are attended by all the stars of magic. These conventions often include seminars, lectures, demonstrations, and even teach-ins, many of which are invaluable for the novice. There are also magic clubs and societies, large and small, all over the world. As you read this book you will also soon realize that there are many branches of magic and that each branch suits particular personalities.

The Magic Book covers the major branches of magic, giving details of important techniques and a host of individual tricks for you to perfect. It also gives advice on the way you should present your tricks before audiences, both large and small.

Buying a book of magic does not

automatically make you a magician, of course, but with practice and enthusiasm, you can go a long way. When you read the instructions for a trick, do not dismiss the method as being too simple. Some of the simplest of tricks are the most deceptive. Practice each trick, and when you are sure that you can do it well, show it to a friend. You may be amazed as your friend – amazed that such a simple method can fool someone.

Do not try to learn all the tricks at once. By all means read through the whole of the book to get a general idea of what magic is all about and of the kinds of tricks that there are. Then pick just one or two and learn them thoroughly. Only when you are confident that you can do these tricks well should you go on to learn another trick. It has been said that "slow but sure wins the race," and slow but sure is certainly the way to achieve success in performing magic.

SUCCESSFUL TRICKS

Many of the props and mechanical gadgets used by magicians are incredibly simple to work. It is even possible to buy tricks that are advertised as "self-working" – that is, the magician isn't meant to have to do anything because the trick "does" itself. Tricks are often sold to novice magicians with the assurance that "no skill is required" or that the trick is "completely self-working." Don't believe it. There is no such thing as a self-working trick, even some of the straightforward card tricks. If you want your magic to be successful, you have got to put a lot of work into it – even with a self-working trick. If you don't, you will just be someone performing tricks. But if you work at your tricks and practice making your whole show entertaining, a magical transformation will take place. When you do this, you are no longer someone who knows how to do a few tricks – you are a magician! Hard work pays off in the end.

None of the instructions given in this book is sacrosanct. If you are at all uncomfortable about a particular aspect of a trick, see if you can change it to suit your own style. An obvious example of this is when you are told to take something in a particular hand. If you are happier using the other hand, then do so.

THE RULES OF MAGIC

Every game, profession, and organization has certain rules to which its players or members adhere. Some of these we accept, some we like, and others we dislike intensely. The first – perhaps the only – rule of magic is that a magician never gives away the secrets, because the audience's enjoyment of magic is, to a certain extent, due to the mystery of how the magic happened, and to explain the secret of a trick would be to deny the audience this enjoyment. The audience would feel that although they had at first been entertained, they have now been cheated. And they would be quite right to feel that way. The first rule of magic is to keep the secret. Can you?

MAGIC THROUGH THE AGES

No one knows for certain how old the art of magic is, but it is probably as old as mankind. Records show that as far back as 50,000 BC magic was being practiced by cave-dwellers, but the first known written evidence of a magician appears in ancient Egyptian texts dating from *c*.2000 BC. These writings, known as the Westcar Papyrus, describe a performance by someone known as Dedi of Dedsnefu, in which Dedi cut off the heads of a duck and a pelican, and restored them both without harming either bird.

It seems that in the Middle Ages most people believed in magic, which was still closely connected with religion inasmuch as Christian teaching considered magic practices to be sinful, and practitioners were persecuted. Until the 1700s, many people who practiced "magic" were burned as witches, and the first book on conjuring in the English language was actually called *Discoverie of Witchcraft*. This book explains many of the tricks that magicians still use to this day. One such trick is the Cups and Balls, in which balls appear and disappear beneath three cups. It is performed today using the same basic method.

The first Europeans to make a living by performing magic tricks as entertainment appeared during the Middle Ages. They were known by the French name *jongleurs* (jugglers), and they were strolling players who swallowed

swords, ate fire, sang and danced, and probably performed the famous Cups and Balls trick for anyone who would wager against them.

ROBERT HOUDIN

Gradually, the modern magician's repertoire grew as performers began to appear in local fairs and, for the first time in the nineteenth century, to perform in music halls and theaters. At this time, most magicians wore long, flowing robes, and their tables were draped to the ground. In the mid-nineteenth century a French performer called Robert Houdin (1805–71) did away with all this suspicious drapery and performed in regular evening dress and with very little

Jongleurs (jugglers) first appeared in Europe in the Middle Ages. They traveled from town to village, entertaining their audiences with juggling and acrobatics, sword-swallowing, and fire-eating. The tradition of the street entertainer persists to this day.

Robert Houdin (1805–71), the French conjurer and magician, was celebrated for his optical illusions, and he became known as the Father of Modern Conjuring. Houdin was the first person to use electromagnetism for his effects.

paraphernalia on stage. Originally a watchmaker, Houdin brought a new inventiveness to magic. He built many automata to use in his shows, and he was one of the first people to do a two-person mind-reading act. His magic was so good that in 1856 the French government even sent him to Algeria to counter the influence of the dervishes by exposing their so-called miracles.

HOUDINI

Houdin is regarded as the Father of Modern Conjuring, and it was from his second name that the young Erich Weiss (1874–1926) took his stage name, a name that lives to this day: Harry Houdini, the greatest escape artist ever. His first big success came when he escaped from handcuffs in Scotland Yard, the headquarters of the British police, and from that time on he was constantly in the public eye, making incredible escapes from straitjackets, boxes, jails, handcuffs, chains, and anything else that people could invent to try to confine him.

Contemporaries of Houdini included some of the greatest names in magic: Harry Kellar (1849–1922), known as the Dean of Magic, who ran away from home to become America's best known illusionist; T. Nelson Downs, who produced showers of coins from the air; Harry Blackstone, who was a master showman and whose son is today one of America's best known magicians; and Chung Ling Soo, the renowned Chinese magician. Chung Ling Soo's greatest trick was not revealed until after his death. Everyone thought he was Chinese – he even used an interpreter – but after his death his great secret was revealed: he was really an American named William Robinson.

THE BRITISH SCENE

When Houdini first visited Britain, the top British magician was John Nevil Maskelyne (1839–1917). In addition to being a superb magician, Maskelyne was a genius at making mechanical figures – like Houdin, he had trained as a watchmaker. Possibly the most famous of these was called Psycho. This figure of an Oriental man could play cards so well that it could beat any member of the audience who offered a challenge. As the figure was seated on a plinth of clear glass, there seemed no explanation of how it was operated. Maskelyne did not confine his mechanical genius to magic: he also invented, other things, a lock for lavatories, a typewriter, and a machine for issuing bus tickets.

Maskelyne teamed up with another British magician, David Devant (1868–1941), and together they dominated the British magic scene for many years. Devant wrote *Our Magic* with Maskelyne in 1911; he later wrote *My Magic Life* (1931) and *Secrets of My Magic* (1936). People who saw Devant perform called him the greatest British magician of all time. That accolade has now passed down to Paul

Harry Houdini (1874–1926) adopted his stage name in honor of Robert Houdin; his real name was Erich Weiss, and he read Houdin's memoirs when he was a boy. He was skilled in many fields of magic, but became world famous as an escapologist.

Daniels, who has done more to popularize magic in Britain than almost anyone else. For almost two decades he has had a regular magic series on television, and his shows have also brought some of the best magicians from around the world to the attention of British audiences.

IN RECENT TIMES

Recently many incredible magical spectaculars have been produced, especially in America, where superb magicians such as Siegfried and Roy, David Copperfield, Harry Blackstone Jr., and Lance Burton have transformed the art of magic. The colorful extravaganzas mounted by these performers use all the modern theatrical effects.

In spite of all this high-tech wizardry to excite the public, there is still room for the more intimate performance in theaters, restaurants, or informal gatherings. Magic can be performed for just one person or for many people, but it is effective in any situation provided that the performer has taken the time to learn the art of entertaining people.

PUTTING ON
A PERFORMANCE

In general, all books on magic explain the secret methods whereby the tricks are accomplished and, of course, this book is no exception. But perhaps the greatest secret of magic – a secret that often takes magicians many years to discover and that many never discover at all – is that the least important part of any trick is the secret element of it.

In magic it matters little what you do. What matters most is how you do it. "It's not what you do, it's the way you do it," is an adage that is particularly appropriate to conjuring.

One of the tricks in this book, the Rising Cards, has baffled and entertained audiences all over the world. Many years ago, a book was published describing some two hundred methods of accomplishing the trick, and since that book was published, magicians have devised many more methods. The methods may vary, but the essentials of the trick remain the same: selected cards rise from the pack of their own accord. So, no matter which method is used, the trick remains essentially the same. And that is why the so-called secrets of magic are not the most important part.

One of the most interesting aspects of magic is that its performance is constantly changing. At first, you may go through the motions of a performance like a robot, but gradually, as you gain experience, the "real" you will come to the fore, and your performances will be enhanced as a result.

It has been said that a good magician is really an actor playing the part of a magician. This means that you have got to believe in your magical abilities and to play the part of a magician. You may find this difficult to do at first, because you are concentrating on the mechanics of the trick. That is why so many books on magic urge you to practice as much as possible. The emphasis is on the mechanics because they are unimportant. This may sound paradoxical, but if you practice thoroughly, the mechanics of the trick will become automatic and, in a sense, subsidiary to the overall effect that you achieve.

Some magicians present a mixed bag of tricks and illusions, drawn from many different branches of magic; others specialize in one form – mentalism, say, or close-up magic. When you are selecting a field in which to specialize, you must take care and choose wisely. So often, enthusiastic beginners pick the wrong branches of magic to present, and it ends in disaster.

If you happen to like comedy magic – that is, ordinary magic laced with comedy patter – then stick to it. Think again if you are someone who does not excite people very much and if you cannot tell funny stories or forget the punchline of jokes you try to tell. It could be that, no matter how much you practice, you will never be able to become a comedy magical entertainer.

If, on the other hand, you feel that your approach is better at reaching a more mature audience, a performance based on mentalism may be for you. If so, make sure that you can deliver direct and dramatic lines. Make sure, too, that you look like someone who can read minds and predict the future.

If you simply want to be a jack-of-all-trades, using your knowledge and skill to entertain your friends and colleagues, you cannot be categorized in any way; you are just a general magician. Relax, look at the tricks described in this book, learn them, and select the ones that you like best. Practice each trick and master the various methods of presentation, then use the ones you feel confident about performing – and go out and entertain your public. Choose the times when you want to perform, and never perform under pressure.

Remember to imbue tricks with your own personality and perform in a way that is natural to you. This is not easy, and it may take you some time before you can do it.

Remember, too, that any performance of magic is really a great big confidence trick, with you, the performer, being only one of the con-artists involved. The members of the audience know that you are not using real magic and that you are cheating them in some way, but they are prepared to maintain the fiction in their own minds that you are using abilities not granted to the mass of humankind. At least, they are prepared to maintain this fiction as long as you present your tricks with sufficient charm and vivacity that the audience is persuaded that you are keeping to your side of the unspoken and unwritten bargain: that you are working hard to entertain them. If you work with charm and verve, your audience will *want* to believe you – and that is more than half the battle.

PRACTICE

Practice involves the learning of individual effects and routines, and the rehearsal of a complete act, from start to finish. Theatrical people use the word rehearsal to mean a run-through with a cast or partner, and a dress rehearsal of a performance is just as it should be on the night.

Professionals and amateurs alike often joke that "it will be alright on the night" – but will it? The wise and discerning performer understands that only practice and constant attention to detail make for trouble-free performances, and to achieve this, you must have patience, time, and understanding.

It is not unknown for enthusiastic students of magic to rush into a performance without planning their programs thoroughly. If you do this, you are likely to fumble, drop items, forget patter lines, and generally make something of a fool of yourself. No matter how good you look, and how good the execution of your tricks, your presentation is an essential aspect of the performance. You must remember not only to practice your tricks, but the movements that go with them. While it is admirable to perform a trick cleverly, it is unwise to disregard the way in which movements should be executed. There is nothing worse than seeing a clumsy magician having to bend down in the middle of an act to retrieve a piece of apparatus and setting it up again in front of the audience.

Practicing in front of a mirror is a good way of training yourself, but it is not always the best. When people work to a mirror, they have a tendency to stand in the same position, which means that a public performance could well appear static. Remember, too, that if you always rehearse in front of a mirror in your house, with a table or even your bed in front of you, you will get into the habit of putting down items on the table or bed as you finish with them, and you may find it difficult to stop yourself wanting to discard items in the same way in front of your audience. If you have not rehearsed in a range of conditions, you will be thrown off your stride by having to think about your unaccustomed surroundings.

Slow, smooth, and elegant hand gestures should also be part of your rehearsal routine. A magician should look graceful and compelling. Practice walking on and off a stage, without ever turning your back on the audience – unless, of course, the effect or routine demands it. Taking a bow may seem easy, but it can often look silly when executed by someone who feels uncomfortable or self-conscious. When the trick has come to its climax, the performer needs to signal this clearly to the audience, perhaps by a smile, by opening the arms outward and upward, and by making a slight bow. It is also important to know how to handle the audience and establish a rapport with them. A wise performer will think about achieving the right effect so that he or she can go home at the end of the evening well and truly satisfied with the performance.

The wise student will practice each trick so much that he or she could almost perform it blindfolded. If you are thinking about giving a public performance, you must practice again and again, until every tiny detail of the trick and your patter is embedded in your mind and becomes second nature to you. When you can do a trick without thinking, you can concentrate on presenting your magic in a professional way. It is somewhat similar to driving a car. At first, new drivers think about when to signal or when to change gear, but as they gain experience, it becomes second nature, and they just do it. A better analogy might be tennis players, who do not consciously think about reaching out to hit a ball and putting some top spin on it to fool their opponents. They just do it. It takes practice and experience to achieve that level, but keep practicing, and you will get there.

One top television magician is reported as having said that he has practiced his act so much that now, while he appears in front of a live audience or before the cameras, he is thinking about what he is going to have for dinner after the show!

PATTER

This is your major aid, especially when you are performing a routine that consists entirely or largely of card tricks. Cards do not (usually) jump through hoops or burst into flames or do any of the other things that more elaborate magical props can do; they are just immobile pieces of pasteboard, although often, of course, you will be doing your best to convince your audience that they are anything but. You must, therefore, manage to arrange for the ostentatious

magical effects to take place inside your audience's heads. You must contrive to manipulate their minds; indeed, this is exactly what they want you to do.

Your best tool for doing this is patter, which is also your main ally in directing the audience's attention away from things you do not wish them to notice – that is, misdirection (see below). Every trick can be made to tell a story, and ideally it should be a story that you have invented yourself. Some of the descriptions of the tricks in this book include an indication of the kind of yarn you might tell and give suitably silly fictitious rationales, which you may use in your patter if you wish. Other tricks – the Scurvy Knaves (pages 73–5), for example – have traditionally had such tales attached to them. Best of all, though, is for you to take the basis of a trick, adapt it as you wish, and then invent your own story to go along with it.

An important aspect of your patter is the relationship you establish with the audience. Usually, you will want to make them laugh to get them on your side. You can, if you go about it the right way, even get them on your side by consistently insulting them, just as long as your insults are witty enough. However, never be tempted to make humiliating jokes at the expense of those members of the audience you ask to help you – they are, after all, volunteers. These spectators have paid their entrance money like everyone, and they may have conquered a good deal of nervousness to help you in front of a hall full of people, so to hurt their feelings would be unforgivably discourteous. Your audience would soon turn against you – and quite rightly.

Work on building up the sequence of tricks you want to perform to make a full routine. One line of patter should not end at the finish of one trick, to be replaced by a quite different line at the start of the next. All through your routine, the various elements of your patter should flow naturally into one another. Deciding on a theme is a good way of achieving this, and a running joke can be helpful.

MISDIRECTION

Misdirection is the art of drawing the spectator's attention in a particular direction at critical moments in your performance – to flourish an empty hand in which an object is believed to be concealed, for example, while secretly disposing of the article with the other hand. You may have seen magicians who produce billiard balls in one hand, holding them up in the air for all to see, while at the same time carefully using the left hand to steal a live dove from a pocket, ready for the next startling effect.

Ask someone to look up in the air – and they will. Hold something in your hand and elevate it into the air for everyone to see, and their eyes will almost certainly follow. That is misdirection. Get ready to steal something away from your person, and in comes your attractive assistant, toward whom all eyes will turn. Misdirection helps all magicians obtain the very best from their magic.

Misdirection can also be executed by word alone – a certain line in your patter, for example, or a change in your tone of voice. The spectator or audience perceives this subtle change, and their attention is directed away from the maneuver you want to keep secret.

PROPS AND EQUIPMENT

By far the majority of the tricks in this book can be done by a solitary performer using simple props – many use standard packs of cards – and the tricks can be done almost anywhere.

For many performances, however, it is desirable to have on stage with you a table and a couple of chairs. For your table, a simple folding card table is perfectly adequate. If you put a tablecloth on it, do not use one that drapes generously to the floor on all sides – that would immediately make your audience think that the table was rigged with all sorts of gadgets and gimmicks, and they would become suspicious every time you approached it. A thin, small tablecloth, of an area about the same as the tabletop but set crosswise on it so that the corners hang down, is perfectly sufficient. You might think of using a patterned tablecloth, since you will, on occasion, be dropping or picking up things that the audience should know nothing about. For the same reason, it is wise if there are a few bits of "clutter" on the table – empty card boxes, perhaps, or even a vase of flowers.

The chairs are especially useful when you are performing card tricks in a fairly small, intimate venue. Many of these tricks work best when you and the volunteer are seated on opposite sides of your table.

Employing accomplices can be tiresome and can entirely defeat your purpose. In very many cases, the relationship between yourself and the accomplice will be either immediately guessed or already known.

Gimmicks and gadgets can likewise bring down your performance, especially if almost every trick you do relies on them. You know – better than anyone else – that your assumed cleverness is a complete sham, and this awareness is likely to communicate itself to the audience. Use such artifices sparingly.

When you begin, most of the props you need will come readily to hand – packs of cards, for example, can be bought inexpensively in shopping malls everywhere. However, as you gain more experience and begin to want to try out more unusual tricks, you may need some special magic props, and these are usually obtained through specialist dealers.

Magic dealers are makers of magic. They make magic in various materials, market their products, and then sell their wares through various outlets. Most dealers offer a mail-order service, which they advertise in magazines. Some larger concerns issue their own catalogs or magazines, in which they advertise their ranges of theatrical properties.

There are three main types of magic dealer. First, is the magic store, often little more than a joke store, which sells whoopee cushions, novelties, and toys. Only a small section of the store may be devoted to magic or to the sale of professional conjuring props. The selection of items is usually very basic. Although some professional equipment is available, only classic effects are ordered by the proprietor who, incidentally, very rarely knows anything about the art of magic.

Second is the small mail-order firm, which usually advertises in magic magazines. Many do not have proper premises, and it is often hard to find those who do. Most magic dealers work from one room of their homes – even from a spare bedroom that they have turned into a stockroom. Some mail-order dealers provide a fast and efficient service, even if they advertise only a small number of products within their range.

Third are the more professional magic dealers who work on a much larger scale. Such dealers have a good knowledge of what customers require, and they carry a wide range of products, both classic and modern. Some publish their own magazines to promote their products. The professional magic dealer never relies on the sales of jokes and novelties to enhance sales of professional theatrical equipment.

"YOU"

Your choice of dress on stage is something that you will work out for yourself, and it is probable that you will dress differently for different occasions. For most tricks it does not matter what you wear, but sometimes you will need pockets and, occasionally, sleeves. For the sake of simplicity, it has been assumed that the magician – you – will wear trousers (not tight ones, like jeans) with standard pockets, an opaque shirt or blouse, and a jacket with side pockets and a top (breast) pocket.

A few tricks also require that you carry a handkerchief. This should be large, opaque, and – don't forget – clean and freshly ironed. The best way to carry it, unless it would clash entirely with the rest of your presentation, is formally folded in the top pocket of your jacket.

ADVERTISING AND PUBLICITY

The subject of promoting yourself as a performer will arise once you have brought together a complete series of tricks, have practiced them until you are perfect, and have built them up into a show ready for presentation to the public.

There are many ways in which you can promote and advertise yourself, the most obvious being a classified advertisement in a local newspaper or telephone directory. Such advertisements are relatively inexpensive and will reach the local community, which is, initially at least, likely to be your target audience.

Wherever you choose to place your advertisement – in magazines or newspapers, or even in the window of a nearby store – it must be clear, informative, and attractively laid out. Poor advertising material never leads to bookings, and an overly complicated advertisement will only confuse people.

An excellent way of obtaining superb advertising at no cost is to supply a story of news interest to the local or national press. Not only does a news story act as free advertising, but it takes up more space than the average advertisement. One magician advertised every week in his local newspaper but without success. One week he concocted a story about his magic rabbit having vanished from its hutch, and this received both local and national coverage. He obtained more show bookings from the single story than from all the advertisements he had paid for over the years.

Photographs, pictures, business cards, leaflets and flyers, and give-away trivia can all help to promote you and your show. Balloons printed with your name, magic posters for children to color in, or magic "money" to give away will amuse and excite a potential audience. An appealing picture of the rabbit that helped you in the show will make your audience want to take home a card or program rather than leave it behind on their seats.

Promoting your show can be as much fun as practicing the tricks and presenting your act. But you must always remember that in promoting the show, you are promoting yourself – you are the commodity. Always aim to emphasize your best features and talents, but always tell the truth.

SLEIGHT OF HAND

ALL ACCOMPLISHED MAGICIANS

MAKE SURE THAT THEY HAVE MASTERED SLEIGHT

OF HAND. FIRST, YOUR MOVEMENTS WILL APPEAR MORE

POLISHED, EVEN WHEN YOU ARE USING OTHER PROPS. SECOND IF

your props let you down, you can rely on sleight of hand to get you through a

trick. Third, your routines will be more varied and entertaining if can you

introduce sleight-of-hand sequences between other effects. A great deal of

time and effort must be devoted to perfecting techniques, but, once

they are mastered, the skills will be a source of great amusement to all.

CARDS

Almost all magicians begin by trying card tricks. There are packs of cards in most homes, and they are available in stores everywhere. Although some more complicated card tricks are described in the following chapter, it is worth spending some time on perfecting the simple movements and routines here. If you practice shuffling cards and making them appear and vanish you will increase your manual dexterity, which will be of benefit in all kinds of other tricks, and will boost your confidence.

STRAIGHT SHUFFLE

This is the shuffle that most of us ordinarily use when we play with cards. The shuffle is open to various deceptions, for all of which you should have the basic shuffle sufficiently practiced that you can do it very quickly and easily and that no one watching you can really keep track of the cards.

1 Start with the pack in the left hand, with the cards facing toward the inside of the hand – that is, toward the ball of the thumb. The fingers and thumb of the right hand grip the ends of most of the pack, lifting it up so that a small packet remains in the left hand.

2 The right hand then drops a few cards into the left hand, on the inside of this packet, then a few to its outside, then a few on the inside, and so on, until all the cards are once more in the left hand.

STRAIGHT SHUFFLE
DECEPTIONS

The straight shuffle is more open to simple fakery than any other type of shuffle, with the possible exception of the Hindoo Shuffle (see page 17).

It is very easy to keep the original top card of the pack at the top. You simply make sure that the final few cards are dropped from the right hand always to the rear of the packet in the left hand. Similarly, you can also keep several cards – up to 15 or even 20 cards – at the top of the deck, in order.

You can likewise keep the pack's bottom card or cards at the bottom. Merely start the shuffle with the cards facing not inward toward the ball of the left hand thumb but outward, facing away from it.

You can, in fact, not shuffle the cards at all. Although you go through all the motions of an ordinary shuffle, you actually consistently drop the cards from the right hand behind the growing packet in the left hand. You cannot hope to get away with this every time if you perform the maneuver directly in front of the audience, but it can be handy to know that you can do it while turning away or while you are distracting the audience's attention elsewhere, simply to add to the illusion that you really are shuffling the cards thoroughly.

You can shuffle a card from the bottom of the pack to the top. In your first pick-up with the right hand, leave only a single card in the left. For a preliminary shuffle, always drop the cards on the inside of the growing packet in the left hand. Immediately, start a second shuffle, to disguise the paucity of the first one, this time shuffling normally, except retaining the new top card in its place.

You can shuffle a card from the center of the pack to the top, assuming that you have located the chosen card through having made a break in the deck (perhaps with a fingernail). Here, the first packet you carefully pick up with your right hand contains all the cards down to the break (that is, not including the chosen card). Your procedure is then as for the previous shuffle.

You can use a shuffle to arrange that there is no face-up card at the bottom of a face-down pack.

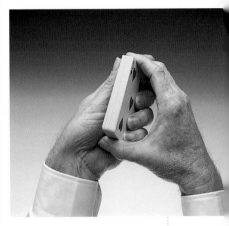

❶ At the end of an orthodox shuffle, wrap the fingers of the left hand around the pack to grip the last card.

❷ Pick up the rest of the deck with the right hand, and at once seemingly use both hands to square up the pack.

RIFFLE SHUFFLE

The riffle shuffle is another move that is frequently used when card games are played.

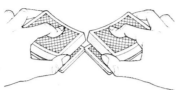

1 You cut the deck into two packets, place both face down on a flat surface with their corners adjacent, bend the corners up with the thumbs, move the two packets still closer together, and release the cards in such a way that the corners of the two packets interlock with a satisfying riffling sound. You then use both hands to carefully merge the two packets, so that the pack is restored with its cards thoroughly rearranged. Alternatively, you can make the shorter edges of the two packets overlap, rather than just the corners. This variant is often called the dovetail shuffle.

2 Rather more difficult is the riffle shuffle performed without recourse to a flat surface. The two packets face toward each other as you start, one in each hand, the cards being held between the thumbs and the first joints of the fingers. Bring the index finger of each hand around and press its back against the rear of each respective packet. Then bring the thumbs closer together, and riffle the ends of the cards into each other. You may require a lot of practice to master this – and you may not consider the practice worth it, since the two simpler methods look better.

HINDOO SHUFFLE

This method of shuffling is rarely used in playing card games, but it is more widely employed by magicians, since it looks slick and allows for deceptions that are not possible with other shuffles. This shuffle requires a lot of practice, so you must decide for yourself whether the effort is worthwhile.

As noted, a well-executed Hindoo Shuffle looks slick, because it is obviously a difficult maneuver. For that same reason, no one will be surprised if the amassed cards in your left hand look a bit ragged. This leaves the way open for one of the deceptions possible with this shuffle. At any stage during the shuffle you can irritably use the cards still remaining in your right hand to tap those in the left into better order, and this gives you the opportunity to glimpse the bottom card of the packet in the right hand. It is clearly simple thereafter to make sure that this card becomes the top card in the pack when the shuffle is completed.

1 To begin, the pack is held horizontally, face down, by the fingers and thumb of the right hand.

2 Advance the pack toward the cupped left hand, and grip the top cards of the deck between the fingers and thumb, with the index finger moved around the end of the received pack for the purposes of control (if it is not there, there is a danger that you are going to throw cards over the floor – enough of a danger, when you are learning the maneuver).

3 The right hand takes the bulk of the pack from beneath this top packet, which you let fall from the fingers of your left hand toward the cupped palm as the right hand advances the deck to repeat the process.

THE PASS

The object of this trick is to bring a card to the top or bottom of the pack unbeknownst to the audience. Typically you will have asked a member of the audience to pick a card and then return it to the center of the proffered pack. There are two common methods whereby you can then immediately bring that card to the top, and once you have mastered them, try adapting them, especially the first, so that you can allow spectators to return their cards to a fanned pack.

The first method requires that you have at least one long fingernail on the hand in which you hold the pack, preferably on the little finger of the left hand. Although the member of the audience thinks that he or she is putting the selected card back into a random place in the pack, in fact, hidden from view by the cards, you have already inserted your fingernail into the deck's rear corner, splitting it into two packets. As you offer the deck to the spectator with both hands, it is easy, with your right hand, to displace the two packets just a trifle sideways from each other as the card is being pushed toward it. The card in place, you can swiftly begin to give the pack a straight shuffle, beginning by cutting the pack at the position of your fingernail so that the selected card is brought to the top.

The previous technique requires only a little practice. The second method is much more difficult. You must be prepared to put in a lot of effort if you are to get this technique right, so that you can perform it smoothly and quickly enough for it to be undetectable to the spectator, who is likely still to be close in front of you. You should also practice it for transferring just a single card from the bottom to the top of the pack – this is, perhaps, its most useful application. Don't be discouraged if you keep dropping the cards all over the floor in your early attempts. Your aim is to become so accustomed to the maneuver that it is almost instinctive, so practice on train journeys or anywhere you find you have some spare time. If your hands are large enough, you may eventually find that you can execute the Pass one handed.

① As the card is inserted, the fingers of your left hand, holding the pack, should crimp the sides of the packet beneath that card, putting a slight bend on those cards, so that the two packets become quite distinct from each other.

② The middle fingers of your left hand can then reach across the top of the pack to pull the upper sideways away from the lower.

3 As if you were merely tidying the cards, you then use the fingers of your right hand further to separate the packets, forcing the edges of the lower packet into the base of the left thumb.

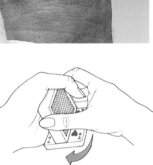

4 By putting the fingertips of your left hand over the top of the upper packet and flexing the thumb as you close your left hand, you can bring the lower packet over the upper.

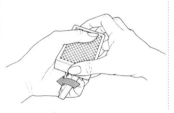

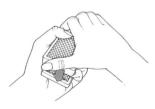

5 This brings the selected card to either the top or the bottom of the pack, depending on whether you chose to crimp it as part of the lower packet or leave it as part of the upper packet.

PALMING CARDS

Many of the card effects performed by magicians and manipulators are achieved by palming cards. There are two principle techniques of palming used in card tricks, one of them involving the palm of the hand and the other, confusingly (and much less usefully), not. Both methods are designed to make it possible for you to have cards in your hand when the audience believes that your hands are empty.

The first technique is when a card is held on the inside of the hand, curved into the palm and braced, usually between the ball of the thumb and the second joints of the fingers. The exact location of the upper end of the card will depend on the size of your hands. People with large hands will have the card braced against the second joint of all four fingers (or even, if their hands are very large, against the base of the fingers). People with smaller hands can brace the edge against the second joints of the three fingers other than the index finger. Practice until you find out the position that suits you and feels comfortable. If your hands are small, try the exercise using patience (solitaire) cards – in fact, you may find it better to use such cards for all tricks that require palming.

Two versions are shown here: the flat-palm version and the curled-in version. Practice them both, then practice palming the top card from the pack so that it looks as if your hand has merely glided over the surface. You might also try palming more than one card at a time.

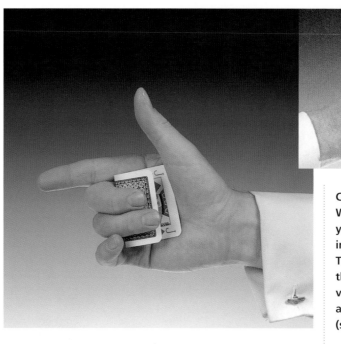

FLAT-PALM VERSION
Place the card in the palm of the hand and hold the card so that it faces toward you. From the audience's point of view (seen in the inset), the card cannot be seen and the hand position looks natural.

CURLED-IN VERSION
With the card held flat in your palm, curl your fingers in, bending the card over. The card is then invisible to the audience, but this version allows you to adopt a different hand position (see inset).

The other technique of palming cards allows you to display the open face of your hand to the audience, showing it to be empty when, in fact, you are holding a card. The card is held, by one of its short ends, between the second and third fingers and almost all of it sticks out at the back of the hand. The thin edge of the card does not show between the fingers, either because of the line between them already naturally there or because their flesh touches in front of the card's edge, obscuring it. It is not at all difficult to hold cards in this way. What is difficult is getting them there in the first place.

Although this technique is not really used for palming cards – unless you are really proficient, you are likely to drop or show the card at the most embarrassing moment, thereby destroying the effect – it can be used as part of a larger maneuver to produce cards, which can be entertaining in its own right.

PRODUCING CARDS

Dexterity with cards can be the basis of some imaginative and amazing routines. Practice the following sequences and, when you are confident with each one, build them up into longer, more complex movements.

Producing Single Cards from the Hand

First, a card is seen between the fingers. Then it is made to vanish, only to reappear again.

1 Display the card to the audience.

2 Grip the sides of the card with the first and little fingers, bend the middle two fingers down behind the card, and use the thumb to pivot the card over . . .

3 . . . like this. Using the middle fingers to control the card, continue the action so that the card disappears from view, to be held . . .

4 . . . in the back-palm position.

5 Hold the hand side-on to the audience and then reverse the pivot.

6 Use the fingers to draw the card into the palm position.

7 Hold the back of the hand toward the audience to show that the card has, once again, disappeared from view.

8 Repeat steps 1–3 to bring the card to the back-palm position again.

9 To produce the card, reach up into the air and, at the same time, pivot the card up into the hand.

Producing Several Cards from the Hand

The same pivoting action can be used to produce a succession of cards from a stack held secretly in the hand. Again, the effect of this is of cards being plucked from the air.

1 Hold the stack in the back-palm position and pivot the stack into the hand . . .

2 . . . like this.

3 Peel off the first card from the stack and pivot the stack to the back-palm position . . .

4 . . . like this.

5 Repeat the sequence, discarding the first card and producing a second and so on, until the stack is exhausted.

Producing Cards – A Variation

Most magicians produce cards with the palm of the right or left hand facing the audience, so that they apparently pluck cards out of the air. In this variation, however, the cards are produced while the hand is clenched with the back of the hand facing the audience.

2 Grip the pack with the fingers. Peel off the first card with the thumb . . .

1 Conceal a stack of cards within the palm.

3 . . . and produce it to the audience, held between the thumb and first finger.

4 The audience's view of the produced card. Repeat the sequence to produce more cards, discarding each in turn until the stack is exhausted.

Producing Fans of Cards

The back-palm position plays a major part in producing fans of cards. The effect is that the magician produces a fan and drops it into a receptacle and then magically produces further fans from thin air, discarding each. In fact, each fan that is produced is split, with the majority of the card being pivoted to the back-palm position, ready to produce the next fan, and the next, while just a few of the cards are discarded.

1 Fan the stack of cards toward the audience.

2 Curl the third and the little fingers around the bottom of the fan to pivot the majority of the stack to the back-palm position . . .

3 . . . like this.

4 The start of the pivoting move seen from the back.

5 The completion of the pivot, again seen from the back, with the stack in the back-palm position.

6 Discard the remaining few cards in the fan, then pivot the stack back into the hand to produce the next fan.

VANISHING HALF A PACK

During card-manipulation routines, a neat vanish of half a pack is visually effective.

1 Display a half a pack of cards, squared up, in the left hand, and fan the remainder of the pack in the right hand.

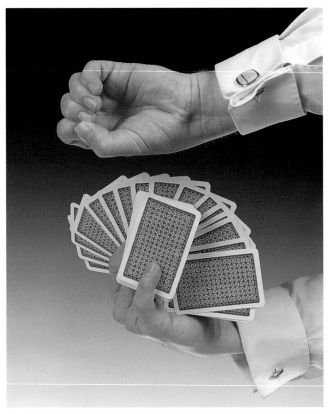

3 The back view shows the half pack held in the right hand behind the fan.

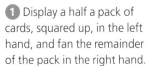

2 Obscure the left hand with the fan of cards, and secretly grip the half pack with the free fingers of the right hand. At the same time, turn the left hand and form it into a fist.

4 Open the left fist to show the audience that the half pack has vanished, and gather the entire pack together in the right hand.

FLYING CARDS

The magician is able to throw a card accurately and quickly, to a member of the audience. In fact, this can be done in quick succession, each time to a different member of the audience. This is not so much an individual trick as an embellishment that you can use at any stage of your performance. In fact, no deception is involved – it is just a knack you can acquire.

Note: Be careful that you don't throw the card too hard. It will be traveling through the air at a fair speed and also rotating horizontally as it goes, so if you were unlucky, it could cut someone's face.

Tricks of the Trade

• New cards work better than worn ones.

• Try holding the card between the thumb and first finger to see if that suits you better.

1 The technique is to hold the card with one of its shorter edges between the first and second fingers of your hand.

2 To throw it, you extend your arm suddenly, while at the same time giving the card a backward flick out of your fingers so that it skims horizontally through the air. The movement as a whole is much the same as if you were hitting a backhand shot in table tennis. The first few times you try this, the card will merely flutter in the air in front of you, but sooner or later – it may come on your third attempt or after 30 minutes – you will suddenly find that you manage to throw the card perfectly. Practice for a little longer and you will get it right every time.

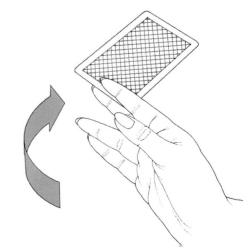

FLYING CARDS – A VARIATION

A card is selected in the customary way, and then returned to the pack. To show that a perfectly standard pack of cards is being used, the magician starts throwing cards toward the audience. Apparently to the surprise of the magician as much as to anyone else, one card pauses over the heads of the audience and comes back to the magician. This proves to be the chosen card.

1 Use the Pass (see page 18) and a Straight Shuffle (see page 15) to get the selected card to the bottom of the pack.

2 Throw the first few cards from the top of the pack, using the technique outlined under the first version of Flying Cards. When you feel that you have done this enough, choose as your next card the one from the bottom of the pack – that is, the selected card – but you need to grip it in a different way.

3 Hold the near corner of one of its shorter sides between your thumb and all the fingertips, except that of your index finger. The index fingertip rests on the corner further away from you.

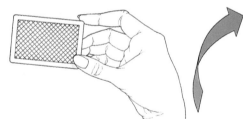

4 Your throw is not horizontal but upward at an angle of about 45°. You must throw gently. As you release the card, give it a flick with the index fingertip. When the card reaches the top of its arc, it will come spinning back to you.

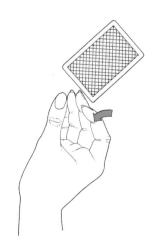

FLYING CARDS –
A FURTHER VARIATION

Although this does not require much manual dexterity, it is an entertaining effect. The magician asks a member of the audience to select a card at random. When all the cards are tossed into the air, this particular card has been miraculously persuaded to return to the magician's hand just as if it were a homing pigeon.

YOU WILL NEED

PACK OF CARDS

HONEY

1 Ask a volunteer to select a card. While it is being shown to the audience in the usual way, you explain that playing cards have always reminded you of pigeons, except that, for the obvious reason that cards have no brains at all; It is more difficult to teach them to "home" as birds will do. Encourage your volunteer and the audience to inculcate the principle into the chosen card by singing to it: "You're the cleverest playing card in the pack, so show us you are by flying right back."

2 While the audience is watching the spectacle of adults trying to teach a card how to behave, you should touch the back of your right hand with a blob of something sticky (honey is useful), which you had earlier placed on your table.

3 Ask the spectator to return the chosen card to the pack. Shuffle the cards and make the Pass (see pages 18–9) to return the card to the top of the pack.

4 Throw the pack of cards into the air, so that they flutter down around you, but in the process of turning to toss the cards upward, find an opportunity to press the sticky back of your hand against the back of the chosen card, which is not, of course, at the top of the pack. With your hand turned so that its back is away from the audience, throw the rest of the pack into the air.

5 In the confusion of the falling cards, simply turn over your hand to reveal the chosen card. If you turn your hand too soon or too late, the audience will see what is going on, so time your move very carefully.

> ### Trick of the Trade
> ● Because of the stickiness involved, it is a good idea to make this the last trick of your program or to switch packs before progressing to your next trick.

FLYING CARDS – 4

This version of the Flying Cards does require a certain amount of dexterity – and it is certainly less sticky than the previous effect.

1 Repeat the previous trick until you have got the stage of shuffling and using the Pass to get the selected card to the top of the pack. Secure the chosen card between your first and second fingers.

2 Very quickly, move to throw the cards into the air, but at the same time use your thumb to push the selected card back between your fingers so that it protrudes to the back of your hand. Then, as the cards fall all around your outstretched hand, make a lunge with your hand (as if you were trying to catch it) and turn the card so that it is revealed. (See Producing Single Cards on page 21 for some guidance.)

THIMBLES

For small gatherings, tricks with thimbles can be effective. Make sure that the thimbles you use are not so tight that they cannot slip easily on and off your fingers. You do not want them, however, to be so loose that they fall off at the wrong moment.

PRODUCING THIMBLES

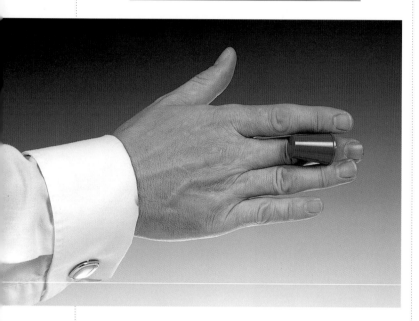

Producing a Single Thimble
A thimble is apparently plucked from the air to appear on the magician's thumb.

1 Secretly hold the thimble at the back of the hand in the finger-palm position, gripped between the first and third fingers, and present the hand palm-on to the audience.

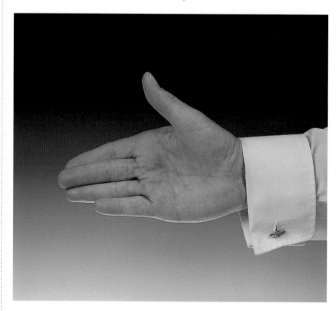

2 The thimble is not visible to the audience.

3 Pivot the thimble into the hand . . .

4 . . . and onto the thumb as you apparently pluck the thimble from the air.

Producing a Succession of Thimbles

Use the thumb-crutch position – also known as the thumb palm – to conceal a stack of thimbles in the fleshy part of your hand between the thumb and first finger. To produce a succession of thimbles, one after the other, simply pivot a finger down onto the thimble on top of the stack, and repeat, passing the thimbles from one hand to the other.

A THIMBLE HOLDER
The thimble holder is an aid that allows you secretly and easily to acquire one or more thimbles while leaving your hands free. The thimbles slide easily from the holder, which is usually attached to and concealed inside your jacket.

VANISHING THIMBLES

Learn these techniques for making thimbles vanish, then practice them until you can do them without thinking.

Poke-in Thimble Vanish
This method is very hard to beat when it comes to making a thimble vanish in a convincing manner.

1 Display the thimble on the first finger of the right hand and poke this finger into the left hand.

2 Seen from the rear, as you close the left hand to form a fist, curl the thimble finger inward, bringing the thimble into the thumb-crutch position.

3 To the audience, your left hand appears to be holding the first finger of your right hand and the thimble.

4 Remove the first finger of your right hand and point toward the closed left fist to reinforce the suggestion that you have retained the thimble in your left hand.

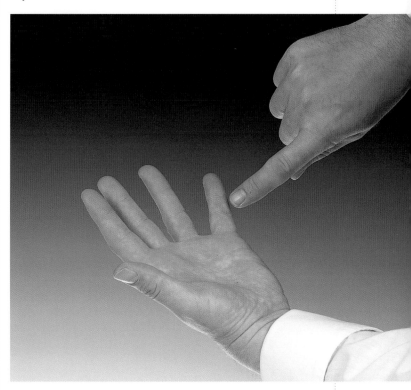

5 Open your left hand to complete the vanish. The thimble is still concealed in your right hand.

A Simple Thimble Vanish

A thimble is thrown high up into the air and then magically vanishes.

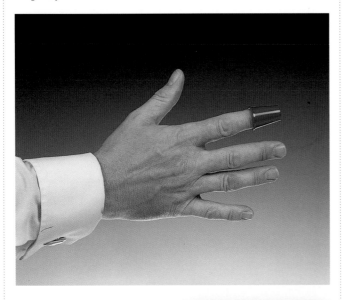

1 Display the thimble on the first finger of one hand.

2 Make an upward throwing motion with the hand and, at the same time, secretly curl the first finger inward, toward the crutch of the thumb.

3 Immediately release the thimble from your finger and hold it in the thumb-crutch position.

4 To the audience, the hand, having just completed the throw, appears to be totally empty.

Showing the Hands Empty

This technique can also be applied to the thumb tip (see pages 144–154).

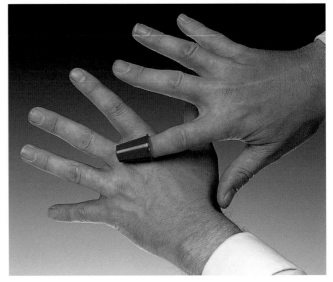

1 Conceal your first finger, which is wearing the thimble, behind the back of your other hand.

2 From the audience's viewpoint, your hands are completely empty.

BALLS

Tricks with small, light, brightly colored plastic balls are a great standby. Remember that apparently simple tricks with props like this are a great way of rescuing your performance if anything begins to go wrong, and, because you will have practiced them so much, they are a good way of building your own confidence, perhaps at the beginning of a routine.

PALMING A BALL

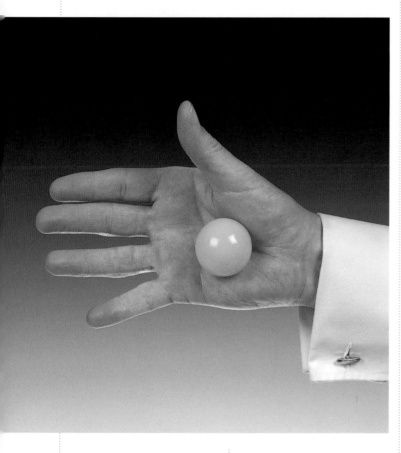

2 This variation, the finger-grip palm position, allows you to adopt a slightly different hand position. As can be seen from the rear view, firmly grip the ball between your palm and the lower three fingers of your hand.

A ball will adhere to the palm of your hand if your hand is moist or has been smeared with a moisturizing cream.

1 Seen from rear, the ball clings to the palm. When you do this, keep your hand in a natural position, making sure that the ball cannot be seen by the audience.

3 From the audience's viewpoint, your hand position will look natural, with your index finger pointing at something else on the stage. The ball is completely hidden.

VANISHING A BALL

Here are three different ways to make the ball vanish. Practice them until you can do them without thinking.

Take-away Vanish

1 Clench your right fist and rest the ball on top of it. Bring your left hand, held in a somewhat cupped fashion, toward the right, as if to take the ball.

2 Pretend to take the ball away from the right fist, and at the same time . . .

3 . . . as this rear view shows, drop the ball into the right fist.

4 With the ball in the finger-grip palm position in your right hand, point to your left fist.

5 Slowly open the fingers of your left hand to show that the ball has vanished.

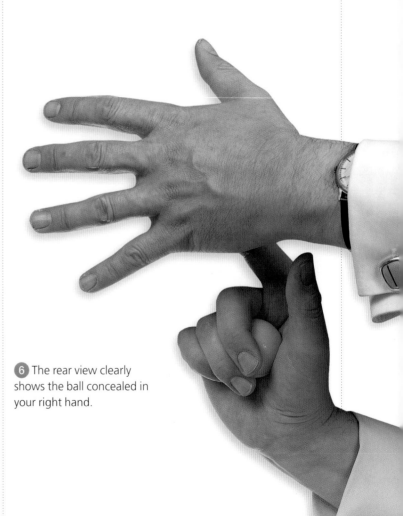

6 The rear view clearly shows the ball concealed in your right hand.

Poke-in Vanish

1 Clench your left hand firmly around the ball, holding it with your fist side-on to the audience so that the ball is visible. Bring your right hand up, underneath your left hand.

4 With the ball held in the finger-grip palm position in your right hand, use your right index finger to "poke" the ball into your left fist again. This will reinforce the audience's belief that the ball is still held in your left hand.

5 Turnover your left hand, still clenched as if it is holding the ball, which is now held in the palm-grip position of your right hand.

2 Poke the ball into your left fist with the thumb of your right hand. At the same time, allow your right hand to cup under your left.

3 As can be seen in this rear view, as your right thumb pushes the ball into the left fist, allow the ball to drop into your right hand.

6 Slowly open the fingers of your left hand to reveal that the ball has disappeared.

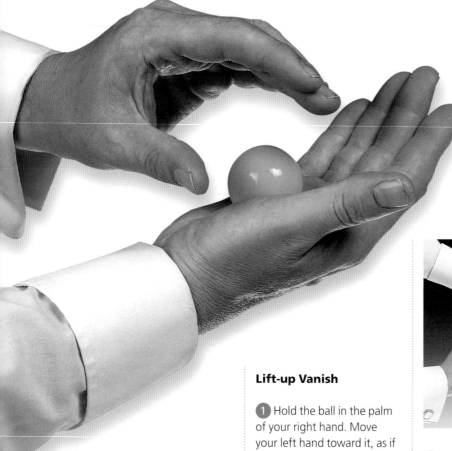

Lift-up Vanish

1 Hold the ball in the palm of your right hand. Move your left hand toward it, as if you are going to take the ball in it.

3 With the ball in the finger-grip position in your right hand, point to your clenched fist with your right index finger.

4 Slowly open the fingers of your left hand to show that the ball has vanished.

2 As your left hand apparently grips the ball and lifts it away, turn your right hand so that the back of the hand is toward the audience. Keep the ball in this hand.

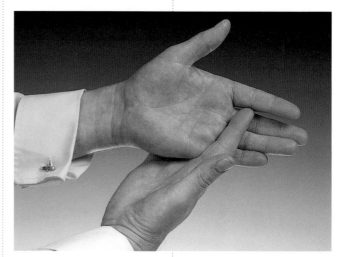

5 An additional effect with this sequence involves partially turning your right hand toward the audience, pivoting the ball behind the back of your open left hand so that it remains invisible to the audience.

CIGARETTES

LIKE CARDS AND BALLS, CIGARETTES ARE READILY AVAILABLE AND, COMPARATIVELY, INEXPENSIVE. HOWEVER, A CLOSER LOOK AT THE PHOTOGRAPHS IN THE FOLLOWING SEQUENCES WILL REVEAL THAT PLAIN WHITE PLASTIC STICKS, TRIMMED TO THE APPROPRIATE LENGTH, HAVE BEEN USED. THIS IS PARTICULARLY USEFUL IF YOU HAVE SMALLER THAN AVERAGE HANDS, BECAUSE ALTHOUGH YOU DON'T WANT YOUR AUDIENCE TO THINK THAT THERE IS ANYTHING UNUSUAL ABOUT THE CIGARETTES, YOU NEED TO BE ABLE TO HIDE THEM IN YOUR PALM.

THE TRIMMED PLASTIC STICKS ALSO HAVE THE GREAT ADVANTAGE OF NOT BEING PRONE TO ACCIDENTAL CRUSHING WHILE YOU WORK, AND, OF COURSE, THEY DON'T SMELL OF TOBACCO.

PRODUCING CIGARETTES

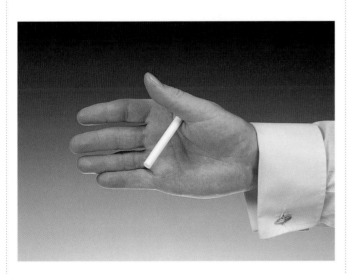

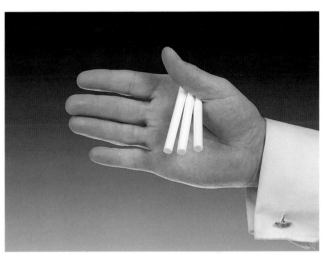

Producing a Single Cigarette
A cigarette can be secretly palmed and produced, as if from thin air, using the following method.

1 Grip the cigarette in the thumb-crutch position. From the front, your hand will appear natural but the cigarette will be completely concealed.

Repeat Production
The same technique you used to produce a single cigarette can be applied to make several cigarettes appear.

1 Secretly conceal a stack of cigarettes – as many as you can comfortably hold – in the thumb-crutch position.

2 To make the cigarette appear, curl your fingers inward to grip the cigarette.

3 Then, in one swift and elegant movement, display the cigarette between the first and second fingers.

2 Curl your fingers inward and grip the first cigarette between your first and second fingers. Repeat to produce the entire stack.

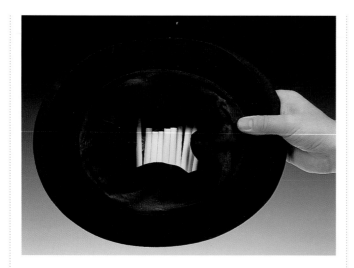

Hat Production

For this trick you will need a folded opera hat, which you open with a flourish. You then produce, one by one, a whole stream of cigarettes, which are discarded, one by one, into the hat. You then empty the hat out onto your table to reveal the pile of discarded cigarettes. In fact, you have produced only one cigarette – the same one, over and over again.

1 Before you begin, take an opera hat and then insert as many cigarettes as you wish between the springs.

The Rising Cigarette

In between your routines of making cigarettes appear and vanish, introduce a little variety with a flourish or two. This particular routine can look good, and can be blended with most cigarette sequences to build up an entertaining program. In effect, a cigarette mysteriously rises out of your hand.

1 Hold a cigarette in your hand, with your thumb tucked inside your fist and resting on the base of the cigarette. Stand with the back of your hand toward your audience.

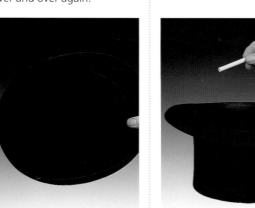

2 When you begin the performance, display the top of the hat to the audience. Because the hat is folded flat, the audience will assume that it is empty. With a simple striking motion, open the hat, thereby secretly releasing the cigarettes between the springs so that they fall into the bottom of the hat.

3 Produce a cigarette from the air, and as you appear to discard it into the hat, pivot the cigarette into the thumb-crutch position. Repeat the action, producing the same cigarette, until you have "produced" and "discarded" the required number.

2 Slowly push up the cigarette with your thumb so that it rises steadily from your clenched fist.

Stealing Cigarettes from a Matchbox

This technique makes it possible for you to keep your hands free before producing cigarettes from a stack. The cigarettes are placed in a matchbox, which has been prepared by cutting away one end of the inner tray. The matchbox is kept at the back of the working area, hidden by other props on your table.

1 Pick up the matchbox and hold it so that the cut-away end and the protruding cigarettes point into the palm of your hand. The audience cannot see the cigarettes and think you are holding a genuine matchbox because your hand position looks natural, especially when you make as if to strike a match

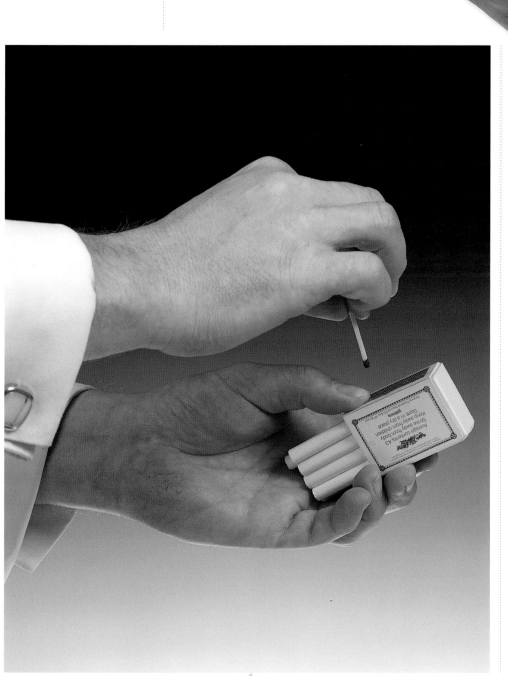

2 As can be seen from the rear, you should tilt the box slightly so that the cigarettes slide out, ready to be produced, one by one.

VANISHING CIGARETTES

Take-away Vanish

1 Hold the cigarette between the thumb and index finger of your right hand and display it to your audience.

3 Form a fist with your left hand and at the same time, secretly bring the cigarette into the thumb-crutch position in your right hand.

Poke-in Vanish

This movement is accomplished in exactly the same way as balls are made to vanish (see page 32). The effect is that a cigarette is poked into your left fist with your right thumb, only for your left hand to open to show that the cigarette has vanished. Your right hand then plucks the vanished cigarette out of the air. In fact, the cigarette is secretly dropped into your right hand and concealed there until you want to produce it.

2 Cup your left hand over the cigarette as if you are going to take it in your left hand, and as you do this, pivot the cigarette into your right hand.

4 Rub the back of your clenched fist with your, apparently, empty right hand.

5 Open the fingers of your left hand to reveal that the cigarette has vanished.

6 Viewed from the rear, the cigarette can be seen held firmly in the thumb-crutch position of the right hand.

COINS

Finally, in this introduction to simple sleight of hand, we look at two sequences for producing and vanishing coins. These simple routines are perfect for children's parties – who can resist having a coin magically produced from behind their ear?

PRODUCING AND VANISHING A COIN

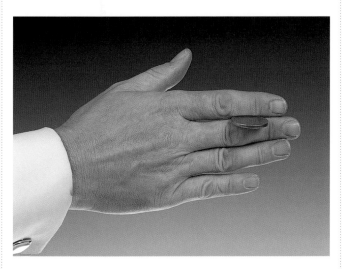

This is a simple and effective movement to produce a coin out of the air, or even from someone's clothing or hair. The coin can be vanished by reversing the procedure.

1 Secretly hold the coin at the back of your hand, firmly gripped between your second and third fingers.

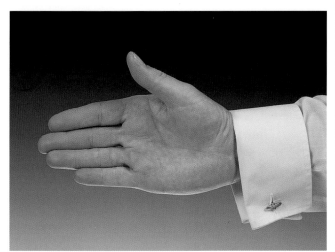

2 Show the hand to the audience palm-on, so that your spectators see that it is apparently empty.

3 To produce the coin, pivot your fingers inward and . . .

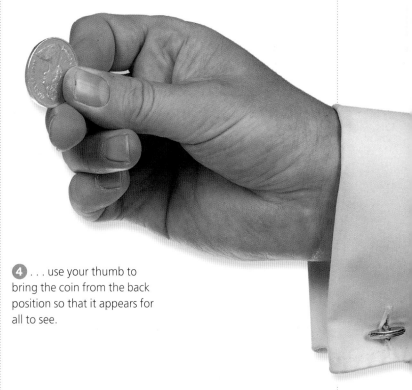

4 . . . use your thumb to bring the coin from the back position so that it appears for all to see.

PRODUCING SEVERAL COINS

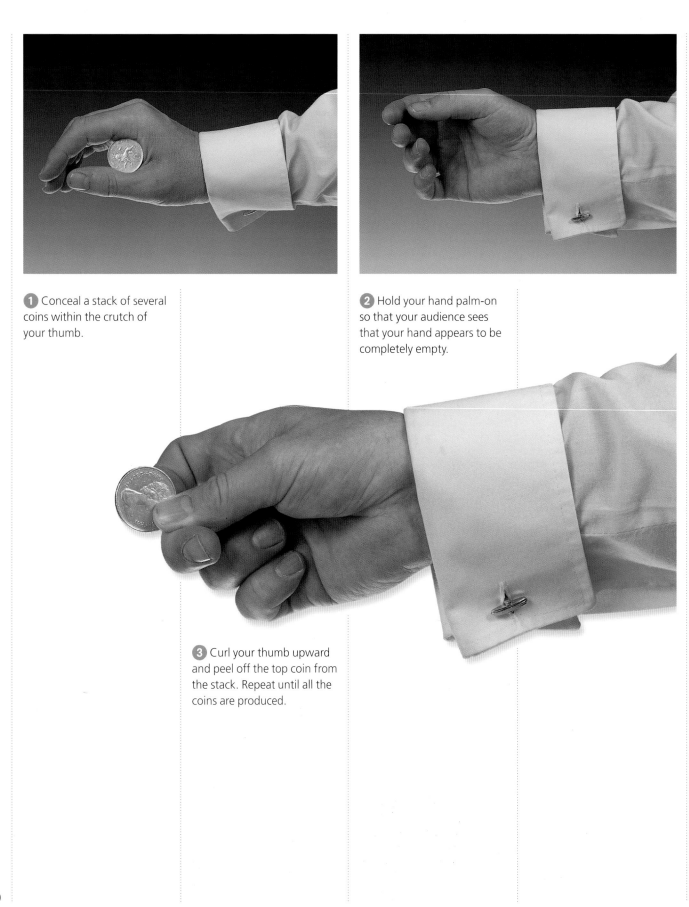

1 Conceal a stack of several coins within the crutch of your thumb.

2 Hold your hand palm-on so that your audience sees that your hand appears to be completely empty.

3 Curl your thumb upward and peel off the top coin from the stack. Repeat until all the coins are produced.

2 ◆

FORCING CARDS

AS WE HAVE ALREADY NOTED,

IT IS NOT UNUSUAL FOR NEWCOMERS TO MAGIC

TO START WITH CARD TRICKS. A PACK OF CARDS IS

INEXPENSIVE, AND YOU WILL PROBABLY FIND ONE AT HOME

anyway. Card tricks can be presented almost anywhere – on a table, on the

floor, or even in the performer's hands. Some magicians like to use a close-up

mat to work on, the spread of cards showing up well against the contrasting

color of the flock-covered surface. Other people prefer an ordinary table.

For the most part, all you need is a single deck of cards although preferably you should possess two decks, with matching fronts but different designs on the backs. Buy the best quality cards you can sensibly afford. Cheap, badly made cards usually turn out to be a complete waste of money: they tend to crack when even slightly bent and do not wear well. Some magicians prefer to use plastic-coated cards; others prefer those with a "linen" finish. This is largely a matter of personal preference, but those with a plastic finish are durable and their surfaces glide easily over each other. It is handy to have an extra deck identical in all respects to one of your two main decks but with a textured "linen" finish rather than a smooth one.

When one or both of your main decks gets scruffy through overuse, replace the pair – remember that bent, torn, or defaced cards never help the performer, because your audience will automatically think that they are obvious markings to help you with your act. Do not throw away your old cards, however. Not only can they be useful for practice (better, often, than nice, clean, new ones), but you can cannibalize them to make fakes or to replace cards that have accidentally got destroyed or damaged. Sometimes, too, you need an extra copy of a particular card in a trick.

In selecting a pack, try to choose one that does not have an unusual design on the back – stick to patterns that will be familiar to your audience – and buy those with designs that incorporate a white margin all the way round. Often you will want to persuade a member of the audience that you are offering a face-down pack,

when, in fact, it is a face-up deck with only the topmost card turned face down. A white margin allows you to splay the deck, to aid the deception.

Specially faked cards can be bought from conjuring stores and through mail-order suppliers, and these can, on occasion, be useful, although you are probably most often better off manufacturing your own. If you are performing in larger venues you might think of buying Jumbo Cards (also known as Giant Cards), but these can be extremely expensive and can be used for only a limited repertoire of tricks. Think of trying to shuffle a pack of Jumbo Cards!

One special type of cards is worth considering. If you have small hands, you may find it difficult to do many of these tricks with a standard size pack. Try them again using a deck of patience (solitaire) cards. These little cards are generally very attractive, largely because of their smallness, and you could make the fact that you use them a distinctive and appealing feature of your act.

There will be times when you may have to "force" a card or cards onto a spectator to achieve certain effects – that is, the spectator takes a card apparently at random, but it is the card of your choice. The ability to force cards is a valuable addition to the magician's repertoire, and while many methods rely only occasionally on sleight of hand or dexterity, some depend on it entirely. For the benefit of the general magician who wishes to learn these important techniques, a few of the most practical have been included in this chapter.

FORCING A CARD

The object of all techniques of forcing cards is, as we have noted, to make a volunteer from the audience think that he or she has selected a card at random, whereas in fact the card that is chosen has been predetermined by you. The simplest method of forcing is also the most fallible, and you should use it only when you are certain of your audience. Ideally, they should be casual and laughing, already convinced by other tricks that you are more or less infallible. It is even better if you are performing at a party or in a bar, so that everyone has had a few drinks.

All you do, while fanning out the pack or immediately afterward, is to edge forward a little with your thumbnail or thumb the predetermined card, which should be roughly in the center of those that you have fanned out. (Note that, in fanning out a complete deck of cards, you need only proffer the central cards of the pack, with the others to either side being more bunched up.) A casual volunteer will probably opt for the card that is protruding slightly from the rest. If not, it is easy to rotate your wrists a little to bring the pre-determined card gradually under the descending fingers. If you are still unsuccessful, suddenly "remember" some part of the trick you have forgotten to set up, and retreat to your table. Either try this technique of forcing on a different member of the audience or try one of the alternative methods – the Bridge, the Riffle Force, Cut It Yourself, Deal It Yourself, or the Shuffle-stop.

THE RIFFLE FORCE

To execute this force, you need to make sure that the predetermined card is at the top of the pack. This is a good technique to use when you want to force more than one card simultaneously.

1 Holding the cards face down in your right hand, with your fingers wrapped around them, riffle one corner of the exposed end with your thumb. Do this a few times through the pack, and then ask a member of the audience to stop you at any time mid-riffle. When this happens, reach across with your left hand and remove the cards of the upper packet, offering the lower packet to the spectator. Remind your audience that the top card of

this lower packet is the one that the spectator's call has selected.

2 In fact, when you draw the upper packet away from the lower, the tips of the wrapped-around fingers of your right hand have pressed against the back of the top card so that, as you draw away the packet to give to the spectator, that card stays in your right hand and falls naturally onto the lower packet. With a little rehearsal you will find that you can perform the whole maneuver so swiftly and naturally that it is undetectable.

THE BRIDGE

In this technique of forcing a card, the predetermined card is at the bottom of the deck.

You can perform this maneuver at your table rather than offering the cards in your hand. However, this is much more risky. Not only are you giving the spectator much more time to think, and hence to cut at somewhere other than the obvious place, but you are also not in control of which way he or she habitually takes the cards when cutting a pack. Most people grip the cards at the sides, but people grip them at the ends, and you may, therefore, have crimped the bridge in the wrong direction – widthwise when it should have been lengthwise, or vice versa. By offering the cards in your hand, you determine the way the spectator cuts the cards, whatever he or she would normally do.

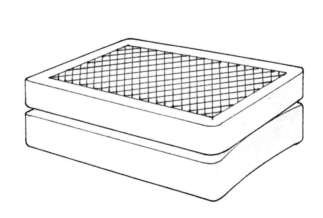

1 Cut the pack yourself first, crimping the (original) upper packet as you do so to form a bridge. As you complete the cut, there will be a distinct gap between the upper and lower packets.

2 Offer the deck in your hand to the spectator and ask him or her to cut the pack. If you do this quickly and offhandedly enough, the spectator will invariably cut at the gap, and thereby at your predetermined card.

CUT IT YOURSELF

THIS IS A VERY SIMPLE WAY OF FORCING EITHER ONE OR A PAIR OF CARDS ON A SPECTATOR. YOU
NEED TO PERFORM THIS FORCE QUICKLY AND WITH THE MAXIMUM OF DISTRACTING PATTER.

YOU WILL NEED

PACK OF CARDS

1 Ask the spectator to cut the pack at random and then either you or the spectator can lay what was the bottom half of the pack crosswise over the top.

2 Because you involved a member of the audience in this, your spectators will believe that the two crossed cards at the new center of the pack have been randomly selected. In fact, of course, they are the cards that were originally at the top and bottom of the pack.

IN THE PALM OF YOUR HAND

NEWCOMERS TO MAGIC WHO WOULD LIKE TO RESORT TO SLEIGHT-OF-HAND TECHNIQUES TO
ACCOMPLISH A CARD FORCE MAY WELL APPRECIATE THIS TRICK. STUDY THE SLEIGHT-OF-HAND
METHODS USING CARD PALMS DESCRIBED ON PAGE 20 BEFORE ATTEMPTING THE TRICK. THE BEAUTY
OF THIS TRICK IS THAT NO SPECIAL APPARATUS IS NEEDED – YOU CAN USE A BORROWED PACK OF
CARDS IF YOU WANT – AND NO PREVIOUS PREPARATION IS NECESSARY.

YOU WILL NEED

PACK OF CARDS

1 Before you begin, make sure that the card to be forced is on top of the pack. False shuffle the cards, keeping the top card on top of the pack.

2 Announce the value and suit of the card to your audience. Grip the pack between the fingers and thumb of your right hand. Transfer the pack from your right hand to your left hand, allow the top card to pivot upward into palm position. This maneuver is executed as the pack is placed on the table. Keep the palmed card in a natural hand position.

3 Invite a member of your audience to cut the pack into two piles. When this has been done, use your right hand (containing the concealed palmed card) casually to reach over and lift up the bottom section of the cut. In doing so, add the palmed card to the top of this section of cards then transfer these cards into your left hand.

4 Ask the spectator to remove the card where the cut was made and to reverse it, revealing its identity.

SHUFFLE-STOP

THIS IS A VARIANT OF THE STRAIGHT SHUFFLE (SEE PAGE 15). IT IS MUCH EASIER THAN IT SOUNDS, BUT IT CAN BE TRICKY WITH NEW CARDS OR WITH EXCESSIVELY OLD AND GREASY ONES, SO BOTH IN PRACTICE AND FOR THE PERFORMANCE, USE A MODERATELY WORN PACK. YOU CAN BEGIN THIS FORCE WITH THE PREDETERMINED CARD EITHER AT THE TOP OR AT THE BOTTOM OF THE PACK.

YOU WILL NEED

PACK OF CARDS

1 Tell a member of the audience that you want him or her to call out at any moment when you are shuffling. Begin to shuffle, using what seems to the audience to be a normal shuffling action, but it is in fact a close variant.

2 If the predetermined card has started at the top of the pack, perform a straight shuffle to take it to the bottom of the pack.

3 For the variant shuffle you use from now on, pick off a packet not from the outside of the pack but from inside – that is, from the side of the deck that is closer to the ball of your thumb. The cards you then drop to either side of the new, central cluster come in groups from the rear, not the front, of this packet, so that the bottom few cards of the packet are retained firmly between your fingertips until, at last, you drop them at the bottom of the pack.

4 Repeat this action over and over while you tell the member of the audience who is helping you what to do. Whenever the spectator calls out to you to stop, the face-out card at the bottom of the packet in your upper hand will always be the one you selected in advance.

DEAL IT YOURSELF

BEGIN THIS FORCE WITH THE PREDETERMINED CARD AT THE TOP OF THE PACK.

YOU WILL NEED

PACK OF CARDS

1 To prove to your audience that the selection process is random, keep shuffling, but making sure that you keep the predetermined card in its place, while asking a member of the audience to think of any number between 1 and 52.

2 When the spectator has selected a number, stop shuffling and explain that you want the spectator to count off the cards from the top of the pack until he or she reaches that number. Demonstrate this yourself to make it absolutely clear what you want done. If the number were 17, say, count off 16 cards and show the audience the 17th card, which is, of course, of no interest. Put this card, the 17th, on top of the heap you have counted off, and then return this heap to the top of the pack.

3 Pass the pack to the spectator and ask him or her to repeat the exercise. Obviously, because of your "demonstration," the card that started at the top of the pack, your predetermined card, is now the 17th down from the top.

CARD PHOTOGRAPHY

THE MAGICIAN ASKS A MEMBER OF THE AUDIENCE TO SELECT A CARD FROM THE PACK AND TO SHOW IT TO THE REST OF AUDIENCE, BUT NOT TO THE MAGICIAN, WHO IS, IN THE MEANTIME, BUSY CUTTING THE PACK ON THE TABLE. THE CARD IS RETURNED TO THE MAGICIAN, WHO PLACES IT IN THE CENTER OF THE CUT PACK, WHICH IS THEN SHUFFLED. THE MAGICIAN TELLS THE AUDIENCE THAT CARDS CAN SOMETIMES ACT LIKE TEMPORARY PHOTOGRAPHIC FILM, RETAINING FOR A SHORT WHILE THE LAST IMAGE TO WHICH THEY WERE EXPOSED. TURNING UP THE CARDS ONE BY ONE, THE MAGICIAN AT LAST POUNCES ON A CARD, DECLARING THE SPECTATOR'S FEATURES ARE VISIBLE ON IT. THE MAGICIAN HURRIES TO SHOW THE CARD TO THE SPECTATOR BUT, SADLY, BY THEN THE IMAGE HAS FADED IN THE LIGHT – ALTHOUGH, MAGICALLY, IT IS THE CHOSEN CARD.

YOU WILL NEED

PACK OF CARDS

1 Peep secretly at the bottom of the pack, either before beginning the trick or while the spectator is showing the card to the rest of the audience. Say it was the 6 of spades.

2 When you return the spectator's chosen card to the cut pack, place it on the pile that was previously the top half of the pack. When you set the other half of the pack on top of this, the 6 of spades is, obviously, brought to the position directly above the selected card.

3 Give the cards a fake shuffle or two and begin to turn up the cards. The one after the 6 of spades is, of course, the one you seek.

Trick of the Trade

• Without the patter, this technique can be used as part of other tricks when you need to know the location of a card selected by a volunteer from the audience.

46

HAT FORCE

MAGICIANS ARE FAMOUS FOR PULLING THINGS OUT OF HATS, AND THIS CARD TRICK IS IN THAT TRADITION. THE TRICK IS SPECTACULAR BECAUSE THE MAGICIAN IS BLINDFOLDED – EVEN SO, THE SELECTED CARD IS SUCCESSFULLY REMOVED FROM THE WELL-SHUFFLED PACK IN THE HAT. ALTHOUGH HATS ARE CUSTOMARY AND USEFUL PROPS, YOU COULD USE ANY CONTAINER FOR THIS TRICK.

YOU WILL NEED

PACK OF CARDS

HAT, SMALL BOX, OR CYLINDRICAL CONTAINER

1 Before your performance, conceal the card that is to be forced in the right sleeve of your jacket.

2 When you do this trick, ask a member of the audience to shuffle the cards thoroughly and to put the shuffled pack inside the hat.

3 Announce the value and suit of the chosen card to the audience, then ask to be blindfolded or simply turn away. Hold the hat in your left hand or place it on the table.

4 As you reach inside the hat to make your selection, allow the card secreted in your right sleeve to drop into the hat. This move is executed under cover of the hat itself. Because the card will be lying loose on top of the other cards, it is a simple matter to pick it up and reveal it to the audience as the predicted card.

CRISS-CUT FORCE

A SPECTATOR MAKES A FREE CUT IN A PACK OF CARDS AND THE MAGICIAN CORRECTLY PREDICTS THE CARD BENEATH THE CUT.

1 Before you begin the trick, secretly note the value of the top card of the pack.

2 Ask a spectator to cut the pack somewhere in the center and then to carefully place the two stacks side by side on the table.

3 State that you are going to mark the cut by laying the cut stack across the bottom stack. At this point, you need to misdirect your audience's attention, perhaps by flourishing an envelope in which, you say, you have written down the name of the card in question, if you have not already announced this at the start of the trick. The misdirection will divert attention from the next move, which is to mark the cut but by crossing the bottom stack on top of the cut stack.

4 Ask the spectator to reveal his or her cut by lifting the top stack and reversing the card immediately below it. This card will therefore be the top card you noted before the performance and successfully predicted.

UNDERCOVER CARD

THIS IS A POPULAR FORCE AMONG BEGINNERS. AGAIN, THE MAGICIAN SUCCESSFULLY PREDICTS AT WHICH CARD A SPECTATOR WILL MAKE A FREE CUT OF A SHUFFLED PACK. THE TWIST IS THAT THE ACTUAL CUT IS MADE UNDERCOVER OF A POCKET HANDKERCHIEF.

YOU WILL NEED

PACK OF CARDS

POCKET HANDKERCHIEF

1 Before beginning the trick, secretly note the value of the top card of the pack.

2 As you hand the pack of cards to a spectator to inspect and shuffle, secretly palm off the top two cards of the pack with your left hand.

3 Take back the pack from the spectator and place it in your left hand so that the palmed cards are face up at the bottom of the pack.

4 Display a pocket handkerchief to the audience and carefully drape it over the pack, which is still held in your left hand.

5 Ask a spectator to cut the pack through the material of the handkerchief but not to lift the cut stack away completely.

6 With your right hand, take off the cut stack and, as you draw this top stack and the handkerchief upward and away, under cover of the handkerchief, reverse the bottom stack that is still in your left hand. The original top card of the pack is now face down and on top of the bottom stack.

7 The spectator now reverses this card to reveal the cut, and it is the card you originally predicted. The card immediately below it is also face down, concealing the fact that the rest of the bottom stack is now face up.

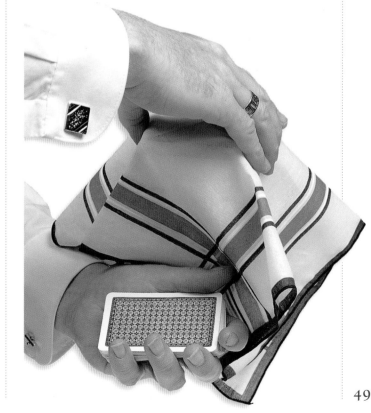

★ ★ ★

ON THE TIP OF THE TONGUE

THIS COMEDY CARD TRICK IS SIMPLY AN ELABORATION OF THE PREVIOUS TRICK. REMEMBER THAT YOU
CAN EMBELLISH QUITE SIMPLE TRICKS WITH BITS OF BUSINESS AND PATTER. THIS TIME THE MAGICIAN
TRIES SOME MIND-READING AND FAILS . . . BUT NOT FOR LONG.

YOU WILL NEED

PACK OF CARDS

PIECE OF PAPER ON WHICH IS
WRITTEN "6 OF CLUBS" (OR
ANOTHER CHOSEN CARD)

HANDKERCHIEF

Note: for the sake of clarity,
the handkerchief has been
removed in the photographs.

3 Tell the audience that you
want a volunteer to lift off a
portion of the cards through
the material of handkerchief
and then to reach beneath
the handkerchief to take the
next card from the pack. You
demonstrate this by lifting off
some cards, but in fact you
actually lift all the cards
except the bottom one,
which is quite easy to do
because the bottom card is
out of alignment.

1 Put the 6 of clubs (or
whichever card you decide to
use) on the bottom of the
pack. Put the pack and the
handkerchief on the table
and conceal the piece of
paper somewhere you can
retrieve it quickly and easily
without anyone noticing.

2 Pick up the pack in one
hand and cover it with the
handkerchief. As you are
arranging the fabric of the
handkerchief, use your
fingers to pull the bottom
card slightly to one side.

4 This then gives you the
opportunity to turn the
bottom card, which is still
lying on your left hand,
face up.

5 Put the pack together
again and let the spectator lift
off some cards. As soon as
this is done, you secretly
turnover the bottom half.

6 When the spectator reaches beneath the handkerchief to take the "next" card, it is the reversed card that is taken.

7 As soon as the card has been taken, turn the bottom half of the pack back the right way, and let the spectator replace the top half. It appears that the spectator has had a free choice of card, but the card has actually been forced.

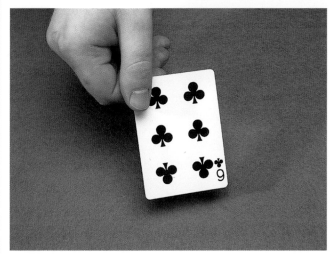

8 Place the pack and handkerchief down on the table, and ask the spectator to show the chosen card to the audience. While all attention is on this action, retrieve the piece of paper and put it in your mouth so that it rests on your tongue.

9 Announce that you will now read the spectator's mind and will reveal the name of the chosen card. You then make a few inaccurate guesses as to the identity of the card. Annoyed at this lack of success, you say: "I don't know what's wrong with me today. A second ago I had the name of the card on the tip of my tongue." As you say this, put out your tongue to reveal the paper. Take the paper from your mouth and show the writing – you really did have the spectator's card on the tip of your tongue!

CLIP IT

THIS CARD FORCE, RELIES FOR ITS EFFECT ON A SIMPLE PREMISE AND ON THE USE OF A COMMON
OFFICE ACCESSORY – THE HUMBLE PAPER CLIP.

YOU WILL NEED

PACK OF CARDS

2 PAPER CLIPS

1 Before the performance begins, decide which card you are going to force and attach one of the paper clips to the card, positioning the clip midway along the bottom edge of the card. Place the card somewhere in the center of the pack, with the paper clip facing into your hand so that the top edges of the fanned cards appear genuine and unmarked to your spectators.

2 At the beginning of the trick, announce to the audience the suit and value of the card that is to be forced.

3 Ask a spectator to select a card from a pack, held fanned out and face down in your hand. Hand the spectator a paper clip and, with the selected card kept face down, ask the spectator to slip the paper clip onto the middle of the top edge of the card and then to return it to the pack.

4 As you close up the pack, give it a half-turn, bring the opposite ends toward the audience. Cut the pack several times, and as you do so, recap on what has happened so far.

5 Fan out the pack again, so that your audience can clearly see that one card has a paper clip on it – this appears to be the one that the spectator selected and marked earlier. Remove this card and hand it to the spectator, discarding the remainder of the pack. The spectator then reveals that you did, indeed, successfully predict which card would be actually selected.

Trick of the Trade

● If the spectator happens, against the odds, to select the card to which you have already attached a clip – it is unlikely, but possible – simply remove the card, revealing the paper clip that is attached to the card. Show the rest of the pack to the audience, proving that there is only one card with such a clip and proving that you have correctly predicted the card that would be chosen.

CLEVER CARD TRICKS

THIS CHAPTER INCLUDES SOME

CLASSIC CARD TRICKS. THE SLEIGHT OF HAND

AND FORCING TECHNIQUES LEARNED IN PREVIOUS

CHAPTERS WILL STAND YOU IN GOOD STEAD FOR THESE TRICKS,

and they can also be combined with all the effects that are described here to

build up a very entertaining performance.

TOPSY-TURVY GAMBLE

THE MAGICIAN ANNOUNCES THAT, AFTER ONE DRINK TOO MANY BEFORE THE PERFORMANCE AND BUOYED UP BY THE DUTCH COURAGE THIS HAS GIVEN, HE OR SHE IS GOING TO BET WITH A SPECTATOR ABOUT THE VALUE OF A CARD SELECTED PURELY AT RANDOM FROM A JUMBLED DECK. STRESSING THAT THERE IS ONLY ONE CHANCE IN 52 OF GETTING THE RIGHT ANSWER, THE MAGICIAN SAYS THAT WAGER WILL BE A WORLD CRUISE AGAINST A VOLUNTEER'S WATCH. WHEN NO ONE IN THE AUDIENCE APPEARS TO WANT TO WAGER THEIR WATCH, THE MAGICIAN RAISES THE STAKES: A WORLD CRUISE WITH THE STARLET OF THE SPECTATOR'S CHOICE AGAINST ANY OLD SCRAP OF PAPER HE OR SHE HAPPENS TO HAVE ON THEM.

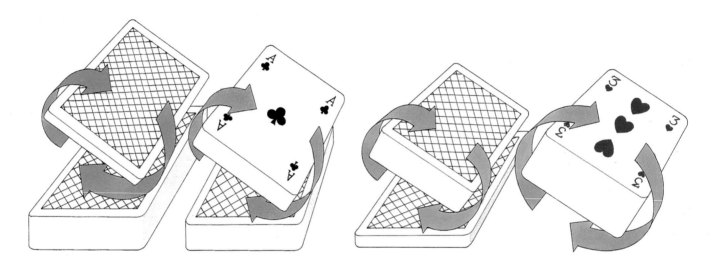

1 Ask a volunteer to shuffle the cards for you. Because the card on which you are betting is the top card of the deck before you begin to manipulate the cards, the best way to determine the card is to glimpse the bottom of the pack as the spectator gives the cards back to you. Use the Pass (see page 18) to bring the bottom card to the top of the pack.

2 Tell the audience that not only are you going to jumble the order of the cards but also the way they are facing. Pull off a packet from the pack, turn it over the replace it face up on the top of the pack.

3 Repeat this maneuver with a second, larger packet.

4 Repeat the maneuver with a third, still larger packet.

5 Finally, turn over the whole pack, so that everything will be well and truly muddled.

6 Announce that the card is, say, the 2 of clubs, and that it will be the first face-down card you come to as you fan through the pack. Sure enough, that card will be the 2 of clubs. The effect of your manipulating is nowhere near as jumbling as it appears – the result is merely to ensure that the initial top card in the pack will prove to be the first face-down card exposed as you fan out the pack.

Tricks of the Trade

• Practice the manipulation until you can do it naturally, without having to pause and count how many times you have flipped the packets over.

• Bearing in mind the size of the stakes involved, it is a very good idea indeed to make sure that you do not have one drink too many before the performance!

THE WHITE RABBIT'S CARD TRICK

THE MAGICIAN INVOLVES THE AUDIENCE IN SELECTING A CARD, WHICH, AMAZINGLY IS DISCOVERED BY REFERENCE TO THE MAGICIAN'S WATCH! THE BEAUTY OF THE TRICK IS THAT, AS LONG AS THE SELECTED CARD IS NOT PLACED IN THE PACKET THAT IS SET ON TOP OF THE OTHER, THE CHOSEN CARD WILL ALWAYS BE 28TH FROM THE TOP, BUT, BECAUSE YOU HAVE INVOLVED THE AUDIENCE IN CHOOSING THE CARD AND IN SELECTING WHICH PILE IT SHOULD GO ON, YOUR AUDIENCE WILL BELIEVE THAT YOU CANNOT HAVE CALCULATED THE POSITION BEFOREHAND. A MOMENT'S THOUGHT, WILL SHOW THAT THEIR DECISION MAKES NO DIFFERENCE TO THE CARD'S ULTIMATE POSITION.

YOU WILL NEED

PACK OF CARDS

1 Explain to your audience that this trick was taught to Alice by the White Rabbit but that Alice forgot about it when she was telling Lewis Carroll of her adventure in Wonderland. Then ask for four volunteers to choose a card each.

2 When the cards are chosen, ask the four spectators to decide among themselves which one of those four cards they like best. While they discuss this, deal the rest of the pack into two equal packets.

3 Take back the cards from the spectators, but do not look at them. Ask the volunteers to select the packet on which they would like the chosen card to be placed. Then ask them to choose which pile they would like the other three cards to be placed on.

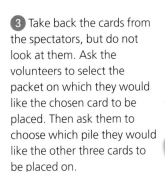

4 This done, you pick up the packet with the three cards on top and place it on top of the other packet, so that the single card, chosen by the spectators, is in the middle of the pack. Glance at your watch, which is what the White Rabbit did when he showed the trick to Alice, and announce the time – 23 minutes past 5, for example. Ask one of the spectators to add the two numbers together, to give the result 28, and then count down through the pack to reveal that the 28th card is, indeed, the one that was chosen.

Tricks of the Trade

• The trick works itself but can only be performed at certain times of the day – 12:16, 13:15, 1:27, 14:14, 2:26, 15:13, 3:25, 16:12, 4:24, 17:11, 5:23, 18:10, 6:22, 19:09, 7:21, 20:08, 8:20, 21:07, 9:19, 22:06, 10:18, 23:05, and 11:17. In fact, it can be done at any time within a couple of minutes of one of these times, because you are the person who checks your watch, and for all the audience knows, it could be a little fast or slow.

• Depending on the size of your audience, you can have the volunteers select from among not four but six or eight cards – the trick will not work with an odd number of cards. With six cards the chosen one will end up 29th from the top, with eight cards it will be 30th. Obviously, you must recalculate the time of your performance accordingly. With a very large audience you could give out even more cards – 16, say, in which case the card would be 34th down – and organize a game among different groups of the audience to determine the final choice. However, you must be confident of your ability to control the audience so that the game ends at about the designed time.

CARD CONTROL

THIS TRICK REQUIRES YOU TO ASK FOR SOMEONE FROM YOUR AUDIENCE TO SELECT A CARD FROM THE PACK OF CARDS. THE SPECTATOR THEN RETURNS IT TO THE PACK. EVEN THOUGH THE PACK IS SHUFFLED, THE MAGICIAN REVEALS THE IDENTITY OF THE SELECTED CARD IN A SURPRISING MANNER.

YOU WILL NEED

PACK OF CARDS

1 Shuffle the cards and then fan them out, face down, between your hands. Ask a person in the audience to take any card.

3 Replace the top portion of the cards, but first place the tip of the little finger of your left hand on the chosen card. Although the pack is now reassembled, your little finger holds a "break" at the rear end of the pack.

4 Immediately lift off about one-third of the cards with your right hand, and place them on the table.

5 Next, lift off about one-third of the cards with your right hand, and place them on the table.

2 Gather the remaining cards together and hold the pack in the left hand. As the spectator is looking at the card, lift off about two-thirds of the pack with your right hand. Ask the spectator to return the chosen card to the lower portion of the pack.

6 Finally, place the bottom portion of the pack on top of the cards that are on the table. It appears that the chosen card is now completely lost in the pack, but unbeknown to the audience, it is actually the top card.

8 The remaining cards are then shuffled on top of the first card. The shuffle looks perfectly normal, but the chosen card is now on the bottom of the pack.

7 Pick up the pack and give it an overhand shuffle. This is a perfectly fair shuffle, except for the fact that the first card (the top card) is taken singly from the pack into the left hand.

9 Shuffle the cards again until you reach the bottom portion of the pack. As you finish the shuffle, make sure that the final part of the shuffle consists of a single card (the bottom, chosen card) only. Unbeknown to the spectators, the chosen card is now back on top of the pack.

10 Because you know the location of the chosen card, there are several ways in which you can reveal its identity. First, fan the faces of the cards toward yourself for a second, as if you are concentrating. You simply look at the top card of the pack, and you can now appear to read the spectator's mind as you name the chosen card. Second, hold the pack behind your back and say that you will try to locate the chosen card through the power of your magic finger. Pretend to be searching through the cards, and then bring forward the top card – it is the spectator's selection! The third option is to ask another member of the audience to choose a card. But this time you do not allow a free choice – you force the top card. When both spectators are asked to name their chosen card, they both name the same card – an amazing coincidence!

Trick of the Trade

• As with all tricks, you must practice this until you can do all the moves naturally. Do not give the appearance of doing something difficult. The shuffling process must be exactly the same as you would use if you were shuffling the cards normally.

IN THE DARK

IN THIS TRICK A SPECTATOR IS ASKED TO SELECT ANY CARD FROM A WELL-SHUFFLED PACK BUT IS TOLD NOT TO LOOK AT THE CARD AT THIS STAGE. TO MAKE IT EVEN MORE DIFFICULT, THE LIGHTS ARE SWITCHED OFF SO THAT EVERYTHING IS IN THE DARK. THE CHOSEN CARD IS PLACED FACE DOWN ONTO THE PALM OF THE SPECTATOR'S HAND. THE MAGICIAN THEN DRAMATICALLY ANNOUNCES THE NAME OF THE CARD, AND IS THEN ABLE TO REPEAT THE TRICK TWICE MORE, WITH SIMILARLY STARTLING RESULTS. YOUR AUDIENCE WILL CERTAINLY BE IN THE DARK WHILE THEY WATCH THIS PUZZLING TRICK.

YOU WILL NEED

PACK OF CARDS

---

1 Ask a spectator to select a card from the shuffled pack but not to look at its suit or value at this stage.

2 The lights are switched off, and you take the card, which you then apparently place on the palm of the spectator's hand. In replacing the card, however, you secretly exchange the chosen card with one from your pocket. Of course, this is all done in the dark. Unknown to the spectator, a quick switch has been made.

3 Announce the value and suit of the chosen card. When the lights are switched on and the spectator looks at the card, it is found to be the very one that you have named!

Tricks of the Trade

● This effect is best performed as part of a series of other card tricks. When the time comes, secretly palm off three cards from the pack, note their values, and pocket them. See page 20 for the various ways of palming cards.

● To avoid confusing the unwanted cards with the palmed cards within your pocket, a simple method of keeping them apart is to have a folded pocket handkerchief acting as a divider. Cards that are secretly placed into the pocket on one side of the handkerchief, and those that are being removed go on the other. This means that the card effect can be repeated several times without any complications arising.

CARDS THAT SPELL

The magician asks a member of the audience to select a card at random from the pack. When the magician "spells" out the card from the pack it is, annoyingly, not the correct card, but when the spectator does it, the selected card is the one that is found.

> **YOU WILL NEED**
>
> PACK OF CARDS

1 Ask a volunteer to select a card and to return it to the pack without you having seen it. Use the Pass (see page 18) in the normal way to bring the card – the 3 of clubs, for instance – to the top of the pack.

2 Explain to your audience that you have managed to teach the cards in this particular pack to spell – well, they can spell their own names – and then, beginning with the top card, ask the volunteer to spell out the card selected while you peel off the cards and place them in a packet on the table. The volunteer spells the card – T-H-R-E-E-O-F-C-L-U-B-S.

3 At the end of the exercise, however, it is found, to your annoyance that the last card to be turned up is not, in fact, the 3 of clubs. Put the discarded heap back on top of the rest of the pack and berate the cards – or your volunteer for an inability to spell – and repeat the exercise, spelling out the card yourself. The card that is turned up when you reach the "s" of clubs is, of course, the selected card.

> **Tricks of the Trade**
>
> • When the first attempt proves to be a failure, you can initially blame the spectator, accusing him or her of being unable to spell the card's name correctly. The by-play will distract the audience from thinking about the fact that the card spelled out the second time must inevitably be the one that was at the top of the pack earlier. You can ask the volunteer to "prove" his or her ability by doing the deal for you.
>
> • This trick should not be performed more than once in your routine, but you can follow it up with Cards That Spell – A Further Variation.

A VARIATION

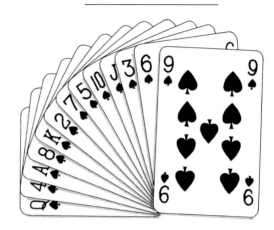

The magician sorts out all the cards of one suit – spades, for example – and tell the audience that this is the cleverest of suits. Each card can spell its own name. As the magician counts through all 13 cards, each one appears as its name is spelled.

1 Select just one suit – the spades, say – from the pack and put the other cards to one side. As you are sorting out the spades, scatter them fairly widely over your table. This will make it less obvious that you are not picking them up at random.

2 Pick up the cards in the following order: queen, 4, ace, 8, king, 2, 7, 5, 10, jack, 3, 6, 9. That is, the queen is at the top of your face-down packet and the 9 at the bottom. Thereafter the trick works itself.

3 Begin by spelling out A-C-E, putting the first two cards at the bottom of the pile. The third card you turn up is the ace, and you should put this to one side.

4 Next spell T-W-O. When you get to the third card, you will turn up the 2. Discard this card.

5 Continue in the same way – the next card is the 3 – until the final card left in your hands is the king.

CARDS THAT SPELL –
A FURTHER VARIATION

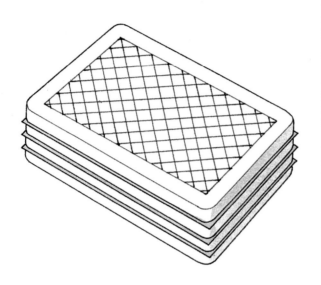

3 Ask the spectator to blindfold you, and while this happens, put the displayed deck in your pocket, announcing that you are making doubly sure there can be no deception. As the blindfold is put on and checked, it is natural that you might keep your hand in your pocket. You are, in fact, picking out the correct card from the duplicate set. The business of the blindfold tying should help distract the audience's attention from any movement of your arm as you select the correct card.

4 Then spell out random cards from the "real" set, through the T-H-R-E-E-O-F-C-L-U-B-S, producing the duplicate 3 of clubs as you get to the final "s".

YOU WILL NEED

2 PACKS OF CARDS

BLINDFOLD

PIECES OF CARD SLIGHTLY
BIGGER THAN PLAYING
CARDS

1 Before the performance, secrete a duplicate deck in your pocket, sorted into suit and rank order. Furthermore, divide the suits off from each other with pieces of card just a little bigger than the playing cards.

2 Invite a member of the audience to draw a card at random from the pack and to announce its value and suit. The volunteer is then asked to return the card to the pack and then to shuffle the pack as thoroughly as he or she wishes.

Tricks of the Trade

• It may seem obvious, but remember that you should not set down the earlier cards of the spelling face-side up. There is a reasonable chance that one of them really will be the 3 of clubs from the "real" pack.

• This trick is an ideal follow-up to the previous tricks. It seems natural to explain that, this time, you will put the chosen card to the sterner test of being able to spell its name in the dark.

The magician announces that the cards in this particular pack of cards have been taught to spell their names. To make doubly certain that there is no deception, the magician announces that not only will he perform the trick blindfolded but, to make doubly sure, will put the cards in a jacket pocket and count from there. As the cards are spelled out, the final card does, indeed, correspond to the selected card.

CARDS THAT SPELL –
YET ANOTHER VARIATION

YOU WILL NEED

PACK OF CARDS

The magician asks a member of the audience to shuffle the pack and deal out the cards into two equal piles. From one packet, the volunteer selects a card and gives it to the magician, who then spells out a sentence to reveal the chosen card.

1 Invite the spectator to shuffle the pack thoroughly and then to deal it into two equal piles on your table. Give the spectator one of the packets and ask him or her to choose one card from that packet.

2 While the spectator is choosing a card, squeeze the packet in your hand so that the 26 cards in it are all slightly curved. This will be sufficient for you to keep this group of cards separate from the cards returned to you by the spectator.

3 Ask the spectator to put the selected card on top of your packet, followed by the rest of the other packet.

4 Cut the deck twice, the first time so that the chosen card goes to the bottom of the pack, the second time so that it is returned to its original order, in 26th position down from the top. While you do this, ask the spectator the name of the selected card – the 3 of clubs, for example.

5 When you know the name of the card, you need to use a phrase that will bring the sentence you use up to the numerical value of the card. The name of any card in the deck is spelled using between 10 and 15 letters – T-H-R-E-E-O-F-C-L-U-B-S, F-O-U-R-O-F-H-E-A-R-T-S, and K-I-N-G-O-F-S-P-A-D-E-S have 12 letters, for example, so need a 14-letter prefix, such as "Your card was the." A 15-letter card – S-E-V-E-N-O-F-D-I-A-M-O-N-D-S, for instance – needs an 11-letter prefix, such as "You chose the." A 14-letter card – J-A-C-K-O-F-D-I-A-M-O-N-D-S, for example – needs a 12-letter prefix, such as "The card is the." A 13-letter card – Q-U-E-E-N-O-F-S-P-A-D-E-S, for example – needs a 13-letter prefix, such as "Your card is the." An 11-letter card – A-C-E-O-F-H-E-A-R-T-S, for instance –

needs a 15-letter prefix, such as "You picked out the." And a 10-letter card – the S-I-X-O-F-C-L-U-B-S, for instance – needs a 16-letter prefix, such as "Here's your card, the." To avoid having to calculate the number of letters in a card's name each time from scratch, memorize the facts that "of diamonds" has 10 letters, "of hearts" and "of spades" both have eight letters, and "of clubs" has seven letters.

Trick of the Trade

● While you are cutting the deck, seemingly at random, you may be able to glance at the chosen card and thus not need to ask the volunteer what it was. This obviously adds to the whole dramatic and magical effect.

ON REFLECTION

YOU WILL FIND THAT YOU CAN REPEAT THIS AMAZING TRICK SEVERAL TIMES WITHOUT THE SPECTATORS DETECTING THE SECRET. ONE OF YOUR SPECTATORS IS ASKED TO SELECT A CARD BY PUSHING THE BLADE OF A TABLE KNIFE INTO THE PACK AND NOTING THE CARD ABOVE THE BLADE. NEEDLESS TO SAY, THE MAGICIAN IS ABLE TO REVEAL THE NAME OF THE CHOSEN CARD.

YOU WILL NEED

PACK OF CARDS

TABLE KNIFE WITH A SHINY BLADE

1 Ask a member of the audience to shuffle the pack of cards and then to hold the pack in his or her left hand, facing downward.

2 Hand the knife to the spectator and ask him or her to select a card by pushing the blade between any section of the cards they wish. Ask the spectator to note the selected card above the knife blade.

3 Take the pack from the spectator, making sure that the knife is still lodged between the cards. Then carefully lift the top portion so that you can secretly glimpse a reverse reflection of the suit and value of the selected card. The polished blade makes this possible, and you need only lift the portion of cards slightly.

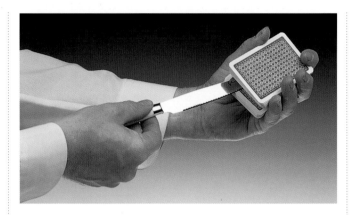

However, it is important to position the knife toward the bottom left-hand corner, where the card's suit and value are shown.

4 You can now reveal the name of the selected card to the audience. Declare the color of the suit first, then the value of the card to make the presentation more effective.

FAST FIND CARD TRICK

FINDING A CHOSEN CARD QUICKLY AND WITHOUT FUSS OR BOTHER CAN OFTEN BE A DIFFICULT TASK. THIS SOLUTION IS CLEVER IN PERFORMANCE. YOU ASK A MEMBER OF THE AUDIENCE TO SELECT A CARD AND RETURN IT TO THE PACK. YOU IMMEDIATELY LOCATE AND IDENTIFY THE CHOSEN CARD.

YOU WILL NEED

WELL-SHARPENED PENCIL

PACK OF CARDS

1 Before your performance, secretly run a pencil line down one side of the pack of cards. The line should be fairly light but should, nevertheless, be clearly visible to you.

2 When you come to perform the trick, fan the pack of cards, face down, toward a spectator, and invite him or her to select any card at all from the pack.

3 When the card has been removed and while the spectator is showing it to the audience so that you cannot see which card has been chosen, secretly turn the pack around before the card is returned.

4 Because the pack has been reversed, the chosen card is the only one showing a pencil mark against the plain white edges of the rest of the pack. It is now an easy matter to break the pack at the card and to remove it to show to the audience that you have, amazingly, identified the selected card.

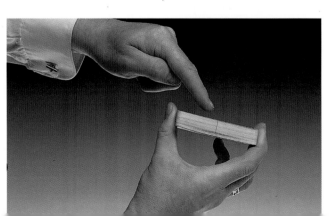

RED UNDER THE BED

THE MAGICIAN DEALS OUT SIX CARDS, ALTERNATELY FACE DOWN AND FACE UP, THEN WRITES DOWN A
PREDICTION ON A SHEET OF PAPER. THE PREDICTION IS GIVEN TO A MEMBER OF THE AUDIENCE TO
GUARD AND READS: "YOU WILL PICK THE ONLY RED CARD OUT OF THE SIX," WHICH IS WHAT HAPPENS.

YOU WILL NEED

2 PACKS OF CARDS WITH
DIFFERENT COLORED DESIGNS
ON THE BACK

SHEET OF PAPER

PEN OR PENCIL

1 Only two cards are
important: the 6 of either
hearts or diamonds and the
ace of either spades or clubs.
The ace is taken from a deck
with a red design on the
back; the other five cards are
taken from a non-red-backed
deck. Apart from the two

specified cards, the other
cards can be any value from
seven upward as long as they
are either clubs or spades.

2 Before you begin the
trick, arrange the cards in the
following order at the top of
the pack: other, ace, six,
other, other, other.

3 Lay the top six cards face
down, face up, face down,
etc. Ask the volunteer to
select a card. If the number
chosen is 1, swoop on the ace
and show that it alone has a
red back.

4 If the number is 3, count
from left to right to get to the
6 of diamonds or hearts. If it
is 2, count from left to right
to get to the ace again.

5 If the number chosen is 4,
count from right to left to get
to the 6 of diamonds or
hearts.

6 If the number chosen is 5,
count from right to left to get
to the ace.

7 If the number chosen is 6,
then pick up the 6 of
diamonds or hearts.

Tricks of the Trade

• Face the spectator
across the table while you
are performing this trick.
That way, counting from
left to right or from right
to left will not seem so
unnatural. You can even
ask your volunteer to do
the counting for you.

• Never be tempted to
encore this trick.

CLEAN CUT

THIS IS ANOTHER TRICK THAT USES A TABLE KNIFE. A SPECTATOR IS ASKED TO SELECT ANY CARD
THEY WANT FROM A PACK, THE MAGICIAN INSERTS A KNIFE INTO THE PACK, THEN ANOTHER MEMBER
OF THE AUDIENCE FINDS THAT THE CARD ABOVE THE BLADE IS THE CHOSEN CARD.

YOU WILL NEED

PACK OF CARDS

TABLE KNIFE

1 Ask a member of the
audience to select any card
they wish from the pack.
Then request that the
spectator displays the card to
the audience.

2 While the card is being
displayed, secretly buckle the
pack of cards, gently
squeezing it with your right
hand so that all the cards are
slightly curved.

3 Ask the spectator to cut
the pack and then replace the
chosen card, returning it to
the top of the bottom pile.

4 Thoroughly shuffle the
pack. Then, holding the pack
in your left hand, take the
knife in your right hand. Force
the knife through the slight
gap in the pack that has been
created by the flat card being
inserted among the slightly
bent ones.

5 Invite another spectator to
remove the portion of the
pack above the knife and, lo
and behold, the card beneath
the blade of the knife is
revealed to be the chosen one.

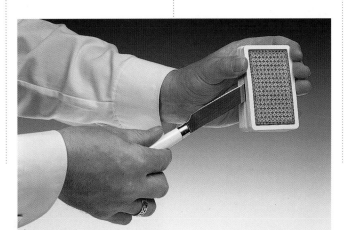

THE VAIN CARD

THE MAGICIAN ASKS A MEMBER OF THE AUDIENCE TO PICK A CARD FROM THE PACK, SHOW IT TO THE REST OF THE AUDIENCE, AND RETURN IT TO THE PACK. THE MAGICIAN SHUFFLES THE CARD AND EXPLAINS TO THE AUDIENCE THAT CARDS CAN BE AS GUILTY AS HUMAN BEINGS OF THE MINOR SINS, ESPECIALLY THE SIN OF VANITY. IN PARTICULAR, THE CARD THAT HAS JUST BEEN SELECTED HAS BECOME OVERLY PROUD OF THE FACT THAT IT WAS SELECTED FROM AMONG THE OTHER 51 – INDEED, THE MAGICIAN SAYS, THERE IS NO WAY OF STOPPING IT FROM RISING FROM THE MIDDLE OF THE PACK TO ACKNOWLEDGE THE AUDIENCE'S APPLAUSE. AS THE MAGICIAN HOLDS THE PACK OF CARDS TOWARD THE AUDIENCE, THE SELECTED CARD SLOWLY AND MYSTERIOUSLY APPEARS.

Tricks of the Trade

• You can enhance the effect by touching a fingertip of your right hand to the top of the card as it rises, giving the illusion that the fingertip is pulling, or is being pushed up by, the card.

• If it is hot, you can press the deck hard against your forehead, as if you are concentrating, and then remove the rest of the pack to leave the rear card – that is, the chosen one – stuck to your forehead.

• You can link this trick neatly with your next one, by continuing your patter along the lines of: "You think that this is just a trick? You don't believe me? Well, look, I'll speak sternly to the cards, but it won't do any good." You should then force the same card onto another member of the audience – it doesn't matter too much if your attempt is unsuccessful – and then proceed at once with your next trick.

YOU WILL NEED

PACK OF CARDS

1 Ask a spectator to select a card. When the card is returned to pack, use one of the methods described under the Pass (see page 18) to bring it to the top.

2 Shuffle the cards, but make sure that the selected card stays at the top of the pack.

3 Display the shuffled pack to the audience, with the selected card at the rear, holding the deck between your thumb on one side and your third and little fingers at the other. This leaves your middle two fingers behind the cards, hidden from view, and you can then use them to "walk" the card slowly upward.

4 To the audience, a little distance from you, it looks as if the chosen card is emerging from somewhere in the center of the pack, an illusion you will have reinforced with your patter.

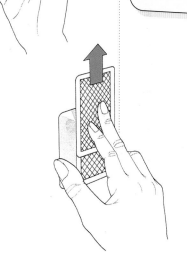

THE VAIN CARD –
A VARIATION

This trick is best done in conjunction with the first version of the Vain Card. In the customary way, the magician invites a member of the audience to select a card and examine it, then to return it to the pack. As the magician shuffles the pack, he or she explains that cards are as vain as humans and that this particular card will now regard itself as superior to its 51 fellows. As proof, the magician fans out the deck face down and, sure enough, the selected card has turned itself the opposite way from the rest, so that it shows face up.

YOU WILL NEED

PACK OF CARDS

❶ While the audience is looking at the card and showing it to the rest of the audience, you simply turn over the bottom card of the pack so that it is face down against the face of the next card (see Straight-shuffle Deceptions on page 16 for one way of doing this).

❷ When you proffer the pack to the spectator so that he or she can push the selected card into it, the cards look as if they are face down, but in fact, all the cards, except the one on top, are face up.

❸ You again shuffle the cards, this time turning the card at the top the right way round, then fan out the pack face down, revealing the chosen card to be face up.

Tricks of the Trade

• It is advisable not to repeat this trick too often, because someone is bound to cotton on to what is happening if you do it too many times.

• You can adapt the patter of I'm It (see page 66) to make it a brief flourish to conclude a set of three tricks involving the vanity of cards.

I'M IT

THE MAGICIAN SHOWS THE AUDIENCE THE TOP CARD OF THE PACK AND EXPLAINS THAT THIS CARD IS OFTEN FOUND AT THE TOP OF THE PACK BECAUSE IT IS SUCH A VAIN CARD. THE MAGICIAN PUSHES THE CARD INTO THE CENTER OF THE PACK, PUTS THE CARDS ON THE TABLE, WAVES A WAND OR MAKES A MAGIC PASS OVER THE CARD, AND REVEALS TO THE AUDIENCE THAT, ONCE AGAIN, THE SAME CARD IS AT THE TOP. THE TRICK DEPENDS ON THE SPEED WITH WHICH THE MAGICIAN EXECUTES THE SECOND VERSION OF THE PASS (SEE PAGE 18) TO BRING A SINGLE CARD FROM THE BOTTOM OF THE PACK TO THE TOP.

YOU WILL NEED

PACK OF CARDS

1 Take the first card from the top of the pack – in this example, say the 10 of spades – and then show it to the audience.

2 As if absent-mindedly, return the card to its place, while continuing with your patter, along the lines "Funny thing about the 10 of spades, incidentally . . . look, I'll show you" and so on. At the same time, pass the bottom card of the pack to the top.

3 Do not show the card to the audience, but take what is now the top card (which your audience will believe still to be the 10 of spades) and push it at random into the deck. The trick is done, although it will be while before you let the audience know this.

I'M IT – A VARIATION

A simpler variant of the first version, relies on your having a long fingernail on the little finger of your left hand.

1 Holding the pack in your left hand, slip the fingernail under the second-top card.

2 When you show the audience the "top" card, in fact, peel off both the first and second cards together, as if they were a single card. Return the two cards to the top of the pack.

3 It is a simple matter then, to take the real top card and push it at random into the pack, leaving the second top card (the card you showed to the audience as the top card) at the top of the pack.

Trick of the Trade

• The first version of I'm It can be done as a finale after the two versions of the Vain Card. Take the card that has already twice demonstrated its vanity – in our examples the 10 of spades – and put it on top of the deck. As if as an afterthought, address some taunting remark toward it (you will already have made the Pass) to the effect that *this* time it is destined for obscurity. Matching your actions to your words, draw off the top card and push it into the pack. Then, looking annoyed, peel off the new top card and show that the 10 of spades has apparently returned immediately to its preeminent position. You can do this two or three times, very quickly (practice!), getting crosser and crosser with each attempt, before abandoning the whole thing as a lost cause.

SWAP

A PACK OF CARDS IS DIVIDED INTO TWO PACKETS, AND FROM ONE OF THESE THE MAGICIAN SELECTS A

CARD, WHILE A SPECTATOR SELECTS A CARD FROM THE OTHER PACKET. THE NAMES OF THE CARDS ARE

ANNOUNCED BEFORE THE TWO PACKETS ARE GATHERED UP. WHEN THE SPECTATOR CHECKS HIS CARDS

AGAIN, HE FINDS THAT THE CARD SELECTED BY THE MAGICIAN HAS APPEARED NEXT TO HIS CARD.

YOU WILL NEED

PACK OF CARDS

1 Shuffle the pack thoroughly and give half of it to a member of the audience, asking the spectator to spreads the cards in that packet out on the table and to draw a single card from somewhere near the middle. As you shuffle, make sure you know the card at the bottom of the pack, and make sure you give the lower half of the pack to the spectator.

3 Both you and the spectator put your respective cards on the top of the respective packets. Gather the packets and cut them, so that the two cards are in the centers of their respective packets.

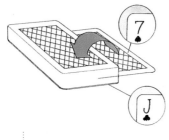

2 Say that you will do the same. Announce that the card that you have chosen is, say, the jack of clubs – that is, no matter what card you draw from your packet, name it as the bottom card in the spectator's packet. Ask the spectator to name the card he or she has selected – for example, the 7 of spades.

Tricks of the Trade

● Although it is easier to ascertain the value of the card at the bottom of the pack, it is easier to retain the top card in its position while performing the shuffle. There is a possibility that the volunteer may notice the bottom card of the packet you hand over. It is better, that the jack of clubs is at the top of the pack. You can give the cards a genuine shuffle, glimpse the bottom card, and then make the Pass (see page 18) to take it to the top.

4 Ask the spectator to fan out his or her packet of cards, just to check that everything is in order and that the selected card is, indeed, in that packet. By completing the cut, of course, the spectator will have placed the selected card next to the bottom card which is the jack of clubs.

5 When the spectator fans out the cards in his or her packet, the jack of clubs is found to be next to the 7 of spades.

S W A P – A V A R I A T I O N

Two cards selected at random by a member of the audience unaccountably appear in and

1 Before the performance, prepare a double-sided card, which you can make by very carefully pasting back-to-back, say, the 3 of spades and the king of hearts from an old pack. Use a warm iron to make the fake as thin as possible. Have the dummy card, with the king-side face down, ready on your table.

2 Ask a member of the audience to select two cards. In fact, use the Riffle Force (see page 17) or Cut It Yourself (page 44) to get the spectator to accept the 3 of spades and the king of hearts. Invite the spectator to show these cards to the audience, then hand over the open-ended box and ask your volunteer to put the two cards inside it. At this point, it is worth adding a little patter. Tell your audience that you know what intelligent and observant people they are and that you are just a little nervous of performing in front of such a discerning crowd. Could they help with the simple task of keeping track of just two cards?

YOU WILL NEED

PACK OF CARDS

OPEN-ENDED BOX SUCH AS AN EMPTY CARD BOX

DOUBLE-SIDED CARD (SEE STEP 1)

---

3 Take back the box, pull out one card – the king of hearts, say – and place that card, face down, on the table. Obviously, the card left in the box is the 3 of spades, so, you say to the audience, there is no need to check. Just to be doubly sure, however, you ask the spectator to look in the box and, sure enough, there is the 3 of spades. Picking up the king of hearts and showing it to the audience, you pick up the box and take out the 3 of spades, which you show the audience, face on, as you return to your table. In fact, when you pick up the king to return it to the box, you pick up the dummy instead. Take the box from the spectator so that you can put the dummy into it and remove the 3 of spades.

---

4 Begin to give the box to the spectator, but appear to change your mind halfway. This gives you the opportunity to turn over the box.

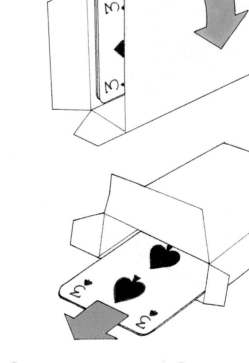

5 The card in the box, you say, is the king of hearts – everyone saw you put it in. But to make sure, you ask the spectator to check – and he or she finds the 3 of spades.

Tricks of the Trade

• Although you can buy ready-printed double-sided cards, they rarely look convincing, and it is better to make your own.

• When you pick up the dummy from your table you are also, as far as the audience is concerned, turning up a card that you laid there face down. To turn up the correct face of the dummy, take it by the edge that is closer to the audience, otherwise you risk giving a glimpse of the wrong side.

6 Look surprised and turn to the card that you put on the table, which has now turned into the king of hearts! At the final revelation, simply pick up the real king of hearts from your table so that both cards and the box can then be safely examined by the audience.

SWITCHEROO

THE MAGICIAN ASKS A VOLUNTEER TO SELECT TWO CARDS. THE CARDS ARE INSERTED IN A SHUFFLED
PACK, AND MAGICALLY, THE TWO SELECTED CARDS APPEAR FACE UP IN THE PACK. THE TRICK RELIES
ON TWO THINGS – ON THE ABILITY TO FORCE TWO CARDS (SEE PAGES 41–52) AND ON PREPARATION
OF THE DOUBLE-FACED CARD.

YOU WILL NEED

PACK OF CARDS

DOUBLE-FACED CARD
(SEE STEP 1)

1 Before the performance, glue together, back to back, two cards from another deck. If the two faces on the dummy card are, say, the king of spades and the ace of diamonds, all you must do in advance is to make sure that, at the outset, the real king of spades and ace of diamonds are placed appropriately for the force used.

2 Ask a member of the audience to select two cards (the cards you have forced) and to memorize them without showing them to you.

3 In the meantime, shuffle the cards, telling the spectator that, at any time, he or she can ask you to stop the shuffle so that the first of the cards can be inserted. The same applies to the second card. Continue to shuffle for a while longer to make absolutely sure that the cards are randomized. In fact, the double-faced card should start near the bottom of the deck – second from bottom, for example – both to make sure that the spectator does

not cut at it and so that you know where it is. Your shuffling can be as thorough as you like, but keep the double-faced card near the center of the pack.

4 Without stopping, lay out the whole deck, face down, in a fan on your table. The first card that the spectator is shown to be face up, and this is hardly surprising (to you, at any rate).

Tricks of the Trade

• The easiest way of making sure that the deck is set up correctly is to prepare a deck in advance. You can then use this trick as the first one in your routine, covertly jettisoning the double-faced card when the trick is over.

• Alternatively, make this the last trick in your program, having the double-faced card and a duplicate of both the king and the ace in your pocket. Find some pretext for popping the pack in your pocket for a moment, and withdraw it with the extra cards.

5 Gather up the rest of the cards, face up, in your hand reinsert the double-faced card in the middle of the pack, also "face-up." Shuffle the cards again, for long enough to make it seem that the shuffling is a significant part of the trick, and fan the cards again – when the second card will show.

PRINTER'S DREAM

IN THIS TRICK, THE MAGICIAN FANS A PACK OF PLAIN WHITE CARDS, SHOWING THAT THE CARDS REALLY ARE BLANK ON BOTH SIDES. WHEN THE CARDS ARE NEXT FANNED TOWARD THE AUDIENCE, THE PACK APPEARS TO BE FULLY PRINTED.

4 Turn over the pack, wave your hand over the front card, and it appears to be printed. Fan the pack, but this time in the usual manner – from left to right – showing that the faces of the cards are now printed.

YOU WILL NEED

PACK OF CARDS THAT IS PRINTED WITH INDICES ON ONLY TWO CORNERS OF EACH CARD AND ON WHICH THE DESIGN ON THE REVERSE OF THE CARDS IS PRINTED WITHIN A BROAD WHITE BORDER

2 DOUBLE-BLANK PLAYING CARDS (WHITE ON BOTH SIDES), WHICH CAN EITHER BE OBTAINED (AS PART OF AN ENTIRE PACK) FROM A MAGIC DEALER OR MADE BY NEATLY COVERING THE FRONT AND BACK OF BOTH JOKERS FROM A PACK WITH WHITE CONTACT ADHESIVE MATERIAL

1 Before you begin your performance, arrange one double-blank card at the top of the pack and the other at the bottom. Place the pack carefully in its case.

2 When it is time to perform the trick, remove the cards from the case and "reverse fan" the pack. In other words, instead of fanning the pack as normal, from left to right, fan from right to left. The reverse fan covers the indices on the cards and, with the blank white card on the face of the pack, the whole pack appears to be blank. The pattern on the backs of the cards has a broad white border, so the other face of the fan appears blank.

3 Square up the pack, turn it face down, and remove the blank card from what is now the bottom of the pack. With a flourish, show both sides of this card to the audience their impression that all the cards are blank on both sides. Then replace this card, but placing it on top of the other double-blank card, which is already on top of the pack.

5 Cut the pack so that the two double-blank cards are now approximately in the middle of the pack, then fan the cards again to show the printed back designs, but being careful not to expose fully the two blank cards in the center. You have just printed a complete pack of blank cards by magic!

YOUR CARD IS

THE MAGICIAN DEALS OUT THREE PACKETS, EACH OF SEVEN CARDS, AND ASKS A MEMBER OF THE AUDIENCE TO SELECT ONE CARD FROM ONE OF THE PACKETS AND TO MEMORIZE THE NUMBER AND SUIT OF THE CARD BUT NOT TO TELL ANYONE WHAT IT IS. THREE TIMES THE PACKETS ARE GATHERED AND DEALT OUT, BUT, FINALLY, THE MAGICIAN FINDS THE SELECTED CARD.

YOU WILL NEED

PACK OF CARDS

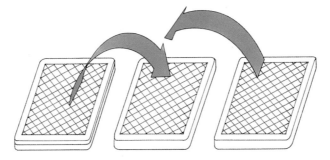

1 Count out three packets, each of seven cards – laying down the cards as one, one, one, two, two, two, rather than as one to seven three times. Put the remainder of the pack to one side.

2 Ask a member of the audience to pick out any one of the packets and to remember the card but not to say aloud what it is.

3 Gather up the three packets, making sure that the packet containing the selected card is between the other two packets, then deal them out again, into three groups of seven cards.

4 Ask the spectator to inspect each group and to indicate which packet contains the selected card.

5 Gather up the packets as before, and once again deal them out into three groups of seven.

6 Again ask the spectator to indicate which group contains the selected card and gather them up in the correct order.

7 Removing one card for each letter, spell out Y-O-U-R-C-A-R-D-I-S and the next card will be the chosen one.

Trick of the Trade

• You can add to the effect by asking the spectator to do most of the work him or herself – all you have to do is make sure that the packets are always gathered in the correct order. As the spectator spells off the cards at the end, spell out the letters of H-E-R-E-'S-M-Y-C-A-R-D, the card corresponding to the D will be the one the spectator originally selected.

RED AND BLACK

THIS TRICK MAKES IT SEEM AS IF THE MAGICIAN CAN ACCOMPLISH THE IMPOSSIBLE – A MIRACLE THAT CAN BE PERFORMED WITH A NORMAL PACK OF CARDS. THE MAGICIAN SHOWS A PACK OF CARDS TO THE AUDIENCE AND SHUFFLES IT, THEN SKILLFULLY DIVINES THE COLOR OF EACH CARD, RED OR BLACK.

YOU WILL NEED

PACK OF CARDS

1 Before you begin, arrange the pack so that the cards that belong to the hearts and diamonds suits are separated from the black cards, spades and clubs. With both blocks of cards held separately, secretly bend them, red cards up and black cards down.

2 Shuffle the cards in full view of the audience, then spread out all 52 cards, face down, on your table.

3 Point to a card and say whether it is red or black. You will find it quite easy to see which are the red cards and which are the black ones.

4 Afterwards, secretly remove the curves by gently flexing the pack.

THE SCURVY KNAVES

THE MAGICIAN TELLS THE TRADITIONAL STORY THAT ACCOMPANIES THIS TRICK, EXPLAINING THAT THERE USED TO BE NOT ONE BUT FOUR SCURVY KNAVES WHO STOLE THE QUEEN OF HEARTS' TARTS. ALTHOUGH THESE CARDS ARE DISTRIBUTED THROUGH THE PACK, BY THE END OF THE TRICK, THE MAGICIAN MYSTERIOUSLY FINDS THAT ALL FOUR OF THE JACKS ARE AT THE TOP OF THE PACK.

YOU WILL NEED

PACK OF CARDS

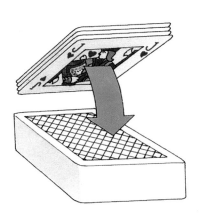

1 As you tell the story, pull out the four "criminals" – that is, the jacks – from the pack. Continue telling the story of how the royal guards chased the knaves until finally they were trapped in a single tower. Show the jacks to the audience and place them on top of the pack.

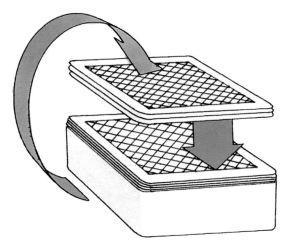

2 Swiftly execute the Pass (see page 18) three times to bring three random cards from the bottom of the pack to cover them.

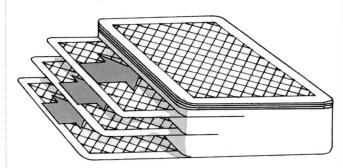

3 Go on to explain that the first of the knaves hid on the ground floor (put one of the cards from the top of the pack at the bottom of the pile), and next hid on the next floor (put the next card in the lower part of the pack), while the third knave hid in the upper part of the tower (put the third card toward the top of the pack). The fourth knave was so terrified that he shinned right up the flagpole (the final jack remains the top of the deck).

4 When the queen's guards came charging to the base of the tower, the thief at the top was so frightened that he jumped from his perch. You peel away the top card, which is a jack, and then show it to the audience.

5 The other knaves, you continue, moved up a floor, and as the guards came up through the tower, each of the thieves in desperation, in turn, climbed the flagpole and jumped off. As you say this, you peel away the three remaining jacks, one by one.

6 Alternatively, when you are showing the four jacks to your audience, have three palmed cards ready behind them. Either way, the trick then works itself.

Trick of the Trade

• The technique of using three already palmed cards is so well known that it is advisable to use either the Pass (see page 18) or, by contrast, to use the palming technique (see page 20) and then, as the trick ends, to grin and say something like: "Of course, every schoolchild knows that trick – but the story really did happen, and it happened like this." And then you can proceed to perform either (or even both) of the following variations.

THE SCURVY KNAVES – A VARIATION

Once upon a time, says the magician, four scurvy knaves stole the queen of hearts' tarts and fled from her wrath. They were chased into the palace gardens by four royal guards, and although they tried to hide in different parts of the garden and to pull bushes over themselves to hide from their pursuers, they were, nevertheless, found hiding together in a single flower bed.

YOU WILL NEED

PACK OF CARDS

1 Show the four jacks to the audience and return them to the top of the pack. As soon as the four jacks have been shown and placed on top of the pack, use the Pass (see page 18) repeatedly to place three cards on top of them.

2 As you explain that each thief chose a different part of the garden to hide in, deal out the four top cards, face down and separately. The fourth card you deal will, of course, be the first jack.

4 Move the packets of cards around, saying that the thieves were trying to confuse the royal guards. Your purpose in so doing is to make sure that the pile of four jacks ends up in one of the two middle positions.

5 Now ask the audience to help in the search for the jacks by calling out a number between one and four. A good contingent will almost certainly call for either two or three, and you need only count from left to right or right to left as is appropriate to settle on the pile containing all four jacks.

3 Make something of a palaver about the way the thieves pulled the bushes over themselves as you count out three cards onto each of the four cards dealt out in step 2. You must put "bushes" on the fourth card – that is, the first jack – before you count out the cards onto the other three cards. The first three cards that represent "bushes" are, in fact, the remaining three jacks.

Trick of the Trade

• The final effect depends on your using a bit of selective hearing. If fewer people are calling for two than for three, start saying something like: "Two? Do I hear two?" when it is perfectly obvious that you should be hearing "three." Shrug, and say, "All right, have it your own way." Then count in the appropriate direction.

THE SCURVY KNAVES – A FURTHER VARIATION

The magician tells the tale of the queen of hearts' tarts and of how the royal guards chased the thieves until they were actually cornered in one of the palace towers.

YOU WILL NEED

PACK OF CARDS

1 As in the first version, explain how one of the miscreants fled all the way up the flagpole to the top of the tower, and at this point, show the first jack quite openly to the audience as you place it on the pack. The second thief stayed on the ground floor, you say, and display the next jack as a single card and quite openly place it at the bottom of the deck.

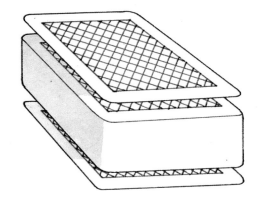

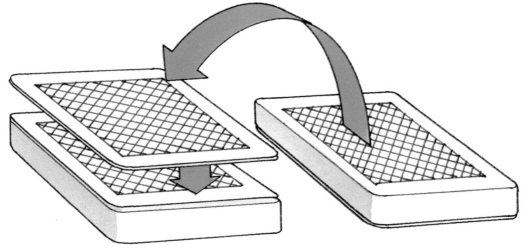

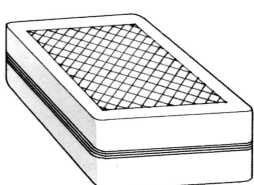

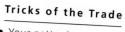

2 Put down the deck on the table in front of you, and, cutting it, tell how the remaining two jacks – both red or both black – were brothers, as can be seen by their colors. They stuck together and, worried equally by the royal paratroopers from above and the royal tunnelers from below, ended up rather indecisively clutching each other for comfort halfway up the tower. Place them in the middle of the pack, which you now pick up.

3 In fact, you say, the brothers were right to worry, because the various divisions of the royal guards drove one thief down from the flagpole and another up from the basement, so that all four were in the middle of the tower when they were finally arrested – which you demonstrate by splaying the pack to show all four jacks in the center.

4 The cut made in step 2 is phony, of course, and it is important that your patter is sufficiently involved and entertaining that no one thinks too much about it. When you cut the cards, make sure that you know which packet is which. You put the two "brothers" into the center of the pack by placing them on top of what was the upper packet, and then you place the other packet on top of that. This maneuver automatically brings the four jacks together in the middle of the deck.

Tricks of the Trade

• Your patter is extremely important if the audience is to be distracted from the very simple cheat you are performing. You might even like to plant an accomplice in the audience further to distract their attention – someone who keeps shouting out that they know all about the trick and that they've seen it before and that you are performing the previous trick. This, combined with your feigned innocence, should be sufficient for the real mechanism to go unnoticed.

• If the deception is detected, laugh it off and say you were just performing another demonstration of a well-known trick, in which the thieves fled not to the tower but to the royal gardens . . . and segue into the next trick.

TRIPLE CARD

YOU WILL BE ADMIRED FOR BEING A CLEVER DIVINER OF CARDS IN THIS TRICK, WHICH CAN BE PERFORMED IN CLOSE-UP, WHEN YOU ARE SURROUNDED BY YOUR AUDIENCE. THE TRICK IS ALSO SOMETIMES KNOWN AS THE SPIRITS SPEAK, BECAUSE YOU CAN TELL THE AUDIENCE THAT THE SPIRITS WILL GUIDE THEM IN THEIR SELECTION OF CARDS. IN FACT, THE AUDIENCE SEES YOU SELECT AND NAME THREE CARDS, APPARENTLY TAKEN AT RANDOM FROM A PACK SHUFFLED BY A MEMBER OF THE AUDIENCE.

YOU WILL NEED

PACK OF CARDS

1 Ask a member of the audience to shuffle the pack of cards. When you take the pack back from the spectator, secretly glimpse the bottom card and remember what it is. (For an explanation, say it was the 6 of spades.)

2 Spread the cards over the surface of your table, face down. Although you are apparently spreading them haphazardly, you must be able to locate the 6 of spades, which was at the bottom of the pack.

3 Point to a card (any card), touch its back and say that it is a black card . . . a spade . . . the 6 of spades. Remove this card from the spread and place it to one side, but, before placing it, face down, on your table, secretly glimpse the value of the card.

4 Point to a second card, and divine its value, but this time announce the value of the first card you selected. Place this second card to one side, again making sure that you secretly note its value.

5 Finally, point to a third card, but this time the card you select should be the card that was at the bottom of the pack – in this case, the 6 of spades – but you announce the value of the second card to the audience. Place this card with the other two.

6 Pick up the three cards and display them to the audience to show that they are the three cards that you have just announced.

Tricks of the Trade

• If, by bad luck, the first or second volunteer selects the 6 of spades, display the card at once, saying that this was a demonstration to make sure that the rest of the audience knew what was going on.

• You can repeat this routine as many as five or six times, but always make sure that you select the final card. Remember that the card chosen by the last volunteer from the audience is the one you *say* that you are going to select, but that you, in fact, select the card that you *said* that the first spectator had selected.

HOP FROM THE HAT

THE MAGICIAN, HAVING EXPLAINED TO THE AUDIENCE THAT HE OR SHE HAS ALWAYS HAD A GOOD HEAD FOR CARDS, ASKS A VOLUNTEER TO SELECT A CARD, EXAMINE IT, AND RETURN IT TO THE PACK. THE COMPLETE PACK IS PUT IN A HAT. THE BOTTOM OF THE HAT IS FLICKED, AND THE CHOSEN CARD HOPS UP INTO THE AIR. THE HAT USED IN THIS TRICK MUST BE A TRILBY, OR A VARIETY OF CLOTH HAT WITH A CREASE ALONG THE CROWN, DIVIDING THE INTERIOR INTO TWO SECTIONS.

YOU WILL NEED

PACK OF CARDS

TRILBY HAT

1 Having asked the spectator to select a card, use any technique to identify the selected card and employ the Pass (see page 18) to bring it to the top of the pack.

2 As you drop the deck into the hat, make sure that the chosen card goes into one section, while the bulk of the pack goes into the other.

3 Simply flick or slap the appropriate section from beneath, and the single card will hop out.

Trick of the Trade

● Ideally, the trick should be done with a trilby hat borrowed from a member of the audience, so that all possibilities of fakery are plainly obviated. These days, however, you cannot rely on there being anyone present wearing such a hat, so you should bring one with you. If a friend will bring it, so much the better – but use someone else's hat, in preference to your friend's.

HOP FROM THE DECK

THE MAGICIAN ASKS A MEMBER OF THE AUDIENCE TO SELECT A CARD. IT IS EXAMINED AND PASSED BACK TO THE MAGICIAN, WHO RETURNS IT TO THE PACK. NO SOONER HAS THE MAGICIAN RETURNED TO THE TABLE, HOWEVER, THAN THE CARD JUMPS OUT OF THE DECK. THE MAGICIAN SHRUGS, AND RETURNS TO THE AUDIENCE TO ASK ANOTHER VOLUNTEER TO SELECT AND INSPECT A CARD. THIS, TOO, JUMPS FROM THE DECK – AND THE PROCESS CAN BE REPEATED AS OFTEN AS THE MAGICIAN WISHES. FINALLY, LOSING PATIENCE, THE MAGICIAN PUTS THE CARDS TO ONE SIDE, AND TAKES ANOTHER PACK TO PERFORM THE NEXT TRICK.

YOU WILL NEED

PACK OF CARDS

2 DOCTORED CARDS
(SEE STEP 1)

SHORT LENGTH OF ELASTIC

STAPLES OR CONTACT

1 Take two spare cards from another pack and, between their centers, staple or glue a short piece of elastic. You will have to experiment until you find the right length. It must be short enough that the inserted cards will jump, but not so short that the edges of the cards are damaged when the cards are pushed against it.

2 Place the gimmicked cards about two-thirds or three-quarters of the way toward the bottom of the pack so that you can fan out most of the rest of the deck for the spectator to make a selection without it being too obvious that there is a bunch of cards held together in your left hand.

3 While the spectator inspects the chosen card, casually square up the rest of the deck. It is easy enough to feel the slight gap caused by the elastic.

4 Push the chosen card back into the pack, between the two joined cards, and clutch the deck tightly until you want the chosen card to leap out.

Tricks of the Trade

• To avoid wrecking a good pack of cards, you could use two from an old deck, but do make sure that the patterns on the backs match the pack you are using in case someone catches a glimpse of them as you fan the deck.

• The staples should be in the centers of the cards. Stapling the elastic to their tops may seem tempting – to give a better hop – but it is advisable to get hold of some stronger elastic. A strip from a broad elastic band is good because it will both have the strength and be less likely to cut into the bottoms of the chosen cards.

• You can use this trick as a follow-up from the Hop from the Hat (see page 77) or as a preliminary to Hopscotch from the Deck (see page 79), which also involve the use of a gimmick and therefore a special pack.

HOPSCOTCH FROM THE DECK

THE MAGICIAN GOES AMONG THE AUDIENCE, OFFERING THE FANNED PACK TO THREE VOLUNTEERS AND ASKING EACH TO SELECT A CARD. AS THEY EXAMINE THESE, THE MAGICIAN RETURNS TO THE FRONT OF THE AUDIENCE, SHUFFLING THE PACK. THE CARDS ARE RETURNED TO THE MAGICIAN, WHO INSERTS EACH INTO THE DECK.

THE MAGICIAN GOES TOWARD THE TABLE AND, HOLDING THE DECK IN A FAN, ASKS THE SPECTATORS TO CONCENTRATE ON THE CARDS THEY CHOSE. SLOWLY, ONE BY ONE, THESE RISE FROM THE FAN.

YOU WILL NEED

PACK OF CARDS

BOX (SEE STEP 1)

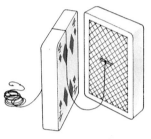

1 This trick involves a quite elaborate gimmick. It is a box, its length and breadth just greater than those of a card and the thickness of six or seven cards. It has a card face stuck to one side of it, and a card back stuck to the other. Its interior is divided into three partitions. Old cards can be used to make the dividers, while the box itself can be constructed of thin card or tin. To the inside of the top center of the box is attached a black thread, at the other end of which is a sharp hook.

2 Offer the fanned cards to the spectators, keeping the box at the bottom of the pack, shielded by a few bunched cards and with the open end toward you. Keep the deck fairly close to your body, with the thread coiled in your hand.

3 As the spectators inspect their cards, give the pack a casual shuffle. This brings the box nearer to the center of the pack and gives you an opportunity to turn the deck around, so that the opening now faces the audience, with the thread running up, over the box's aperture and top of the deck.

5 For a less elaborate gimmick using the same principle, staple the end of a thread to the center of a card, which you retain near the bottom of the deck. Proceed as before, pushing the returned cards into the deck against the thread looped over the ends of the other cards.

4 Push the returned cards into the box in inverse order, with the first above the second above the third. As you return to the table, with your back to the audience, attach the hook to the front of your jacket. Do not fan the deck too broadly as you hold it up. Slowly extend your arm, and the first card will climb up from the rest. As soon as it is about two-thirds of the way out, pluck it from position, gather, and re-fan the cards. Repeat the trick.

Tricks of the Trade

• The advantage of the box over stapling the thread is that you can make the chosen cards arise from the fanned pack. With the simpler gimmick, the pack must be held gathered.

• At the end of the effect, give the cards back to the spectators. This is a pretext for putting the pack to one side, so that you can use a fresh pack for your next trick.

JOKER'S DELIGHT

A VOLUNTEER FROM THE AUDIENCE HELPS THE MAGICIAN WITH A TRICK THAT IS SIMILAR TO FIND THE
LADY, EXCEPT THAT THIS TIME, THEY ARE GOING TO PLAY FIND THE JOKER. THE EFFECT REQUIRES BOTH
A GIMMICK AND A MANUAL DEXTERITY IF THE MAGICIAN IS SUCCESSFULLY TO MAKE THE JOKER VANISH.

YOU WILL NEED

3 CARDS FROM A PACK

JOKER FROM THE SAME PACK
(SEE STEP 1)

CLEAR ADHESIVE TAPE

1 Before your performance,
cut out a thin central section
from a joker and discard it,
leaving yourself with the
card's top and bottom.

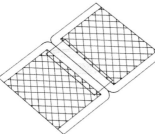

2 Use clear adhesive tape to
fix the top edge of the top
part of the card to the bottom
edge of the lower part of the
card, with the tape on the
wrong side of both pieces
and acting as a kind of hinge.

3 You can now hang the
assembled card over the top
edge of another card, with
part of the joker showing to
the front over the card's own
face.

4 When you perform the
trick, hold the three cards one
above the other and gripped
at the sides. Grip the cards
backhand in your left hand,
with your thumb to the left-
hand side of the packet. The
cards are face on to the
audience, and the dummy
card is in the center so that
from the front it looks as if
that card is a joker.

5 Ask a member of the
audience to help. Tell him or
her to watch the cards very
carefully as you deal them out
on the table. To deal out the
cards, bring your hand down,
so that its back is upward in
front of you. Tap the card
edges quickly on the table to
shove what was the
uppermost card (the back one
of the three) through your
hand level with the rest.

6 Then (again with the back
of your hand upward) pull the
cards one by one from your
hand to lay them on the
table, leaving the assemblage
of half-jokers in your hand.

7 Tell the volunteer to move
the three cards around freely
but to keep an eye on the
joker. Then ask people in the
audience to say where the
joker is, inviting your volunteer
spectator to turn over the
cards as directed by the
audience. No one, of course,
is able to say where the joker
is. While the volunteer is
moving the cards around,
take advantage of this to get
rid of the assemblage as
quickly as you can.

Trick of the Trade

• You might prefer to use
a queen rather than a
joker, so that this really
becomes a case of "Find
the Lady." The point of
using a joker is that you
don't waste a pack of
cards on a single effect.

THE RISING CARDS

THIS IS ONE OF THE CLASSIC TRICKS OF MAGIC AND A VARIATION ON HOPSCOTCH FROM THE DECK.
THREE CHOSEN CARDS RISE FROM THE PACK OF THEIR OWN ACCORD.

YOU WILL NEED

PACK OF CARDS

RAZOR BLADE OR SHARP
KNIFE

BLACK THREAD
(ABOUT 1 YARD)

GLASS TUMBLER THAT WILL
HOLD A PACK OF CARDS

SMALL TRAY

1 Take one of the cards and carefully cut a slit in one end of it, using a razor blade or sharp knife. Push one end of the thread through the slits and tie a series of firm knots in the end.

2 Place one card face down on your table and the prepared card face down on top of it. The slit in the prepared card should be facing toward the back of the table. The thread hangs down from the card onto the floor. The tumbler and the rest of the pack are in front of the face-down cards.

3 When you are ready to do the trick, pick up the pack and shuffle the cards. Ask three spectators to take one card each. They keep their cards, while you return to your table. Place the pack down on top of the two cards already there.

4 Pick up the glass and show it to the audience. Put the glass back on the table and pick up the pack. Place the pack in the glass in such a way that the thread runs from the front of the pack, across the top of the cards, and then down to the floor.

5 Collect the chosen cards on the tray and place them, one by one, into the pack. This action pushes the thread down to the bottom of the pack of cards.

6 Place your foot on the thread on the floor (it may help to stick a small pellet of paper to the end of the thread to enable you to spot it easily). Lift up the glass and ask for the names of the three cards. As the glass is raised, the thread is made taut and the card will rise from the pack one by one.

ELIMINATION

MAGICIANS HAVE BEEN USING ELIMINATION METHODS FOR MANY YEARS. IN THIS TRICK, ELIMINATION
IS USED TO RESTRICT A SPECTATOR'S SUPPOSEDLY FREE CHOICE. IN ORDER TO CARRY THIS TRICK OFF
SUCCESSFULLY, THE MAGICIAN NEEDS PRACTICE AND THE ABILITY TO THINK CLEARLY AND QUICKLY.

YOU WILL NEED

PLAYING CARD

ENVELOPE

1 Display the back of the card to the audience and seal it inside the envelope (for the purposes of this trick, let the selected card be the 3 of diamonds.) Hand the sealed envelope to a spectator to take charge of until the experiment is over.

2 Recruit the help of a second member of the audience and begin to involve them in a conversation. The aim is to make it appear as if you are asking questions, but in fact, as you will quickly realize, you are twisting the spectator's responses. The first question is: "Think of one of the colors – black or red?" If the spectator chooses red, all is well, for that is the color of the card in the envelope. But if the chosen color is black, you will then have to say: "That leaves us with red."

3 The second question is: "A picture or a plain card?" If the spectator chooses plain, all is well. But if the spectator selects a picture, you will then have to say: "That leaves us with plain."

4 Continue with your questions: "Red was chosen – please mention one of the two suits, hearts or diamonds." If the spectator chooses diamonds, all is well. If hearts are chosen, you will have to say: "Well, that leaves us with diamonds."

5 Your next question is: "Now, do you want high or low numbers?" If low numbers are chosen, you say: "Between ace and four, but because the ace doesn't count, we are left with two or three." If the spectator chooses three, all is well, but if four is selected, you will have to say: "That leaves us with three." If the spectator selects high numbers, you again eliminate the choice, by saying: "That leaves us with the low numbers." Whatever the spectator replies, this method always enables you to arrive at the card you have first selected – apparently having allowed the spectator to divine the card for him or herself.

ODDLY EVEN

THIS IS AN IDEAL OPENING TRICK FOR A ROUTINE TO BE PERFORMED IN FRONT OF SMALL CHILDREN.
MOST ADULTS WILL REALIZE THAT YOU MADE SURE THAT YOU PICKED UP AN ODD NUMBER OF CARDS.
EVEN AMONG CHILDREN, THERE IS A CHANCE THAT SOMEONE WILL SPOT THE TRICK. EXPLAIN WHAT YOU
HAVE DONE – AT THE END OF YOUR EXPLANATION, YOU CAN SAY: "THAT WAS OBVIOUS – IT WAS JUST A
TRICK, WITH NO MAGIC. BUT THE OTHER TRICKS I'M GOING TO PERFORM, REALLY DO NEED MAGIC."

YOU WILL NEED

PACK OF CARDS

1 Spread out the pack of cards on the table and ask a member of the audience to select a bunch at random, but not looking at what he or she is doing. The magician asks the spectator to take away these cards to a corner of the stage and to count them.

2 While the cards are being counted, you should scoop up a handful in as casual a fashion as you can manage.

3 Tell the volunteer that, if he or she has an odd number of cards, you will make them even by adding the cards you have in your hand. If the volunteer has an even number of cards you will make them odd by adding the cards you have in your hand.

4 Ask your helper to count out the cards in the packet he or she has selected, then pass over your own cards and ask that all the cards be recounted. The new total will, naturally, be as you predicted.

Tricks of the Trade

• The one person who almost certainly won't realize the principle straightway is your volunteer. Resist all temptations to tease him or her. It would be all too easy to humiliate your helper. Instead, say something like: "It fooled me, too, the first time I saw it."

• Practice scooping up cards so that it is not obvious that you are counting as you do so.

NOT IN THE CLUB

THE MAGICIAN EXPLAINS THAT THE SUIT OF CLUBS DERIVED ITS NAME NOT FROM ANYTHING TO DO
WITH WEAPONRY, OR FROM ONE OF THE SUITS OF THE TAROT PACK, BUT FROM THE FACT THAT THE
CARDS ARE EXTREMELY CLUBBY, BUT, LIKE THE MEMBERS OF A GENTLEMAN'S CLUB, THERE ARE STRICT
RULES ABOUT WHICH CARDS ARE ADMITTED AND THAT ANYONE OF THE WRONG SUIT THAT TRIES TO
JOIN IS BLACKBALLED.

YOU WILL NEED

PACK OF CARDS (SEE STEP 1)

BLINDFOLD

1 Before the performance, prepare the clubs in the pack of cards by gently rounding down the four corners of all 13 club cards with very fine sandpaper. Although the discrepancy will go unnoticed when the cards are used in the normal way, it will be easy to detect any single card in a packet whose corners have not been rounded. Take off a tiny amount, find out if that is enough, then sand off a little more if necessary, and so on.

2 Separate the clubs from the remainder of the pack and pass the two separate packets to a spectator. Ask the spectator to select any card from the main pack and to shuffle it into the clubs.

3 While the first spectator shuffles the cards, ask another member of the audience to blindfold you.

4 When the first spectator gives you the shuffled cards, you will easily be able to identify the intruding card.

Trick of the Trade

• Once you have performed the basic trick a couple of times, vary things. Ask the volunteer sometimes to give you an unadulterated packet of clubs, sometimes to put one "intruder" into the packet, without telling you which he is doing.

4 ◆

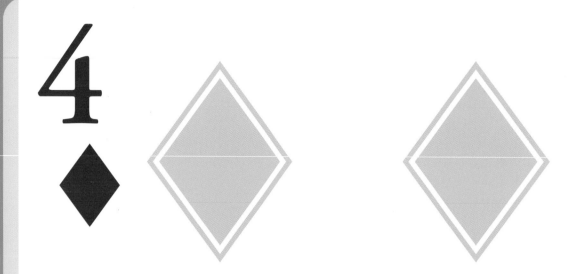

MORE AMAZING CARDS

THIS CHAPTER NEATLY FOLLOWS

ON FROM THE PREVIOUS CHAPTERS AS IT USES

ALL THE TECHNIQUES THAT HAVE ALREADY BEEN MASTERED

FOR EXAMPLE, "FIND YOUR OWN CARD" CAN ALSO BE A

technique for forcing cards. All these tricks can be combined

with the others to produce a very entertaining performance.

★ ★ ★

SHOTGUN MARRIAGE

The magician asks a volunteer to select a card, which proves to be the queen of spades. Becoming whimsical, the magician explains how, long after the other three kings had married the appropriate partners, the king of spades remained unwed, because he had set his heart on the princess of a foreign land, but her father refused his consent to the marriage. How the two came, in the end, to wed, so that she became the queen of spades, is not something that the magician wishes to discuss in what is, after all, intended to be a family show. So . . . on with the trick.

YOU WILL NEED

PACK OF CARDS

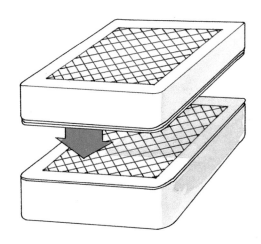

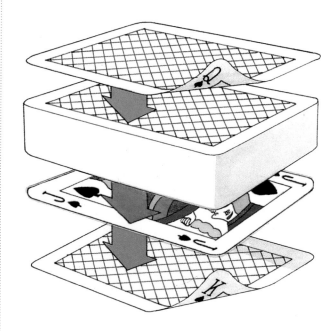

4 Fan out the cards, still face down, and at once discover that one of them – the jack of spades – is face up. Tutting to yourself, pull out this card from the rest, accidentally pulling out the one beneath it as you do so. You pick this up, and it proves to be the king of spades.

5 You say that this turn of events reminds you of the legend of how the king and queen of spades eventually married, and as you speak, you pull out the next card as well, which is, of course, the queen of spades. That was the trouble, you remark, as you gather up the pack ready for the next trick, the jack always came first.

1 Before your performance, have the jack face up at the second-bottom of the pack, the king face down at the bottom, and the queen face down at the top. Shuffle the pack assiduously, but keeping these three cards in position.

2 Force the queen on the volunteer, using the Riffle Force (see page 43). Then shuffle again, still keeping the jack and king in their places.

3 Place the pack face down on your table and ask a member of the audience to cut it anywhere he or she wishes. Insert the chosen card (the queen of spades) and complete the cut.

Trick of the Trade

• The mechanism of this trick is very simple, and it would not take an audience too long to figure it out, were it not for your patter and for the fact that the effect seems to be happening against your will. Practice the patter to make sure you give it the right blend of fluency and impromptu.

MYSTIC FIVE

A MEMBER OF YOUR AUDIENCE SELECTS A CARD FROM THE PACK, NOTES ITS NUMBER AND SUIT, THEN REPLACES IT ON TOP OF THE PACK. THE PACK IS CUT. THE MAGICIAN EXPLAINS THAT ONE CARD WILL MAGICALLY REVERSE ITSELF IN THE PACK AND THAT ITS VALUE WILL DENOTE THE POSITION OF THE CHOSEN CARD. WHEN THE PACK IS FANNED, A CARD – THE 5 OF HEARTS, FOR EXAMPLE – IS SEEN TO BE REVERSED. AND, BELIEVE IT OR NOT, THE FIFTH CARD TO FOLLOW IT IS THE ONE THAT HAS BEEN SELECTED.

YOU WILL NEED

PACK OF CARDS

1 Before you begin your act, remove a five-spot card from the pack, reverse it, and replace it so that it becomes the fifth card from the bottom of the pack.

2 When you begin your performance, fan the cards, making sure that the audience is not aware that one of the cards has been reversed.

3 Ask a spectator to select a card and then to return it to the top of the pack.

4 Make a complete cut of the cards, which will bring the reversed card toward the center of the pack.

5 Fan the pack to show the reversed card, then state that the value of the reversed card will indicate the exact position of the selected card.

6 Withdraw the reversed card and count along five cards from it – and the fifth card will automatically be the one chosen by the spectator.

Five-spot card

Bottom

Top

The set up for Mystic Five shows the correct positioning of the five-spot card.

QUICK STUDY

BOASTING IDLY OF YOUR TELEPATHIC POWERS, YOU FAN OUT THE CARDS, FACE UP, TOWARD A VOLUNTEER, CUT THEM, RIFFLE THE DECK A FEW TIMES, AND THEN ASK THE SPECTATOR TO STOP YOU SOMEWHERE MID-RIFFLE AND REMOVE THE CARD THUS RANDOMLY SELECTED. HAVING EXAMINED IT, THE SPECTATOR SHOULD PUT THE CARD IN A POCKET. CUT THE DECK AGAIN, CONCENTRATE FOR A MOMENT OR TWO, THEN REVEAL THE VALUE AND SUIT OF THE CARD.

YOU WILL NEED

PACK OF CARDS

1 Although the cards appear to be in random order, the deck is stacked. One simple way of doing this is first to have the face-up cards running from the top downward in suit order, with a spade followed by a heart followed by a club followed by a diamond followed by the next spade, and so on. Note the alternating colors. The numerical order, on the other hand, increases by the count of three each time. The net result of these orderings if that, for example, a sequence within the deck might run 5 of spades, 8 of hearts, jack of clubs, ace of diamonds, 4 of spades. Cutting the deck does not affect the ordering.

2 Ask a member of the audience to take a card, then cut the pack at this point and get a glimpse of the new bottom card. This card was the one immediately behind the card that has been removed, so you can quickly work out what card must have been taken. For example, if you see the 4 of spades, you know that the missing card is the 7 of hearts; if you see the 10 of clubs, you know that the missing card is the king of diamonds; and so on.

Trick of the Trade

• This is a very easy way of stacking a deck, and it can be used in lots of other tricks. But there is no need to stick to this principle; try inventing a few different ways of stacking the deck to gain the same result and settle on any that might personally suit you.

CARD THROUGH A HANDKERCHIEF

A CARD IS SELECTED AND RETURNED TO THE CENTER OF THE PACK. THE CARDS ARE THEN SHUFFLED BEFORE BEING WRAPPED IN A HANDKERCHIEF. WHEN THE HANDKERCHIEF IS SHAKEN, ONE CARD PENETRATES THROUGH THE FABRIC – IT IS THE SELECTED CARD.

YOU WILL NEED

PACK OF CARDS

HANDKERCHIEF

① Have a member of your audience select a card and return it to the pack. Secretly bring the chosen card to the top of the pack as described in Card Control (see page 56).

③ Grasp the edge of the handkerchief that is nearest to your body and gently lift it up and forward so that it covers the pack.

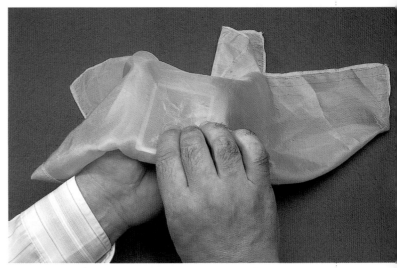

② Hold the pack in your left hand and drape the handkerchief over it. The moment the pack is covered, your right hand reaches beneath the handkerchief, retrieves the pack, and places it on top of the fabric. Unbeknownst to the audience, the top card has been left behind, resting on the palm of your left hand.

④ Now, with your right hand, take the pack between your finger and thumb, holding it firmly through the handkerchief.

5 The selected card remains hidden beneath the fabric, firmly held in position by your right thumb.

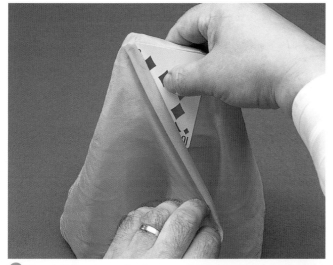

6 Your left hand now firmly takes the left edge of the handkerchief and wraps the fabric backward and around the rear of the pack.

7 Transfer the pack (together with the hidden card) to your left hand, still holding it through the fabric. This leaves your right hand free to drape the right side of the fabric back and around the pack.

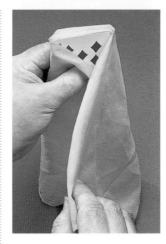

8 Take all the fabric that is hanging beneath the pack, and twist it around several times. The pack is now completely enclosed by the fabric and the selected card is held in a pocket formed by the way the pack is wrapped. Move your right hand upward and your left hand down, then remove your left hand.

9 Ask the spectator to name the selected card, and then begin shaking your right hand. The selected card will gradually come into view, and it appears to be penetrating the fabric.

Trick of the Trade

- You can borrow a handkerchief from the audience if you like, but this is always a bit of a gamble – especially if your audience are children. You need a handkerchief that is opaque, clean, and large enough, so it is best to resist the temptation of gaining an added effect by borrowing one.

JACKS WILD

THE MAGICIAN ASKS FOR A MEMBER OF THE AUDIENCE TO REMOVE THE FOUR JACKS FROM A FULL

PACK AND TO ARRANGE THEM IN ALTERNATING COLORS – RED, BLACK, RED, BLACK. TAKING THE FOUR

CARDS, THE MAGICIAN COUNTS THEM TO MAKE SURE THERE IS NO ERROR AND THEN LAYS THEM OUT

ON THE TABLE. THE SPECTATOR IS THEN ASKED TO PICK OUT TWO JACKS OF THE SAME COLOR –

SURELY A SIMPLE ENOUGH TASK – YET IT PROVES IMPOSSIBLE.

YOU WILL NEED

PACK OF CARDS

1 The trick lies in the apparently simple act of counting the four cards. Normally, you would do this by holding the four face-down cards in, say, the left hand, thumbing the next card onto the top of this one, and so on. This procedure reverses the order of the cards but obviously does not affect the alternation of colors. This action is what you must be seen to be doing.

2 In fact, count the first two cards in the normal way, except that you should hold the cards between the thumb and fingertips of your left hand rather than, more conventionally, further back in your hand.

3 As your right thumb moves to take the third card, you slip the two cards in your right hand and place under the two in your left hand.

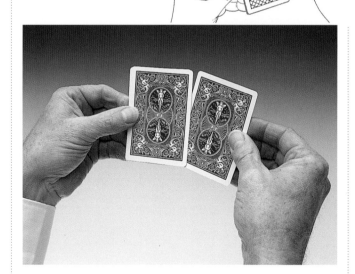

4 Then thumb away not a single card but the top three from the packet of four. Finally, thumb the fourth card in the normal way from your left hand to the top of the three-card packet now in your right hand.

5 The result of your maneuver is that the colors of the four jacks have now become paired, rather than alternating. The trick will seem clumsy at first, but with a little practice you will be able to perform it as swiftly as executing a conventional count.

Trick of the Trade

● You can, if you like, draw attention to the count and thus increase the illusion. When you take the cards, count them normally, keeping them face up. Whether or not the spectator shows any interest in this, josh him or her: "Oh, you're a bit worried about that, are you?" Repeat the count several times in front of the volunteer, still with the cards face up, starting with exaggerated slowness and then increasing to normal speed. Your point amply demonstrated – that the colors still alternate – you are halfway through the final count as you begin to turn toward your table. It is this final count, that is the false one.

POKER CHAMP

THIS IS ANOTHER TRICK THAT WILL MORE OR LESS WORK ITSELF IF YOU PREPARE THE CARDS
CAREFULLY BEFOREHAND AND KEEP UP THE MOMENTUM BY RECOUNTING AN ENTERTAINING STORY.

YOU WILL NEED

PACK OF CARDS

---

1 Announce that you are going to tell the story of how your great-grandfather met his death. He was playing poker in the Te Deum Club with three friends. As you say this, deal out four hands from the top of the pack.

2 Your great-grandfather, you say, easily won the first hand. You turn up the first hand and reveal four 7s. You turn the hand face down again, and then, in turn, show the other three hands, none of which contains anything very special.

3 One of your great-grandfather's friends dropped out of the game, you say. Here, you discard the winning hand and collect up the other three. But, you continue, the three "survivors" played on, and here you deal out three hands from the cards you have just gathered up.

4 Again, you say, your great-grandfather won, and you turn up his hand to demonstrate his winning cards – four aces. Show the other two hands, which, as before, do not contain anything very spectacular.

5 Another member of the group dropped out, leaving just two of them. As you say this, discard the winning hand and gather up the remaining cards. Deal out two fresh hands from these cards.

6 This third time your great-grandfather's win was too much for the credulity of the other members of the Te Deum Club. You turn up the hand and show that this time he had a straight five-flush of spades, from nine through king. He was given, you say sadly, a revolver and told to go off to the library and Do the Decent Thing. That's how he met his end.

7 Your great-grandfather, of course, had rigged the top 20 cards of the pack, from the top down, as follows: ace, any, king of spades, 7, any, ace, any, 7, 9 of spades, any, ace, 7, ace, queen of spades, any, 7, 10 of spades, any, jack of spades, any. This arrangement will give the desired effect if you pick up the used hands correctly. Each should be placed face down after being shown, and for the next deal, you should pick up first the hand to your right, place it on top of the hand to its right, and so on.

Tricks of the Trade

- You can shuffle the cards a little before starting the trick, taking care not to disturb the packet of cards at the top of the pack.

- Experiment a little beforehand with the cards identified as "any" – you don't want to give one of the other hands in the first deal something better than four 7s, but, at the same time, it shouldn't be obvious that all the other cards are garbage.

FIND YOUR OWN CARD

THE PRINCIPLE OF THIS TRICK CAN COME IN USEFUL IN OTHER EFFECTS, AND IT CAN ALSO BE USED AS A WAY OF FORCING CARDS. A MEMBER OF THE AUDIENCE SELECTS A CARD, WHICH IS RETURNED TO THE PACK. AS THE MAGICIAN DEALS OUT THE CARDS, THE SPECTATOR SAYS "STOP" WHENEVER HE OR SHE WISHES – AND THE NEXT CARD TO BE TURNED UP IS THE SELECTED CARD.

YOU WILL NEED

PACK OF CARDS

1 Ask a member of the audience to select a card, examine it, and return it to the pack. Move this card to the bottom of the pack by whatever means you wish.

2 After briefly shuffling the pack, keeping the selected card at the bottom, you deal out the cards face down from the bottom of the face-down pack, asking the volunteer to stop you at any time. Hold the pack face down and tilted slightly toward the spectator. Your grip should be overhand, with your fingers and thumb wrapping around the cards so that the tips of your fingers make a good friction contact with the bottom card. Slide this card an inch or so back toward your wrist while you quite naturally deal out the cards from above one by one.

3 When the spectator does stop you, the next card you deal, you turn face up, and it is, of course, the chosen card, which you have simply eased forward from under the pack and dealt as the next card.

Trick of the Trade

● You may find it easier to deal the cards "wrong handed" – that is, if you would normally hold the pack in your left hand and deal the cards with your right hand, for this effect you might try holding the pack with your right hand and dealing with your left. It all depends on how strongly "handed" you are to the right or left.

FULL FRONTAL

THE MAGICIAN INVOLVES A MEMBER OF THE AUDIENCE IN CUTTING THE PACK, BUT EVEN SO IS ABLE
TO FIND THE CHOSEN CARD.

Trick of the Trade

● Of course, you run the risk that the dummy card – say the 3 of spades – may be close to the 3 of spades belonging to the main pack, a coincidence that would make the deception obvious as you fanned the cards. It may be that the spectator's chosen card was the 3 of spades! You should, therefore, use both hands when fanning the cards, which will look natural enough, because you are fanning the full pack and do not want to drop any cards. If you are holding the base of the pack with your right hand, use the fingers of your left hand at the top of the pack to help fan the cards. Spread the cards quite slowly, and as soon as you notice the dummy card emerging from the bunched cards, let a fingertip drop behind the cards to push the dummy in the opposite direction from that in which you are fanning.

YOU WILL NEED

PACK OF CARDS

DUMMY CARD FROM A PACK
WITH A DIFFERENT BACK BUT
THE SAME STYLE FACE

1 Before the performance make sure that you have in a jacket pocket a card from a separate pack. From the front it must resemble in every way the style of your main pack, but the design on the back must make it easily distinguishable.

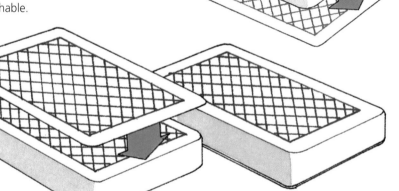

2 Ask a member of the audience to take a card, then shuffle and cut the rest of the pack thoroughly. Palm the face-down dummy card from your pocket (see page 20) into your right hand. Put the residue of the pack on the palm of your outstretched right hand.

3 Ask the spectator to take the top part of the pack from you and to shuffle the cards in this packet before placing them, face down, on the palm of your outstretched left hand. At this point, the spectator should be asked to place the chosen card on top of this packet – that is, the one on your left hand. The dummy card is still, at this point, at the bottom of the packet on your right hand.

4 Now ask the spectator to place the packet that is resting on your right hand on top of the packet on your left hand – in effect, the spectator is completing the cut by transferring the stack from your right to your left hand.

5 Take the cards and fan them, face out, toward the audience, then draw the chosen card from its position in the fan. It is next to the dummy card, which enables you to locate it instantly.

SIMON SAYS

THE MAGICIAN REMINDS THE AUDIENCE OF THE TRADITIONAL CHILDREN'S GAME SIMON SAYS. A
VOLUNTEER REPEATS ALL THE MAGICIAN'S MOVEMENTS, CUTTING AND SHUFFLING A PACK OF CARDS,
AND EVENTUALLY SELECTS THE SAME CARD AS THE MAGICIAN.

YOU WILL NEED

2 PACKS OF CARDS

1 Give a member of the audience one pack of cards and produce another for yourself, which you start to shuffle. Encourage your volunteer to shuffle the cards, by saying, "Simon says shuffle the cards." Use the Hindoo Shuffle (page 17) yourself, and when the volunteer finds this difficult, apologize, saying, "Simon says sorry." Then sit down at your table. The volunteer does likewise. Cut and shuffle the cards a few times. While you are shuffling your pack, notice that the bottom card is, say, the ace of clubs.

2 Exchange packs of cards with the volunteer. Take a card from the middle of the new deck and make a great show of memorizing it, although you do not say what it is. Encourage your volunteer to do the same. Place your chosen card on top

of the pack and cut it to the center. The volunteer does the same. The effect of the volunteer's cutting the pack is to place the ace of clubs directly over the chosen card.

3 Swap packs again, and cut the packs a few time, the volunteer copying your actions. The additional cutting does not affect the order of the cards. Suddenly say, "I wonder if you really did do as Simon says." Turn up your card and pull out one of them – the jack of diamonds for example. Show it to the audience but not to the volunteer. When the volunteer does likewise, the chosen card is, also, the jack of diamonds. You know, of course, that the volunteer's chosen card was the one that was next to the ace of clubs in your pack, no matter where it was in the pack the volunteer was using.

Trick of the Trade

● It is tempting to add all sorts of crazy routines to the basic tricks so that the volunteer ends up making a fool of him or herself attempting to imitate your funny faces and silly stances. However, unless you are performing this trick in front of children, the best effect is usually gained by keeping things simple. The surprise at the end is greater because you have not created so much distraction that the audience thinks that, somewhere in the middle of it all, you must have cheated.

UNFAIR DEAL

THE MAGICIAN MANAGES TO IDENTIFY A CARD SELECTED BY A MEMBER OF THE AUDIENCE, EVEN THOUGH THE CARDS HAVE BEEN DEALT OUT AND RE-GATHERED WHILE THE MAGICIAN'S BACK WAS TURNED.

YOU WILL NEED

PACK OF CARDS

1 Before the performance, set all the 5s as the top four cards of the pack and all the 8s as the bottom four cards of the pack. Practice shuffling so that these eight cards are kept in position.

2 Fan the cards face down and ask a member of the audience to take any card from the pack. While the volunteer is examining the chosen card, you deal out the remaining cards face down in four equal heaps (almost equal: one heap will be one card short, but that is irrelevant).

3 Turn your back on the table and ask the volunteer to place the chosen card on one of the heaps, then to pile the four heaps on top of each other and hand them back to you.

4 As you turn back to the table, fanning out the cards, you immediately pull the selected card from the fan.

5 The secret is, of course, that once the cards have been dealt into four heaps in step 2, each heap will have an 8 on the bottom and a 5 on the top. When you fan out the cards, the selected card will be immediately obvious to you – it will be the only card in the pack to lie between a 5 and an 8.

Trick of the Trade

• You need not choose 5s and 8s – any two numbers will do. Avoid using court cards, however, because a sequence of paired kings and queens throughout the pack will look much more obvious when the cards are fanned out than pairings of nondescript values like 8s and 5s.

UNEXPECTED THIEF

THE MEMBERS OF THE AUDIENCE ARE GIVEN EQUAL NUMBERS OF CARDS, BUT WHEN THE CARDS ARE
RECOUNTED, ONE SPECTATOR IS FOUND TO HAVE LOST ONE. THE MAGICIAN IS NOT TO BLAME – THE
MISSING CARD IS FOUND IN THE OTHER SPECTATOR'S POCKET.

YOU WILL NEED

PACK OF CARDS

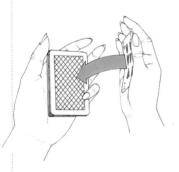

1 Call for two members of
the audience to help you and
ask one to stand on each side
of you. Give volunteer A the
pack of cards and ask him or
her to count out 10 cards
onto your extended left hand.
Tuck this packet of 10 cards
into the spectator's front
jacket pocket and take back
the remaining cards. The
deception is simply the
palming of a card (see page
20). Before you hand the
pack to volunteer A, palm the
top card into your right hand.

2 Transfer the counted
cards from your left hand to
your right hand, carefully
adding the extra one as you
put the packet into volunteer
A's pocket.

3 Turn to volunteer B and
repeat the process of
counting out 10 cards. Once
volunteer B has counted the
cards, again transfer them
from left hand to the right
before giving them back, this
time, palming off one of the
cards from the packet as you
put it in his or her pocket.
Receive the pack from
volunteer B with your left
hand, and immediately
transfer it to your right hand.

4 Ask both volunteers if
they are confident that they
have indeed got 10 cards,
turning to volunteer B and
saying that he or she looks
particularly uncertain. It
might, therefore, you say be a
good idea if the cards are
counted. Volunteer B counts
out the packet and finds only
9 cards. You say something
like: "I suppose you think I
took it, don't you?"

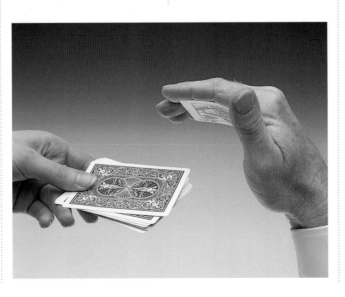

5 To prove your innocence,
count out the remaining
cards to show that there are,
in fact, 32 cards – as there
should be.

6 Point accusingly at
volunteer A and say: "It was
you, wasn't it?" Sure enough,
volunteer A is found to have
11 cards.

Trick of the Trade

• The second act of
palming is the one in
which you are most likely
to be caught out. Use
distraction. Start as if you
are going to tuck the
packet of cards into the
volunteer B's pocket as
you did with volunteer A,
saying something like,
"Oh, you're grown up
enough to do this for
yourself," as you transfer
the packet back from your
right to your left hand to
give to the volunteer. In
almost the same
movement, take the fake
deck from the volunteer's
free hand rather than wait
to be offered – this should
startle the spectator so
much that the other
things that are going on
won't be noticed.

BOXING BACK

A CARD SELECTED BY A MEMBER OF THE AUDIENCE IS NOT ONLY DIVINED BY THE MAGICIAN BUT ALSO
APPEARS IN THE CARD BOX FACE DOWN AMID THE OTHER FACE-UP CARDS OF THE PACK.

YOU WILL NEED

PACK OF CARDS

1 EXTRA CARD

CARD BOX

SILK HANDKERCHIEF

1 The trick involves the use of shaved cards. Before your performance, place the pack in a vice or similar, and prepare the cards by trimming off the long edges at a slight angle with a craft knife or sandpaper. The cards should taper, being wider at one end than the other. You need to include one extra, identical card in this pack.

2 At the beginning of the trick, the cards should all lie the same way. Pull the deck from its box and offer the fanned cards to a member of the audience, asking the spectator to pick one card. The chosen card – say, the 7 of hearts – is returned to the pack, but as the selected card is replaced, turn the deck so that the corners of the chosen card protrude from the rest of the cards. The pack is then shuffled and returned to the box in this same direction – that is, with the wider edge of the chosen card entering the box first.

3 Place the box under a handkerchief. Pause for a moment, saying: "I want you to be absolutely certain that there's no trickery involved here – just magic." Retrieve the box from under the handkerchief, and pull out the face-down pack. When you remove the pack this first time, grip the box between your thumb and first finger so that the selected card is retained in the box as the others are pulled out. If you have longish fingernails, you can wrap those of the thumb and first finger over the edges of the opening to trap the chosen card.

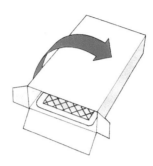

4 Turn the "empty" box over as you put it down so that the chosen card is now face up.

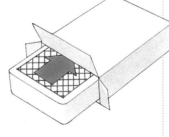

5 Ask the volunteer to count the cards to make sure they are all there. The volunteer's count comes to 52 because you had 53 cards in the pack originally. Once everyone is satisfied that there are 52 cards there, take the pack and return it to the box once more. This time when you return the pack, face down, to the box, glimpse the chosen card, which is face up, and make sure that it is pushed somewhere into the middle of the pack.

6 Put the box under the handkerchief. Guess that the chosen card was 6 of diamonds. "No," the spectator replies. "It was the . . ." But you stop the volunteer from revealing the selected card. Instead, you say, "Let's try this again." Reach for the box, but just before you remove the handkerchief say: "What I meant to say was the 7 of hearts." Pull the pack from the box and spread out the cards face down to show that the 7 of hearts is the only one that is face up among them.

Trick of the Trade

- You may find difficulty in retaining the chosen card in the box while you are drawing the others out. You can make this maneuver easier to accomplish if you doctor the box to reduce the thickness of the cardboard at its sides. Use a sharp craft knife to open out the box and carefully reduce the thickness of the side flaps until they are paper thin. Glue the box back together again. Take great care not to collapse the sides when you grip them firmly to hold the chosen card in place.

SHORT SHRIFT

EVEN WHEN THE MAGICIAN IS BLINDFOLDED, THE CHOSEN CARD IS STILL FOUND IN THE PACK, WHICH THE SPECTATOR HAS CUT AND CUT AGAIN. THE TRICK, IN FACT, DEPENDS ON THE USE OF A GIMMICK: A SHORT CARD – THAT IS, ONE THAT HAS BEEN FRACTIONALLY SHAVED AT EACH END – OR A THICK CARD.

YOU WILL NEED

PACK OF CARDS

EXTRA CARD (SEE STEP 1)

BLINDFOLD

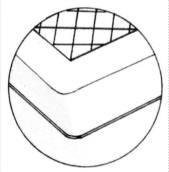

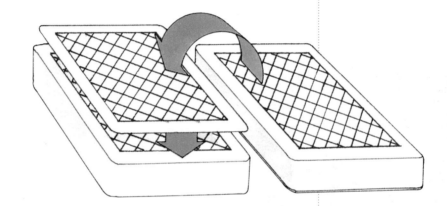

1 Before the performance, prepare the short card. In normal use, such a card, or a thick card, is indistinguishable from the other cards in the pack. But when the pack is squared up, the shortfall can be easily detected – if you are feeling for it.

2 At the beginning of the trick, have the short or thick card at the bottom of the pack and keep it there as you shuffle. Ask a member of the audience to select any card from the pack and to examine it.

3 Tell the spectator to put the card on the top of the pack, which you immediately cut, so that the chosen card is somewhere in the middle. The effect of the first cut is to put the faked card directly over the selected one, and this relationship will remain, no matter how often the pack is cut.

4 "You could do that as well as me," you say, inviting the spectator to cut the pack a couple of times. Then ask the spectator to blindfold you as securely as possible. Once you are blindfolded, suggest that the spectator cuts the pack once or twice more.

5 Ask the spectator to hand the pack to you. Make sure that the pack is well squared up on the table in front of you, riffle the ends once or twice (see page 17), and pull out the chosen card.

Tricks of the Trade

● Short cards and thick cards can be handy for other tricks. For short cards, experiment to find out exactly how little you can shave off a card yet still be able easily to find it in the pack.

● A thick card, easily made by gluing an old card to the back of one of the cards in the pack you intend to use, does not have the advantage of being usable for other purposes.

● Be aware that either type of gimmicked card makes a distinct "click" when you riffle the pack.

TEARING A LADY IN HALF

THE MAGICIAN REMOVES THE QUEEN OF SPADES FROM THE PACK, HOLDS UP THE CARD, AND
ANNOUNCES THAT THE AUDIENCE IS ABOUT TO WITNESS A NOVEL VERSION OF THAT CLASSIC TRICK,
SAWING A LADY IN HALF. JUST LIKE THE MAGICIANS WHO RESTORE THE LADY, THE MAGICIAN WILL
RESTORE THE CARD TO ITS ORIGINAL FORM.

YOU WILL NEED

PACK OF CARDS

DUPLICATE QUEEN OF HEARTS
FROM AN IDENTICAL PACK

HANDKERCHIEF

1 Before you begin, place the second queen, folding it up within the handkerchief, into your top pocket.

2 Remove the queen of hearts from the pack, hold it up to the audience, and tear it in half. Put the two halves, one over the other, and tear them again. Your patter can be to the effect that you are actually tearing the lady into quarters. Hold up all four quarters in one hand, say your left hand, for everyone to see.

3 Pull a folded handkerchief from your top jacket pocket with your other hand and drape it over your left hand. Grip the duplicate card between your fingertips and thumb, holding the card through the cloth, as you shake out the handkerchief. Distract the audience by reminding them that the difficult part of the original trick was not the actual sawing of the lady in half – anyone can do that – the difficult bit is restoring her afterward. The action of shaking out the handkerchief and draping it over your left hand allows you to deposit the whole, duplicate card on top of the torn pieces. Your continued patter allows you to use the thumb and fingers of your left hand, which are now hidden by the handkerchief, to edge the whole card toward the thumb side of that hand, the torn pieces toward the facing side. The aim is to end up with the whole card lying like a bridge across the gap between your thumb and first two fingers.

4 Now, whip away the handkerchief to reveal the restored queen of hearts. Do this quickly and take with the handkerchief the four fragments. Tuck the handkerchief loosely into a side pocket, out of the way, dropping the fragments into that pocket as you do so, ostensibly so that you can use both hands to hold up the restored card.

5 Hand around the card for inspection, and then, as if on an afterthought, pull out the handkerchief so that it can be examined as well.

Trick of the Trade

• If you are concerned that tucking a handkerchief into your pocket might seem too obvious, or that the audience might demand to examine the pocket as well, when you pick up the fragments, make sure that you hold them between your thumb and fingertips near the hem of the handkerchief. Retain both the handkerchief and the fragments in your right hand. Give out the card for examination, then, to give out the handkerchief, pull it from your right hand with the left. You can then ditch the fragments.

TWISTING CARD

A CARD CHOSEN BY A SPECTATOR AND THREADED, WITH THE REMAINDER OF THE PACK, ON A LENGTH
OF RIBBON DESCENDS MAGICALLY, SUSPENDED ON THE RIBBON, TO HANG BENEATH THE REST OF THE
PACK. THE TRICK INVOLVES THE USE OF A GIMMICK, BUT IS SPECTACULAR FOR ALL THAT.

YOU WILL NEED

PACK OF CARDS THROUGH ONE
END OF WHICH A HOLE HAS
BEEN PUNCHED

DOCTORED CARD (SEE STEP 1)

LENGTH OF RIBBON

BLINDFOLD

---

1 Before the performance, take a card from an identical pack – in this instance the 6 of spades – and shave off the opposite end from the hole (see Short Shrift on page 98).

2 Produce the deck of cards with the hole punched through one end and ask a volunteer to choose a card and return it to the pack. Use any of the forcing techniques (see pages 40–52) to make sure that the selected card is, say, the 6 of spades. While the spectator is examining the chosen card, palm the top card of the deck (see page 20) and surreptitiously turn the deck over, returning the palmed card face down to the top of the now face-up deck.

3 Splay the deck a little as you offer it to the volunteer so that the chosen card can be returned. Shuffle the cards, but keeping the top card in place, and go to your table. At this point, again palm off the reversed top card and unobtrusively dump it or reverse it.

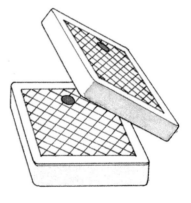

4 Cut the deck casually at the point indicated by the short card, because it is easier to thread the ribbon through two halves rather than the whole pack at once. Pick up the length of ribbon and pass it to the spectator to inspect.

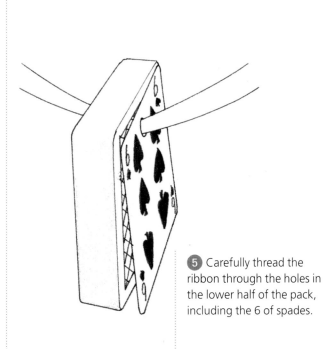

5 Carefully thread the ribbon through the holes in the lower half of the pack, including the 6 of spades.

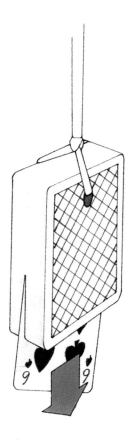

7 Put the knot of the ribbon in the spectator's hand, letting the pack hang beneath. Say to the blindfolded volunteer: "You know what your card is, but can't see it; it's about time you let the rest of us see it, even though we don't know what it is." Ask the volunteer to give the ribbon a jerk, and one card is found to have reversed itself in the deck. When the blindfold is removed, the volunteer confirms that this is, indeed, the card.

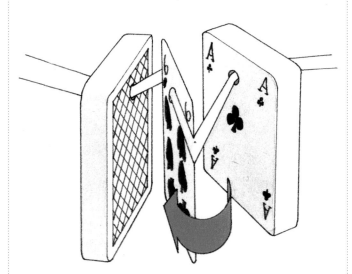

6 Then thread the ribbon through the upper section of the cards. But have a slight difficulty as you are finishing, so that with your non-ribbon holding hand you can rotate the doctored 6 of spades, turning it face down like all the other cards. Grip the deck and ask the spectator to tie the loose ends tightly, making certain that the loop of ribbon around the turned card is tight. The volunteer is the only person who might notice the loop, so, having fanned out the cards to give them one last check, blindfold the spectator or ask a second member of the audience to fasten the blindfold.

Trick of the Trade

• This trick operates much better with ribbon than with string. White ribbon makes the extra loop around the end of the 6 of spades less noticeable than would any other color.

CONFORMIST JACK

A SIMPLE GIMMICK MAKES IT SEEM AS IF A CARD CAN BE PUSHED INTO A PACK FACING ONE WAY AND EMERGE FROM THE OTHER SIDE FACING THE OTHER WAY. THE MAGICIAN HAS PROVED, MYSTERIOUSLY, THAT CARDS REALLY DO BEHAVE LIKE PACK ANIMALS.

YOU WILL NEED

PACK OF CARDS

DUPLICATE JACK OF SPADES FROM AN IDENTICAL PACK

1 Before the performance cut the jack of spades from another pack in half horizontally, and when you are ready to do this effect, have one of the halves palmed (see page 20), face down in, say, your left hand.

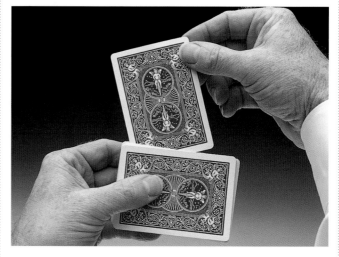

3 Take back the card and, holding the pack so that its back is toward the audience and with the long edges upward, push the jack, face out, into the pack.

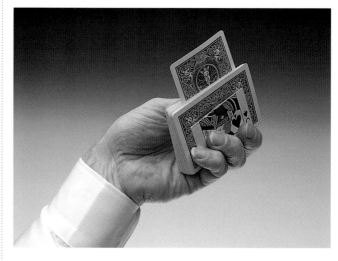

2 Pick out the jack of spades from a pack of cards and tell the audience that this card is well known by all students of cards to be the most conformist of any of the 52. "You wouldn't think so just to look at," you remark and pass it to members of the audience in the front row to look at. While the card is being inspected, palm the face-down top card of the deck in your right hand, turn over the deck, and place the palmed card face down on

the pack, which is otherwise face up in your left hand, with the half-card at its rear. Holding the face-out pack in your left hand, you can keep the half-card at the rear of the deck with the index finger of your left hand.

4 Push the jack down through the pack until its bottom half protrudes below. Give it an extra little tug with your right hand.

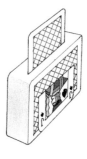

5 While you are giving the extra tug, use your right thumb to transfer the half-card to the rear of the protruding jack, then start pushing the jack upward, simultaneously pushing the half-card a little way into the pack. Turn over the pack, although still keeping the back toward the audience, and push the jack back through the pack. When you turn over the pack, it is easy to turn it around at the same time – if you perform the maneuver with enough panache, the extra move will go unnoticed.

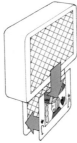

6 The audience will think they are still seeing the face of the jack, but, in fact, it is the half-card, with part of the real jack behind it.

7 Start pushing downward again, and the real jack will emerge, having apparently reversed itself while going through the pack. Give the jack out for examination and put the pack "carelessly" on your table, spilling it a little. If anyone asks to inspect the pack, pick it up equally "carelessly," losing the half-card in the process and "fumblingly" turning over the reversed card.

Trick of the Trade

• As you give the jack out to the audience for inspection, splay the cards in your hand a little, face out, so that the observant people among your spectators will notice that the jack did, indeed, emerge facing the same way as the other cards.

103

UNRELIABLE JUMBO

THIS IS AN EXCELLENT TRICK FOR A CHILDREN'S ENTERTAINMENT. THERE IS NO REAL DECEPTION, BUT THE EFFECT IS STARTLING. THE MAGICIAN EXPLAINS THAT, BECAUSE THEY THINK IT IMPROVES THEIR SHOWMANSHIP, A LOT OF OTHER MAGICIANS HAVE TAKEN TO USING JUMBO CARDS, WHICH ARE JUST LIKE ORDINARY PLAYING CARDS BUT VERY MUCH BIGGER. THIS MAGICIAN, HOWEVER, CHOOSES NOT TO DO SO, NOT FOR REASONS OF TRADITION AND NOT JUST BECAUSE JUMBO CARDS ARE EXPENSIVE, BUT BECAUSE THEY SEEM TO HAVE A LIFE OF THEIR OWN AND DO THINGS THAT NO ONE IS EXPECTING. THE MAGICIAN THEN PROVES THIS BY FOLDING AND UNFOLDING A CARD, WHICH APPEARS TO TURN FROM BACK TO FRONT IN THE COURSE OF THE MANEUVER.

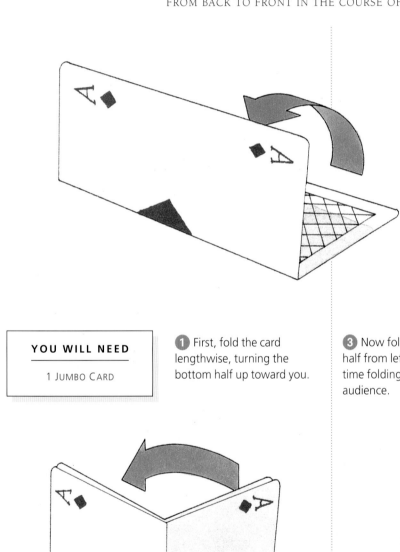

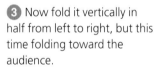

YOU WILL NEED

1 JUMBO CARD

---

1 First, fold the card lengthwise, turning the bottom half up toward you.

3 Now fold it vertically in half from left to right, but this time folding toward the audience.

2 Fold it vertically in half, from left to right, folding the card toward you.

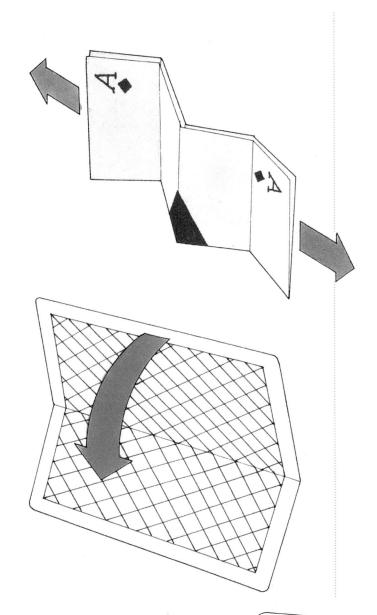

4 Taking the pair of cut ends closest to you, straighten out the folded card in one movement, so that the only fold remaining is the longitudinal one.

5 Straighten out this fold, and the back of the card is now seen to be facing the audience.

Trick of the Trade

• Jumbo Cards, which are available from conjuring stores, are expensive, so it is a good idea to make your own. Even better, especially with children, is to bring a sheet or two of stout paper and some marker pens, and call for volunteers to make the Jumbo Card for you. That way the audience can be absolutely sure that there is no cheating.

KINGS ON TOP

THE MAGICIAN TELLS THE AUDIENCE THAT HE OR SHE REALLY IS A MONARCHIST AT HEART, BECAUSE, DESPITE EVERYTHING THAT APPEARS IN THE NEWSPAPERS THESE DAYS, ROYAL BREEDING DOES SHOW. A PRINCE MAY CHANGE PLACES WITH A PAUPER, BUT NO MATTER WHAT MARK TWAIN WOULD HAVE US BELIEVE, IT WILL ALWAYS BE EASY TO DISTINGUISH THE ONE FROM THE OTHER. TO PROVE THE POINT, THE MAGICIAN PERFORMS THE FOLLOWING TRICK.

YOU WILL NEED

PACK OF CARDS

1 Before the performance, place all four kings at the top of the pack and, in the subsequent shuffling, keep them there.

2 Shuffle the pack and pass it to a member of the audience, asking him or her to cut the cards into four approximately equal heaps. Make sure that you know which heap has the four kings on top of it.

3 Then ask the volunteer to move the cards in an apparently random fashion: "Take three cards from that heap and put it on that one. Now, take two cards from this heap and put one of them on that heap and other over here." The aim of these instructions and transpositions is to make everyone lose track of everything. In fact, because you know where the kings are, the object is to move the three top cards from that heap in such a way that one is left at the top of the other three heaps. The exact transpositions can vary from

performance to performance, and keeping track of the kings is quite easy if you concentrate.

4 Suddenly say, "That's enough," and ask the volunteer to turn over the top card of each pile. Sure enough, they prove to be the four kings, "who will always end up at the top of the heap, no matter what happens."

> ### Trick of the Trade
> • You can adapt this trick using jacks instead of kings if you wish, and use it to form the dénouement of the first version of the Scurvy Knaves trick (see pages 73–5).

KINGS ON QUEENS ON TOP

THE MAGICIAN NEEDS MORE OR LESS THE SAME PATTER AS FOR KINGS ON TOP AND THE RESULT IS
PRETTY MUCH THE SAME – EXCEPT EVEN MORE CONCENTRATION IS REQUIRED.

YOU WILL NEED

PACK OF CARDS

1 At the outset you arrange the four kings and four queens at the top of the pack, and you retain them there as you shuffle.

2 Take the pack from the table, shuffle the cards, and hand them to a member of the audience to cut into four more or less equal heaps on the table. As before, you must remember which heap has the kings and queen at the top.

3 Begin to issue the volunteer with a complex set of instructions about moving the cards around from heap to heap. At first, keep things reasonably simple – you do not want to disturb the nest of queens at the top of one of the heaps. Finally clap your hands and call a halt to the moving around of the cards.

4 Ask the volunteer to turn up the top card of each heap, and, sure enough, there are the four kings. However, before the applause starts, set the kings to one side, quieten the audience, and issue the next set of instructions. During the second part of the trick, the heap with the queens on it may look a little too obviously smaller than the rest, so your first instruction of this second stage might be to move four cards (that is, the four queens) from that heap to another.

5 Finally, reveal the top card of each pile to be a queen.

Trick of the Trade

● It is nice to be able to use this trick as a follow-up to Kings on Top, but the difficulty is that you require a fresh stacked deck. One way round this – assuming you can afford it – is, at the end of Kings on Top, to give the cards you used to the volunteer as a souvenir. It seems natural, as you draw out a fresh pack for the next trick, to call also a fresh volunteer – who must, of course, at the end of the trick likewise be given the cards as a keepsake.

ACES

THIS TRICK RELIES ON THE CAREFUL PREPARATION OF THE STACKED PACK BEFOREHAND, BUT THE RESULT IS THAT BOTH THE MAGICIAN AND VOLUNTEER END UP WITH ACES IN THEIR HANDS, AND ALSO A GROUP OF CARDS THAT ARE A SINGLE COLOR.

YOU WILL NEED

PACK OF CARDS

1 Before you begin, prepare the pack. Decide how many cards you want in each packet – 12, for example – and arrange the top 21 cards – that is, twice 12 = 24 – 3 = 21 – alternately red and black. The values of the cards do not matter but should be as haphazard as possible. The 22nd card should be a black ace, the 23rd card should be any red card, and the 24th card should be a red ace. Place this packet of 24 cards on top of the pack.

2 Hold up the pack and fan it, face out, to the audience. The ordering will not be apparent as the audience briefly sees the fanned cards.

3 Deal out two heaps of cards, face down, one heap for yourself and one for a volunteer from the audience. The dealing, obviously, gives the volunteer all red cards. You have 10 black cards plus a black ace and a red ace.

4 Turn to face the audience and ask the volunteer to do likewise. Putting the rest of the pack to one side, take your packet behind your back, and ask the volunteer to do the same, saying that you are both going to jumble up the cards as much as you wish, although still keeping them face down. While the volunteer is jumbling the cards, you look as if you are doing likewise, but you are, in fact, taking the red ace from the top of your packet, turning it around, and slipping it, face up, into the middle of the packet.

5 When the volunteer is satisfied, still keeping the rest of the packet behind you, bring forward a face-down card. Offer to exchange it for one that the volunteer draws from behind his or her back. The card you offer the volunteer is, of course, the black ace.

6 Ask the volunteer, who is still holding the packet behind his or her back, to insert your card into the packet but face up. You do the same thing with the card given by the volunteer. When you take the card from the volunteer, ostensibly turn it and push it face up into your packet. In fact, you put it into a convenient pocket or into your waistband.

7 Both you and volunteer produce the two packets with the exchanged cards showing face up in the face-down fan. Both cards prove to be aces, the one in the volunteer's hand being black, the one in your hand being red. This seems to be a great coincidence, but when you turn your cards around, all the other cards in your hand are black, while all the other cards in the volunteer's hand are red.

> ### Tricks of the Trade
>
> • It is a good idea to have plenty of court (royal) cards – not too many, though – in the stacked section. The colors will further distract the audience's eyes from the red-black sequence.
>
> • If you are worried that someone might notice that, at the end, there is one fewer card in your fan than in the spectator's, slightly alter your original stacking and then give yourself two cards in the guise of one at the end of the deal.

CHEATING

THIS TRICK REALLY IS A CHEAT. YOU CAN BUY GOOD QUALITY CARDS IN TWO FINISHES, ONE PLAIN AND ONE WITH A TEXTURED "LINEN" FINISH. THE DIFFERENCE IS SCARCELY OBVIOUS TO THE EYE, BUT IT IS CLEARLY DETECTABLE TO THE FINGERTIPS. THE VOLUNTEERS MIGHT SPOT THE DIFFERENCE BETWEEN THE TWO PACKS IF THEY WERE ABLE TO SEE THE FACES OF THE CARDS, WHICH IS WHY THE MAGICIAN KEEPS HOLD OF THE PACK WHILE THEY INSERT THEIR CHOSEN CARDS.

YOU WILL NEED

2 PACKS OF CARDS, ONE WITH A PLASTIC FINISH, ONE WITH A "LINEN" FINISH

BLINDFOLD

1 Offer a deck – the one with the "linen" finish – to the audience and tell them to pass it around among themselves, with three – or even four or five – people each taking a single card from it. Once they have selected both themselves and their cards, these volunteers must stand up, holding the cards so that they are not visible to the magician.

2 Take back the remainder of the pack and return to your table where you put on a blindfold. Pick up the pack of cards – this pack, of course, is the one with the smooth finish and move – carefully – to the front of the stage.

3 Ask the volunteers to come toward you and begin to riffle the cards (see page 17). Ask each volunteer in turn to stop you at any time during the riffle so that he or she can insert their card into the pack. Shuffle the pack thoroughly. Then begin to deal out the cards, face down, but stop suddenly and announce that the next card is one of the chosen ones. Give it to the volunteer whose card it was, and continue, until you have identified and returned all the chosen cards.

Tricks of the Trade

• Make sure that your table is fairly cluttered by this stage of the routine, so that both packs of cards can be behind something else, out of view, without this seeming unnatural. Moreover, you want to keep the volunteers away from the table, which is why you move to the front of the stage.

• As an alternative, you can effect the exchange by rigging one of the pockets of your costume so that it has two compartments. However, this involves you having a pretext to put the pack briefly into your pocket, which might arouse the audience's suspicions.

FLEEING RED

THIS TRICK INVOLVES THE USE OF A SHAVED PACK OF CARDS. SEE BOXING BACK (PAGE 97) FOR
INSTRUCTIONS ON CREATING A SHAVED PACK. A RED CARD VANISHES FROM A PACKET OF BLACK
CARDS, ONLY TO REAPPEAR IN THE MAGICIAN'S POCKET — MYSTERIOUSLY, THE MAGICIAN HAS NOT
BEEN WEARING A JACKET THROUGHOUT THE TRICK.

YOU WILL NEED

SHAVED PACK

1 CARD FROM AN IDENTICAL,
UNSHAVED PACK

HANDKERCHIEF

---

1 Before the performance, plant a card – the 10 of diamonds, for example – from the shaved set in your top jacket pocket, which, at the end of the previous trick, you may have draped over a chair, some distance from your table. Place the unshaved 10 of diamonds in the pack of shaved cards.

2 Deal out some or all of the black cards in the pack and also one red card at random (this red card is, obviously, the 10 of diamonds). Shuffle the cards a few times to show that there is still only one solitary red card – the 10 of diamonds – in the packet.

3 Square up the packet, pull out a handkerchief, and invite a member of the audience to help you with the next part of the trick. The volunteer you choose "happens" to be sitting at the back of the hall, and as he or she comes to the front, you say something reassuring like: "There's no need to be frightened. all I'm going to do is this." At this

point, demonstrate what you are going to be asking the volunteer to do – the deception occurs at this point.

4 Take the packet in one hand, drape the handkerchief over it with the other, hold the packet loosely through the cloth, and then swiftly pull the handkerchief away. In fact, as you hold the packet loosely, grip the edges of the 10 of diamonds through the handkerchief.

5 As you whip away the handkerchief, take the card away too.

6 Holding the handkerchief casually with your hand at your stomach, gesticulate with the hand that is holding the packet toward the advancing volunteer. This will distract your audience's attention long enough for you to slip the 10 of diamonds inside your shirt. The trick then works for itself.

7 When your volunteer reaches the stage, hand over the packet and tell him or her to hold it really tightly. Then shake out the handkerchief, drape it over the deck, and swiftly pull away the handkerchief. Give the handkerchief to the volunteer and ask him or her to look at the cards. Yes, the 10 of diamonds has vanished. You say: "Yes, the 10 of diamonds has fled to my jacket pocket . . . of dear, this wasn't supposed to happen . . ." Look as if you have only just realized that you took off your jacket earlier on in the performance and draped it over a chair.

8 Ask the volunteer to put the cards and handkerchief down and to go to look in the top pocket of your jacket, meanwhile worrying aloud that you do not think that the 10 of diamonds could possibly have fled such a distance. "Cards have very short legs, you know," you tell the audience. However, the volunteer does find the missing card there.

Trick of the Trade

● Experiment, and if you find the edges of the undoctored card insufficiently raised from those of the shaved packet for you to get a confident grip, instead put the plain card in your jacket and have the shaved one in the pack. While you are dealing, make sure that you keep all the black cards with the taper in the same direction. The red card, being separately selected, can be tossed "casually" on top of them, giving it a slight spin as you do, so that it lies with its taper in the opposite direction from the others. It should be easy, to grip it through the handkerchief.

CLASSIC CONJURING

EVERY MAGICIAN SHOULD SPEND TIME PERFECTING SOME OF THE CLASSICS OF MAGIC. THESE TRIED AND TESTED EFFECTS HAVE BECOME FAMILIAR TO AUDIENCES ALL OVER THE WORLD, AND SOME NEWCOMERS to magic make the mistake of passing over these tricks because they think they are too well-known. However, these essential components of the magician's repertoire, including such old favorites as the Multiplying Billiard Balls, Chinese Linking Rings, and the time-honored Cups and Balls, remain popular today, especially when they are combined with imaginative new routines.

20TH-CENTURY SILKS

Ask any practicing magician to explain the working details of this trick and he or she will immediately know, for 20th-century Silks has become a classic magical effect. The special silk squares you need can be bought as a set from a supplier of magic effects, or you can make up your own props from squares of colored silk.

YOU WILL NEED

BAG MADE OF A PURPLE SILK, SQUARE, FOLDED DIAGONALLY AND STITCHED AROUND THE OPEN EDGES, LEAVING A SMALL OPENING IN ONE CORNER

PURPLE SILK HANDKERCHIEF

YELLOW SILK HANDKERCHIEF

YELLOW SILK HANDKERCHIEF WITH A PURPLE CORNER

CLEAR GLASS TUMBLER

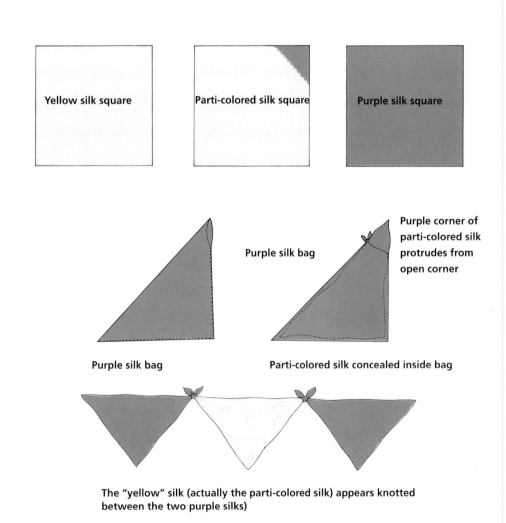

Yellow silk square

Parti-colored silk square

Purple silk square

Purple silk bag

Purple corner of parti-colored silk protrudes from open corner

Purple silk bag

Parti-colored silk concealed inside bag

The "yellow" silk (actually the parti-colored silk) appears knotted between the two purple silks)

1 Take the parti-colored silk square and knot the yellow corner that is diagonally opposite the purple one to the open corner of the silk bag. Tuck the yellow handkerchief with the purple corner inside the purple silk bag, arranging it so that the purple corner protrudes from the open corner. The handkerchief is hidden inside during the presentation. Gather together the other two handkerchiefs so that it seems that only three are actually used.

2 When you come to perform the trick, pick up the two purple silks (one of which is the bag) and knot one corner of the purple silk to the false purple corner protruding from the bag.

3 Tuck handkerchiefs into a clear tumbler so that the corners hang over the edge.

4 Display the yellow silk handkerchief and make it disappear. Some performers use cones, boxes, tubes, and so on to facilitate this vanish, but a pocket is just as effective. Place the silk handkerchief in your pocket and, after uttering some magic words, pull out the lining of the pocket to show that the handkerchief has vanished. It has, in fact, been pushed up into the top section of the pocket, and when the lining is turned out, the handkerchief is secured there and cannot be seen by your audience.

5 Returning to the handkerchiefs inside the tumbler, take the unattached corner of the purple silk and pull it firmly to show that in fact, the missing yellow silk handkerchief has now miraculously reappeared, but now it is firmly tied between the two purple silks.

THE MULTIPLYING BILLIARD BALLS

Often sold in more advanced boxes of magic, this is usually one of the first tricks that newcomers to magic learn. The basic movements involved in producing two balls are shown below, and following are descriptions of some of the variations and alternative maneuvers that can be built upon to develop into a really exciting program. At its basic best, the magician simply reaches into the air – and a red ball materializes! Then the single ball becomes two balls, then three, then four, with all four balls being displayed between the magician's fingers. Just as easily, the balls can be made to vanish, only to reappear somewhere else.

YOU WILL NEED

3 SOLID BALLS AND A SHELL (A HOLLOW HALF-BALL, MADE ESPECIALLY TO FIT OVER ANY OF THE THREE BALLS)

SILK HANDKERCHIEF

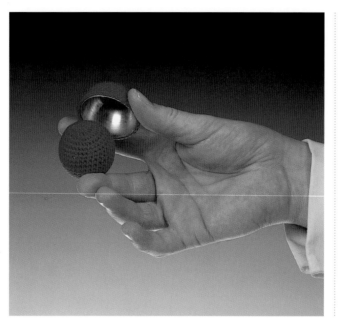

Tricks of the Trade

• It is a good idea to paint the balls with red lacquer, because this color allows audiences large and small to see the balls clearly during your performance.

• The pivoting move, on which the Multiplying Billiard Balls sequence relies, may at first seem awkward to the beginner, but constant practice, preferably in front of a mirror, will enable anyone to master these moves and present a polished and entertaining performance.

1 Before the performance, place one ball, with the shell over it, in the right trouser pocket. Place the second ball in the left trouser pocket. Place the third ball in the left jacket pocket with the silk handkerchief. When you begin the sequence, with your right hand casually resting in the right trouser pocket, palm the ball with the shell over it (see page 30). Remove your hand from the pocket and "pluck" the ball out of the air so that it appears between your thumb and first finger. Show it on both sides as one ball.

2 Lower the second finger of the right hand to pivot the solid ball out from the shell . . .

3 . . . like this.

4 To your audience, you appear to be holding two solid balls.

PRODUCING THREE BALLS

1 Reach inside your left trouser pocket with your left hand, removing the ball you planted there earlier on.

2 As you position this ball between the first and second fingers of your right hand, quickly pivot out the ball within the shell to be held between the second and third fingers. Three balls have now been magically produced.

PRODUCING FOUR BALLS

1 Reach inside your left jacket pocket with your left hand, and produce the ball planted there. Place it firmly between the third and fourth fingers of your right hand. Show the three balls on both sides to the audience.

2 Produce the final, fourth ball from within the shell, as before, using the pivoting action, so that the ball now takes its place between the first and second fingers.

THE VANISH

1 Raise your left hand as if to take away the ball that is gripped between your first and second fingers. But in fact, use your hand as a shield to conceal the following move. Under cover, make a clutching motion with your right hand, allowing the ball to pivot back inside the shell.

2 Withdraw your closed left fist, supposedly holding a ball, from your right hand, where one solid ball appears to remain, gripped between your thumb and first finger.

3 Slowly open your left hand to show that it is empty.

ANOTHER VANISH

1 Shield the center ball with your left hand, pretending to remove it from its position. As you appear to grasp it, pivot the ball back inside the shell.

2 This time, pretend to place the ball, supposedly in your left hand, into your mouth. As your clenched fist moves up in front of your mouth, press your tongue against the inside of your cheek, so that it looks as if you are holding the ball in your mouth.

3 Show your empty left hand to the audience, then, with the first finger of your left hand, push the "bulge" in your cheek inward as if you are swallowing the ball.

VANISHING TWO BALLS

1 Show the right hand holding the four balls. Shake your hand in the air, and one ball appears to have vanished. In fact, of course, you have simply pivoted the ball between your first and second fingers inside the shell, leaving three in view. Show both sides of the remaining balls to your audience.

2 With your left hand, move the ball that is between your second and third fingers and reposition it between the first and second fingers. Under cover of this movement, "steal" away the ball from within the shell with your left hand – allow the ball to drop out of the shell and into the awaiting clenched fist.

3 Make a second vanish with the right hand, pivoting the ball now held between your first and second fingers into the shell. At the same time, pocket the unwanted ball from your left hand.

4 Next, remove the ball from between the third and fourth fingers and place it between your first and second fingers. While you do this, again "steal" away the ball that is within the shell with your left hand as before.

HANDKERCHIEF VANISH

1 Place the ball in your left hand palmed from a pocket) between the first and second fingers of your right hand and, under cover, steal away the one inside the shell.

2 Reach inside your left jacket pocket and remove the silk handkerchief, at the same time, depositing in your pocket the ball you have just taken from the shell.

3 Holding one corner of the silk in your left hand, drape it over both balls in your right hand. Then reach beneath, supposedly to take one away. In reality, pivot the ball into the shell. Withdraw your left hand as if you are still holding the ball.

4 Slowly open the fingers of your left hand to show that the ball has vanished. Then remove the handkerchief to show that only one ball remains in your right hand.

5 Pocket the handkerchief. The remaining ball, together with the shell, can be vanished by any of the sleight-of-hand methods described on pages 14–40. The routine should end, as it began, with your hands completely empty.

THE AMAZING CARD BOX

THE CARD BOX IS ONE OF THE MOST USEFUL AND VERSATILE MAGIC PROPERTIES EVER INVENTED. AS WELL AS PLAYING CARDS, SLIPS OF PAPER, PHOTOGRAPHS, PAPER CURRENCY, AND OTHER FLAT OBJECTS CAN BE INTRODUCED INTO THE BOX. THE BOX IS EASY TO USE – YOU CAN MAKE CARDS DISAPPEAR AND REAPPEAR, CHANGE FROM ONE VALUE TO ANOTHER OR EVEN TO SOMETHING ELSE ENTIRELY.

YOU WILL NEED

CARD BOX, WHICH IS SIMPLY A WOODEN BOX WITH A HINGED LID AND A LOOSE FLAP THAT FITS OVER RECESSES IN THE LID AND BASE (THE FLAP MUST BE THE SAME COLOR AS THE INTERIOR OF THE BOX – BLACK IS THE MOST USUAL COLOR)

Flap fits into either base or lid of box

Hinged box

1 Before you begin your performance, place the object to the produced – a card, for example – under the flap in the lid. This means that the box can be shown to be completely empty.

2 When you close the box, the flap – and the card – fall to the base of the opposite side, and when the box is opened once more, the card appears to be in position on the base.

CHANGING ONE CARD FOR ANOTHER

1 Secretly place a different card from the one selected for display under the flap before the beginning of your performance.

2 The flap is positioned in the lid of the box, and the box is shown to the audience to be empty.

3 The second card is displayed to the audience and then placed inside the box, which is then closed.

4 When the box is re-opened, the card has magically transformed into another one.

VANISHING A CARD

1 The card box is empty at the beginning of your performance, with the flap positioned in the lid.

2 A card is placed in the box, and the lid is closed.

3 When the lid is raised, the flap now covers the card and the box is shown to the audience to be apparently empty.

20 TRICKS USING THE AMAZING CARD BOX

1 A playing card is shown, torn into pieces, and the pieces are dropped into the box. Moments later, the card is seen to be restored.

2 The four 2s of a pack of card magically change into the four aces.

3 A card chosen freely from a pack is dropped inside the box, without the audience being able to see the face of the card. The magician predicts the value and suit of the card before the experiment begins – and reveals this to be the card that is inside the box.

4 A plain white card is placed inside the box, which is closed. The performer then opens the box and places a pencil inside it. When the box is opened a third time and the contents shown to the audience, the card is seen to have ghostly writing on it.

5 The king and queen of hearts are placed inside the box. The jack of hearts is shown to the audience and placed inside the magician's trouser pocket. It vanishes (it is pushed up under the top lining of the trouser pocket), and when the box is re-opened, the jack is found with the king and queen.

6 A blank piece of paper placed inside the box turns magically into a genuine paper currency.

7 A bank note placed inside the box changes magically into a note of a larger denomination.

8 Unknown to the audience, a card is stuck onto the outside base of the box with a thin layer of wax. With the flap in the upper section of the box, a duplicate card is dropped inside the box and the lid is closed. The box is tapped, and the waxed card falls from the base onto the table and is shown to the audience. The box is opened to show that the card has disappeared. This penetration effect is guaranteed to puzzle any audience.

9 Force onto a spectator the 3 of diamonds (see pages 41–53 for forcing). Tell your audience that you will find the chosen card from the pack. Remove, say, the 6 of clubs, dropping it inside the empty box. When you ask the spectator if this is the correct card, he or she will, of course, say "no." But when the box is opened, written on the card are the words: "You will select the 3 of diamonds." So you win in the end.

10 Two spectators each select a card from two different packs, but they do not look at them. These are placed inside the box. An envelope, which has been in full view throughout your performance until now, is opened and the contents read aloud. The prediction states that both spectators will select identical cards from the different packs, and these cards are named. This is achieved simply by changing two cards for another two.

11 Numbers, from one to six, are boldly written on pieces of white card, which are dropped into the box and the lid closed. A spectator is asked to select any number, from one to six, at will. The performer can either predict beforehand or divine at the time which number has been chosen. This is a simple switch of one set of genuine numbers, from one to six, for a set of six that are identical – for example, all fives.

12 Flat, colored counters, such as those used in board games, are mixed up. They are placed inside the box. A spectator is invited to reach inside the box and to remove, without looking, one of the counters. The magician will be able to predict what color is selected.

13 A piece of card is placed inside the box, together with a postage stamp. The performer blows in the box. When the lid is opened, the stamp is seen to be stuck to the surface of the card, ready to be mailed.

14 With a piece of white chalk, mark the name of a card – the 4 of spades, for example – on one side of the flap. Put the 4 of spades from another pack of cards in the lid and cover it with the flap; the marked side of the flap must face into the lid. A card is selected from a pack by a spectator, who does not look at it, and it is then dropped inside the box and the lid closed. Open the lid and drop inside a piece of white chalk on top of the planted card. The spectator opens the box and finds the piece of chalk

and the card, and sees that the name of the card has been mysteriously chalked on the bottom of the box (actually the flap).

15 A piece of white card is placed inside the box. It becomes a photograph of an object that has previously been mentioned.

16 A crossword puzzle, ready to be solved, is placed inside the box and the lid closed. The box is opened and a pencil is dropped in. When the box is re-opened, the answers are all marked in.

17 A card taken from a pack is marked with a bold X on the front. It is placed inside the box and the lid closed. When the box is re-opened again, the card is found to have the X on the back, not the front.

18 Cards taken from a Lexicon pack are dropped inside the box, only to spell the word that the magician has previously predicted.

19 The performer magically prints his or her name on a blank business card and hands it out to a member of the audience.

20 Colored gummed spots magically form a message on the surface of a blank card.

THE INEXHAUSTIBLE BOX

THIS CLASSIC PIECE OF MAGICAL APPARATUS IS USED BY MAGICIANS THROUGHOUT THE WORLD. IT ALLOWS THE MAGICIAN TO PRODUCE NUMEROUS ITEMS – EVEN LIVESTOCK – FROM AN APPARENTLY EMPTY BOX, AND THE BOX CAN BE SHOWN TO BE EMPTY BETWEEN EACH PRODUCTION. THE LOAD CHAMBER OPERATES WHEN THE BOX IS TILTED OVER FROM BACK TO FRONT, SO THAT THE TOP OF THE BOX FACES THE AUDIENCE.

YOU WILL NEED

SPECIAL BOX WITH A PIVOTING LOAD CHAMBER THAT ALLOWS IT TO BE SHOWN ON ALL SIDES, INCLUDING THE BASE

1 Before your presentation, place as many items as required in the load chamber and position the chamber inside the box at the start.

2 Show the box on all sides.

4 The back view shows a rabbit in the concealed load chamber, which now protrudes from the back of the box.

3 Tilt the box forward toward the audience, and lift the lid to display the inside.

5 Position the box so that it is upright again, and then quickly produce the rabbit from the top of the box.

CUPS AND BALLS

THIS IS POSSIBLY THE OLDEST TRICK IN THE WORLD. THE FAMOUS CUPS AND BALLS – KNOWN IN FRANCE AS *LE JEU DES GOBLETS* – HAS BEEN PERFORMED IN EVERY COUNTRY, USING EVERY CONCEIVABLE TYPE OF GOBLET OR CUP. CUPS AND BALLS WAS A GREAT FAVORITE IN VICTORIAN DRAWING ROOMS; FAKIRS HAVE PERFORMED THE ROUTINE ON THE PAVEMENTS; AND IN INDIA IT IS STILL POSSIBLE TO WATCH STREET MAGICIANS PRESENTING IT ALONGSIDE THEIR SNAKE CHARMING. THE ACTUAL EFFECT OF THE TRICK VARIES FROM PERFORMER TO PERFORMER, BUT IN ESSENCE, BALLS VANISH, APPEAR, TRANSPOSE, REAPPEAR, AND EVEN CHANGE INTO FRUITS AND VEGETABLES. SOME MAGICIANS EVEN CHANGE THE BALLS INTO LIVE CHICKS.

YOU WILL NEED

3 GOBLETS OR OPAQUE PLASTIC BEAKERS

4 SMALL SPONGE OR CORK BALLS

Although the routine can be presented with opaque beakers, it is best performed with the correct type of goblet. Magic dealers manufacture sets of three goblets in spun aluminum, brass, and copper. Some types are called "dumpies" – a term deriving from their shape – while others look rather like beakers. All, however, have a "wall" around the mouth of each goblet, and all are made to stack on top of each other. Because of the walls, when the cups are stacked one on top of another, they cannot be pushed right into each other, and a similar amount of space is left between each so that a secreted ball can be hidden with ease. All the cups also have an indentation in the bottom, so that when each goblet is placed mouth down on a table, a ball will rest comfortably on top, without rolling off.

Trick of the Trade

- When you initially work through the different stages of the trick and when you practice, you might want to use clear plastic tumblers so that you can see exactly where each ball is.

THE GALLOP MOVE

Before you begin your act, conceal the three large balls in your right trouser pocket and three of the small balls in the left trouser pocket. Place the fourth small ball in one cup, and stack the remaining two cups on top. The entire set should be displayed with the nesting cups standing upright, mouths upward, neatly on the left-hand side of your table.

2 Invert the bottom cup, which contains the secreted ball, onto the table, so that the ball secretly drops with it to lie underneath the cup.

1 Display the cups, picking them up in your left hand and showing them, still nested and mouths toward the audience. With your right hand, take hold of the bottom cup, ready to perform the gallop move.

3 Remove the two remaining cups from the stack, one at a time and in the same way as before, placing them in a line, mouth down, alongside the first one.

THE PLACE-IN MOVE

Remove a small ball, the first of three, from your left trouser pocket and hold it in your right hand.

1 Move your left hand toward your right hand as if you were going to take the ball from your right hand. In fact, you retain the ball in your right hand.

2 Clench your left fist as if you are holding the ball in that hand. Secretly palm the ball in your right hand, and point to your left hand to reinforce the dummy move.

3 With your right hand (still holding the concealed ball), lift the left-hand cup, tilting it forward, toward your audience. Pretend to place the ball that is supposedly in your left hand under this cup. Throughout this maneuver the ball remains hidden in your right hand.

4 Pointing to each cup in turn, say something like: "Ladies and gentlemen, a transformation. Watch the ball travel from this cup to the one at the other end of the line." Lift up the left-hand cup so that the audience can clearly see that it is empty. Lift up the cup that is in the center, which is also empty.

5 Continue the routine and, with your right hand, lift up the cup at the right-hand side, tilting the top of the cup toward the audience, to show that the ball has actually "transferred" from one cup to another.

6 While the audience's attention is diverted by the appearance of the ball and while you tilt the cup forward, the ball that is palmed in your right hand is secretly loaded into the cup, ready for the next effect. The secret of the maneuver is to tilt the cup to an angle that brings the mouth of the cup into contact with the palm of your right hand so that the palmed ball secretly drops into the mouth of the cup.

7 Execute the gallop move once again, inverting the cup on the table, with the secretly loaded ball remaining underneath the cup ready for the next effect.

121

PRODUCING ONE BALL

1 Take the ball that is now in view of the audience (the one produced in step 5 page 121) in your right hand and, again, supposedly place it in your left hand.

2 Involve the audience in the routine by asking a question like: "Which cup do you wish the ball to reappear under next, Madam?" You should peer at the your clenched left hand while you talk to underline the audience's impression that there is where the ball is being held.

3 If the spectator chooses either the left or the central cup, lift up the chosen cup with your right hand, tilting the top of the cup toward your audience, and release the palmed ball beneath it, so that a ball suddenly appears at this position.

4 If the spectator selects the cup on the right, simply lift the cup to reveal the ball previously loaded at this position. However, because a ball must remain hidden beneath the right-hand cup, ready for the next effect, load the ball that you palmed in your right hand into the cup as it is lifted to reveal the ball that is already there.

5 Execute the gallop move once again, taking care that the mouth of the cup hits the surface of your table and conceals the ball you have loaded inside it.

FURTHER PRODUCTIONS

1 Repeat the gallop move, displaying the cups once again on the table, with the secreted ball now hidden under the center cup.

2 Make the visible ball "vanish" by using any of the sleight-of-hand techniques described on pages 14–40. In fact, retain this ball in the palm of your right hand.

3 Lift up the center cup with your right to show that the ball has appeared under that cup. While the audience's attention is diverted, allow the palmed ball to drop inside the center cup, which is in the loading position – mouth upward into the palm of your hand, ready to receive the palmed ball.

4 Use the gallop move to place the cup over the ball just produced.

5 Take a second ball from your left trouser pocket and vanish it. Every magician has a favorite method for doing this, but basically you need to retain the ball secretly in your right hand.

6 Lift up the center cup to reveal the "vanished" ball – together with the first one. With the cup gripped in the right hand, load the palmed ball inside, ready for the third and final production of the small balls. Invert the cup over the two balls on the table.

7 Repeat step 5, taking the third ball from your left trouser pocket. "Vanish" it and make it "reappear" under the center cup.

8 Casually put your right hand into your right trouser pocket and discard the palmed ball, at the same time obtaining one of the three larger balls, which you need to hold in the finger-palm position. While you do this, arrange the three small balls with your left hand so that they are neatly displayed, one on top of each of the cups.

A PENETRATION

Once you have executed the gallop move, you are ready for the next effect in this sequence. Remember that there is a ball hidden underneath the right-hand cup.

1 Place the visible ball on top of the right-hand cup.

2 Place the center cup, then the left-hand cup on the stack, crashing them down as if to assist in a dramatic penetration.

3 Lift the entire stack of cups to reveal the loaded ball. To the audience, the ball you placed on top of the cup will seem to have penetrated its base and fallen to the table.

TIP-OFF LOADING MOVE

This move is executed three times to vanish the three small balls and to produce the three large balls, one under each cup.

1 Grip the base of the right-hand cup with your right hand, which is holding the large palmed ball, and tilt it over toward the audience, allowing the small ball, resting on the top, to fall into your waiting, cupped left hand. This gesture simply creates the impression that there is a practical way of dropping the ball from the top of the cup into the hand without touching it.

2 While you are presenting this movement with a flourish, allow the large ball, concealed in your right hand, to drop inside the cup. This is the same loading position as used in the earlier tricks. Immediately tilt this cup back, so that it returns, mouth down, to the table.

3 Take the smaller ball in your right hand and put it in your right trouser pocket. Under cover, finger-palm the second large ball from the pocket while you are pointing to the center cup with your left hand, in particular to the ball resting on top of it.

4 Load the large ball inside the cup as before, and again pocket the small ball. Repeat the maneuver, palming and loading the third and final large ball inside the left-hand cup. In pocketing the last of the three small balls, secretly gather all three together and then push them securely under the top lining of your trouser pocket.

5 Announce to your audience that all three balls will vanish from your pocket to reappear under the cups. Reach inside the trouser pocket, withdrawing the lining to show that it is completely empty. All three balls have vanished entirely.

6 Lift up the cups, one by one, to reveal that not only have the three balls reappeared under the cups but they have increased in size! If you want, hand the balls and cups to members of the audience so that they can examine them.

CHINESE LINKING RINGS

THIS CLASSIC PIECE OF MAGIC IS PERFORMED ALL OVER THE WORLD. THE RINGS ENABLE THE MAGICIAN TO LINK AND UNLINK SOLID METAL RINGS. IN THE PAST, THE EFFECT HAS BEEN PERFORMED SILENTLY, WITH A MUSICAL BACKGROUND, BUT IT CAN BE PRESENTED WITH AN AMUSING PATTER TO ACCOMPANY THE MOVES. MANY DIFFERENT ROUTINES HAVE EVOLVED OVER THE YEARS, SOME USING FOUR, FIVE, OR SIX RINGS, AND SOME EVEN USING 16 RINGS. THE MOST USUAL VERSION USES EIGHT SOLID STEEL RINGS, ALL OF WHICH APPEAR TO BE HANDLED BY MEMBERS OF THE AUDIENCE.

COUNTING THE RINGS

YOU WILL NEED

SET OF EIGHT RINGS (CONSISTING OF TWO SINGLE RINGS; A SET OF TWO RINGS PERMANENTLY LINKED TOGETHER; A SET OF THREE RINGS PERMANENTLY LINKED TOGETHER; THE "KEY" RING, WHICH HAS A GAP IN IT)

Trick of the Trade

• Although a professional set of linking rings can be bought from a magic dealer, it is possible for magicians to make their own if they have access to basic metal-working facilities.

1 Prepare for your performance by arranging the rings so that they are resting on your table or over the back of a chair. They should be set in this order, from the bottom of the stack: the key, one single, the chain of three, the chain of two, one single. It is important that you pick up the set in this order.

2 A classic introduction is along the lines: "A trick from China, as old as magic itself, it is called the Chinese Linking Rings. Before your very eyes, you will see these solid rings do incredible things. Ladies and gentlemen, eight solid steel rings. Let me count them." In counting the rings, use the "drop count" – hold the rings in your left hand.

3 Allow the first single ring to drop from the others to be caught in your right hand. Lower this hand slightly so that the ring is quite separate from the others in the set.

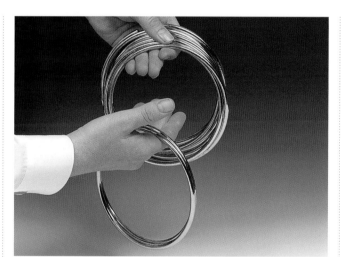

4 Next, allow the two linked rings to drop singly into the

5 Then, in the same way, drop the following three linked rings so that they appear to fall one at a time into your right hand. Finally, drop the second single ring. Then, lower the key ring into your right hand. You have now apparently dropped and counted eight solid and quite separate rings.

waiting right hand, which, as before, is slightly lowered.

6 Keep the rings in their original order when you transfer them back to your left hand. The gap in the key ring must always be at the top of the set and covered by the thumb of your left hand during the presentation.

LINKING THE RINGS

Although this classic effect and routine are easy to perform, a certain amount of practice, skill, and dexterity are necessary if you are to become truly proficient in handling the rings.

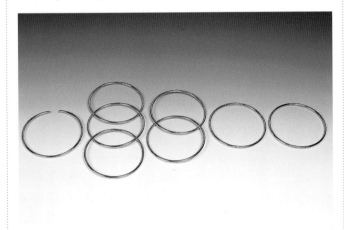

1 With your right hand, remove from the front of the set the first single ring and "crash" it against the others.

At the same time, allow the first of the two linked rings to fall from the first finger of your left hand.

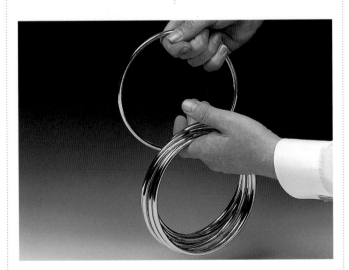

2 To the audience, it appears that you have caused the first ring to penetrate the second. Remove the two linked rings to display a perfectly coupled pair, and hand them to a spectator to inspect thoroughly.

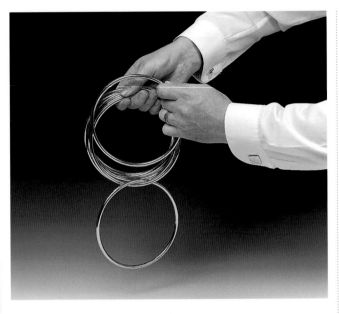

3 Now link three rings. With your right hand, remove the loose single ring, which is still in front position, and again "crash" it against the front of the set. Allow the first of the set of three linked rings to drop and hang. Again, crash the loose single ring against the others, so that the second of the set of three linked rings falls. Take the hanging rings away from the set to show that the three rings are now linked together, and then hand them to another spectator to examine.

4 It is now time to link the last two rings. By this stage of your trick you are holding three single rings, one of which is the key. Place one of the solid single rings over your arm so that it is out of the way then holding the remaining solid ring into and over the gap in the key ring. The rubbing motion should continue for a short period, even after the rings are actually linked together. Suddenly, allow the solid ring to drop, so that it becomes linked to the other ring (the key ring).

5 Turn to the spectator who is holding the chain of two and ask him or her to repeat your actions. Holding the two linking rings in front of your body, rub them together, asking the spectator to do the same, but although your rings will part, those held by the spectator will remain linked and cannot be separated.

6 Remove the solid single ring from around your arm and rub the three rings together, engaging the two solid rings onto the key ring. Gather together your set of three rings, and ask the second spectator to repeat your action. First, remove one loose ring. Alas, the spectator will be unable to do the same. Then, remove a second ring (the key ring), making sure that you cover the gap in it with your thumb, and throw the third ring into the air to prove that all three are completely separate. The spectator's rings will, of course, remain linked together. Link your own three rings together again.

7 Ask the first spectator to hand over the two linked rings. Take these and rub them against your linked set of three. Under cover of the rubbing motion, link them all together, forcing one of the set of two linked rings over the gap in the key ring. Hold the key ring so that the other rings hang from it.

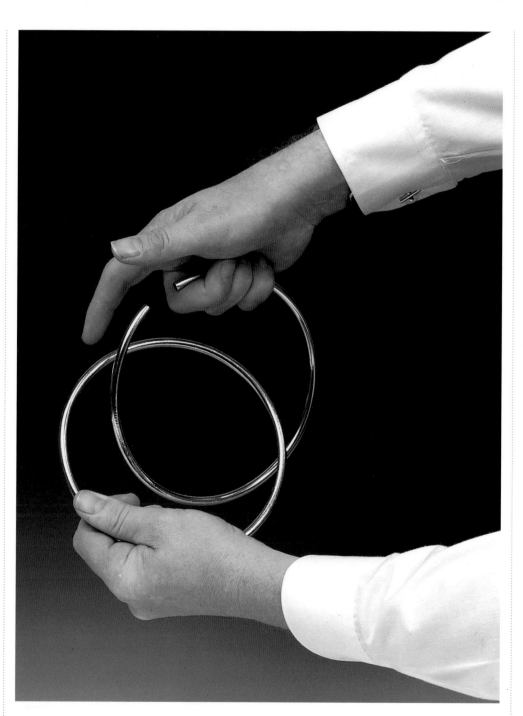

8 Take the set of three linked rings from the other spectator. In the same way, place them alongside the other rings, rubbing them together and, as you do this, forcing one of them over the key ring as before. Display the entire set of rings to your audience so that seven hang from the uppermost key ring, which is gripped in your hand.

9 The climax of your performance needs an introduction along the lines: "Ladies and gentlemen," here you see eight solid rings of steel. In my hands they have become as soft as putty. But, let me prove to you once again that we have, just as we had when I began, eight solid, separate rings." Holding the set high above your head and away from your body, under cover, open the gap in the key ring so that the other rings automatically scatter – apparently all single again – to the floor. Drop the key ring last of all.

CUT AND RESTORED ROPE

MAGICIANS HAVE BEEN CUTTING AND RESTORING ROPES FOR LONGER THAN ANYONE CAN REMEMBER, AND THIS TRICK IS REGARDED AS ONE OF THE GREATEST OF ALL THE CLASSICS OF MAGIC. THE EFFECT IS THAT A LENGTH OF ROPE IS CUT IN THE CENTER, SHOWN AS TWO PIECES, AND THEN RESTORED TO ITS ORIGINAL WHOLE STATE BY THE MAGICIAN.

YOU WILL NEED

SMALL PIECE OF ROPE

TRANSPARENT ADHESIVE TAPE

GOOD LENGTH OF ROPE

HANDKERCHIEF

SCISSORS

❶ Take the smaller length of rope and form it into a loop, using adhesive tape to hold the join. Place the loop over the long piece of rope and lay them both on your table, using the handkerchief or another prop to conceal the loop from the spectators' view. In performance, you pick up the rope with your right hand. Your hand actually goes around the loop, which is toward one end of the rope.

❷ Take the far end of the rope in your left hand and hold the rope between your hands. This gives the audience the impression that you are holding a single length of rope – they have no idea that you are concealing the loop of rope in the fingers of your right hand.

Trick of the Trade

• An alternative approach to this trick is to tuck the dummy loop securely into your watch strap, rather than hiding it in your fist. If you decide to do this, in addition to a watch you must remember to wear a jacket or long-sleeved garment to disguise the loop until you are ready to take it into your palm.

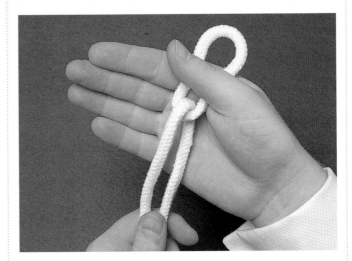

❸ Raise your left hand toward the end of rope held in your right hand. Your left hand now grasps the end of rope above your right hand, while your right hand moves down toward the center of the rope, taking the hidden loop with it. Let go of the ends of the rope held in your left hand as your right hand moves upward, apparently to show the center of the rope. In fact, by this time part of the loop has been allowed to come into view.

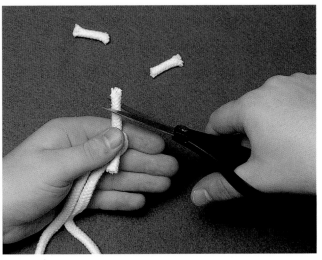

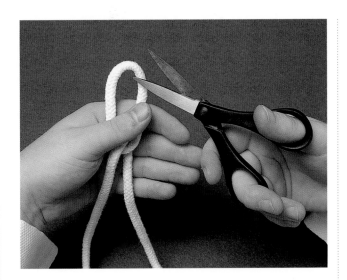

4 Transfer what appears to be the center of the rope from your right hand to your left, taking care that you do not accidentally reveal the loop. Do not make anything special of this movement – it should appear that you have simply transferred the center

of the rope from one hand to the other so that you can pick up the scissors with your right hand. Take the scissors in your right hand and then apparently cut through the center of the rope. You are actually just cutting through the loop.

6 Use the scissors to "trim" the top ends. Actually, you trim off so much that you cut away all of the secret loop.

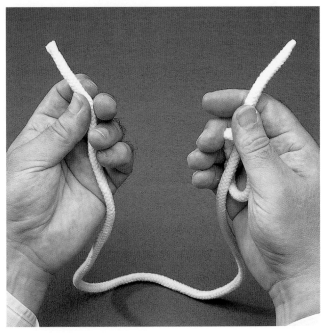

5 It now appears that you have two pieces of rope in your hand because your audience can see two cut ends above your left hand and the two long ends trailing below.

7 Put down the scissors. Wave your right hand over the "cut" center of the rope or blow on your hands. Take

both hands out to the ends of the rope and, as you take your bow, show that it is completely restored.

Trick of the Trade

● It is best to use magician's soft, white rope, which is made without the usual central core. Make sure that your scissors are sharp, so that they snip cleanly through the rope.

THE CLASSIC EGG BAG

THE FAMOUS EGG BAG TRICK WAS A FEATURE OF ARNOLD DE BIÉRE'S MUSIC-HALL ACT, AND IT WAS ALSO A HIT IN THE SHOW *HOW'S TRICKS* PRESENTED BY THE AUSTRALIAN-BORN LES LEVANTE. THE TRICK LENDS ITSELF TO COMEDY PRESENTATION, AND IT CAN BE PERFORMED AT CLOSE QUARTERS WITHOUT DETECTION. FURTHERMORE, DURING THE ROUTINE A NUMBER OF MAGICAL THINGS HAPPEN, AND THERE IS PLENTY OF SCOPE FOR AUDIENCE PARTICIPATION. THE TRICK INVOLVES SHOWING AN APPARENTLY EMPTY FLAT CLOTH BAG TO THE AUDIENCE, INSIDE AND OUT, AND THEN MAKING AN EGG APPEAR, VANISH, REAPPEAR, AND, FINALLY, FIND ITS WAY INTO A SPECTATOR'S POCKET. THE FIRST SIX MOVES DESCRIBED HERE WILL BE AN IMPRESSIVE TRICK, BUT AN ADVENTUROUS MAGICIAN MAY WANT TO ADD TO IT TO GIVE THE ROUTINE A STING IN THE TAIL, AND A POSSIBLE ADDITIONAL ROUTINE IS ALSO DESCRIBED.

YOU WILL NEED

SPECIAL CLOTH BAG WITH A SECRET POCKET ON ONE OF THE INSIDE FACES; THE POCKET HAS AN OPENING TOWARD THE BOTTOM

IMITATION EGG MADE OF PLASTIC OR WOOD (RUBBER JOKE EGGS, AVAILABLE FROM JOKE AND NOVELTY STORES ARE IDEAL, BUT A BLOWN EGG IS NOT SUITABLE FOR THIS TRICK)

1 Before the performance begins, conceal the faked egg inside the secret pocket in the cloth bag.

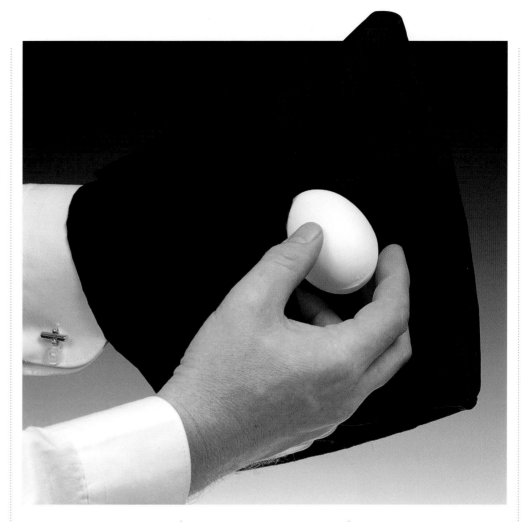

2 Lift the bag from the table, show both sides, then turn it inside out. To do this, grip the egg through the material of the bag as you turn the bag inside out. The egg will stay inside the bag during this procedure, and, from your audience's point of view, everything looks quite convincing – you appear to be holding an ordinary cloth bag. However, when you show the inside of the bag, make sure that you always keep the side with the pocket toward your body and away from the audience. Turn the bag right side out again, and you are now ready to start the routine.

3 Announce that you will now produce an egg from the empty bag by using the magic word "Eggstraordinary." Say the magic word, and place your empty right hand inside the bag. At the same time, release your left hand's grip on the egg through the material of the bag, allowing the egg to drop out of its secret pocket into the bag. With a flourish, withdraw your right hand to reveal the egg.

4 Replace the egg inside the bag, and then ask a member of the audience to shout out the magic word, "Eggstraordinary." Then, invert the bag. Nothing falls out because, when you turn the bag so that its mouth is toward the floor, the egg automatically drops into the pocket. The egg appears to have vanished.

5 To make it even more convincing, turn the bag inside out as before, showing the inside to be empty. Bring the bag back to its original position. Now, insert your empty right hand into the bag – and bring it out, holding the egg, which you display to your audience.

6 Next, put the egg back inside the bag, utter the magic word, and swish your right hand around inside the bag. Pretend to remove the egg, making your hand into a fist as if you were gripping the egg, and further pretend to secrete it under your left armpit. Continue with your presentation. Turn the bag inside out and back again, showing that the egg has completely vanished. When the audience begins to call out "It's under your arm," ignore them at first. Eventually, lift your right arm, showing that the egg is not there. The audience is not impressed, so raise your left arm, showing that the egg is not there either. Then hold the bag open in both hands, and ask a spectator to reach inside and bring out the egg – which, of course, he or she can do.

7 Ask a spectator to open up the side pocket of the jacket he or she is wearing. Tip the egg inside – at least, appear to the audience to be tipping the egg into the jacket pocket, but in fact, as you tilt the bag, the egg will roll into the secret pocket and stay there. Hold the bag, mouth toward the floor, to prove that it is empty.

8 Turn the bag inside out with the mouth upward, so that the egg falls out of the pocket and into your right hand. Palm the egg in this hand and casually take it away while misdirecting the audience's attention toward the spectator's jacket pocket.

Ask if the spectator still has the egg. The spectator reaches inside the pocket, only to find that the egg has mysteriously vanished. Look inside the jacket pocket yourself, and agree that the egg is not there. As you are doing this, secretly drop the palmed egg into the pocket.

9 Pretend to try to make the egg reappear in the bag – but without success. Try again, and reach inside to bring out what you call an invisible egg, holding it between the fingers and thumb of your right hand.

10 Make a movement as if to toss the egg into the spectator's pocket. Then ask the spectator to remove the egg and to drop it inside the bag, completing the routine.

UNEQUAL ROPES

OF ALL THE ROPE TRICKS THAT MAGICIANS PERFORM, THIS IS PROBABLY ONE OF THE BEST. IT IS CERTAINLY ALWAYS POPULAR WITH AUDIENCES, AS THE MAGICIAN SHOWS THREE UNEQUAL LENGTHS OF ROPE, THEN APPEARS TO "STRETCH" THEM TO MAKE THEM THE SAME LENGTH, THEN, MYSTERIOUSLY, THEY REVERT TO THEIR ORIGINAL LENGTH.

YOU WILL NEED

3 DIFFERENT LENGTHS OF ROPE – ONE SHORT, ONE TWICE AS LONG AS THE SHORT PIECE, AND ONE THREE TIMES AS LONG AS THE SHORT PIECE; THE ROPES MUST BE IDENTICAL IN APPEARANCE AND COLOR

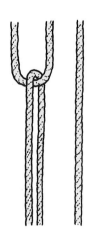

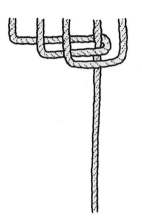

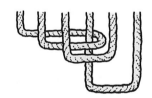

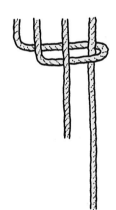

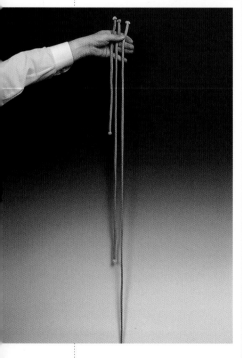

1 Untie the ropes and display them to your audience in order of length to emphasize the difference between them. First, hold up the short length, then place it in your left hand. Take the medium length, and place it in your left hand, to the right of the short length. Finally, hold out the long piece of rope, and place it in the left hand, to the right of the medium length.

2 Pass your right hand between the medium and long lengths, take hold of the short length, and bring it through, over the long length, and then round the back of all the lengths so that the free end is brought into the left hand and held to the left of the other ends. You will now be holding four ends in your left hand.

3 Bring the free end of the medium length up and place it in your left hand, to the right of the other three lengths. You will now be holding five ends of rope in your left hand.

4 Bring the free end of the long length up and place it in your left hand, to the right of the other lengths. You will now be holding six ends in your left hand.

5 You are now ready to "stretch" the ropes into equal lengths. With your right, take hold of the three ends lying on the right. Keep the three ends that are lying on the left in your left hand. Pull the ropes taut, and all three pieces of rope actually appear to be the same length.

6 Drop the ends from your right hand, and hold the ropes up in your left hand, with the fingers of that hand curling around and thus concealing the looped joins in the ropes.

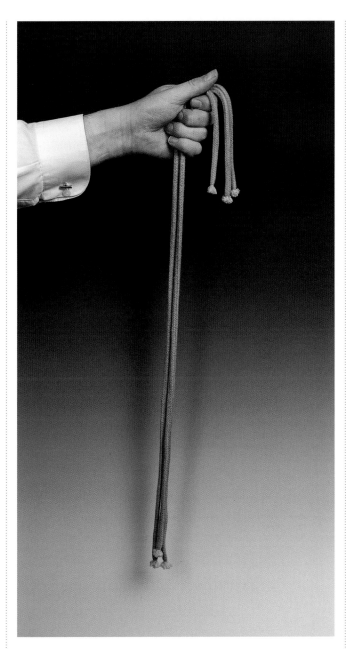

REVERSING THE EFFECT

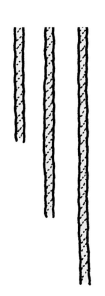

1 Bring the free end of the separate length and place it in the left hand to the left of the other ends.

3 Bring the right-hand portion up to the right.

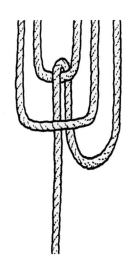

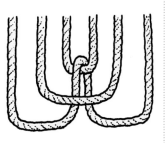

2 Bring the left-hand portion of the long linked length up to the left.

4 Take the first three ends on the right in your right hand, and at the same time drop the remaining ends from the left hand. Give the ropes a dramatic shake. They automatically separate to return to their original lengths – one short, one medium, and one long.

7 You can now count the ropes and show them separately. With your right hand, remove the one separate length (the original medium length), and display it, counting "one" out loud. Go to pick up the second length, secretly depositing the separate length and removing the two linked lengths, counting "two." Finally, pick up the separate length again and count "three." The audience believes that they have seen three separate ropes, each of equal length.

Trick of the Trade
• Keep the three lengths of rope neatly knotted together ready for your presentation so that you do not lose one of them at a vital moment.

THE WONDERFUL CHANGING BAG

THE FLAT CHANGING BAG IS ONE OF THE MOST VERSATILE PROPS THAT A MAGICIAN CAN POSSESS. IT COMES IN HANDY FOR SO MANY EFFECTS THAT IT WOULD BE ALMOST IMPOSSIBLE FOR ANY MAGICIAN TO BE WITHOUT ONE. THE BAG CAN CONTAIN AN ITEM OR ITEMS IN ONE COMPARTMENT SO THAT WHEN YOU WISH TO SHOW THAT THE BAG IS EMPTY, YOU SIMPLY TURN THE OTHER COMPARTMENT INSIDE OUT. THE BAG IS TURNED BACK AGAIN, AND THE ITEMS CAN BE MAGICALLY PRODUCED (FROM THE OTHER SIDE). THE BAG CAN ALSO APPEAR TO CHANGE ONE ITEM FOR ANOTHER. THE EMPTY SIDE IS SHOWN FIRST, AND A SELECTED ITEM IS PLACED INSIDE THIS COMPARTMENT. A COMPLETELY DIFFERENT ITEM (PREVIOUSLY CONCEALED) IS THEN TAKEN FROM OTHER COMPARTMENT. THE ITEM IS SHOWN TO THE AUDIENCE, AND THE NOW EMPTY SECTION OF THE BAG CAN BE DISPLAYED, PROVIDING THAT THERE IS NOTHING ELSE IN THE BAG.

THE MAGICIAN CAN "SWITCH" ONE THING FOR ANOTHER. FOR EXAMPLE, AN EMPTY BOX COULD BE PLACED IN THE BAG, AND THEN A DUPLICATE BOX CONTAINING A RING CAN BE WITHDRAWN. TWO TRICKS THAT USE THE CHANGING BAG ARE DESCRIBED IN DETAIL, AS WELL AS 20 SUGGESTIONS FOR WAYS IN WHICH YOU CAN INCORPORATE THE CHANGING BAG INTO YOUR OWN ROUTINES.

MAKING A CHANGING BAG

> ### YOU WILL NEED
> ───────
> CHANGING BAG

A changing bag is simply a cloth bag in which there is a central divider. Because the audience is not aware of this, it is possible to put something into the bag (into one of the compartments), and then show the bag empty (by showing the other compartment).

1 The easiest way to make such a bag is to take a strip of fabric measuring about 20 × 8 in. and a second piece of fabric measuring 10 × 8 in.

2 Fold the larger pieces in two and insert the small piece inside it. Stitch the edges together and stitch along the bottom so that you have two separate compartments.

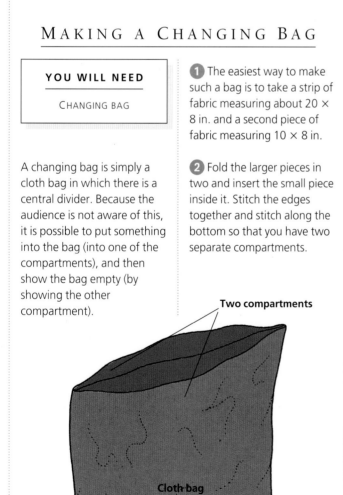

Two compartments

Cloth bag

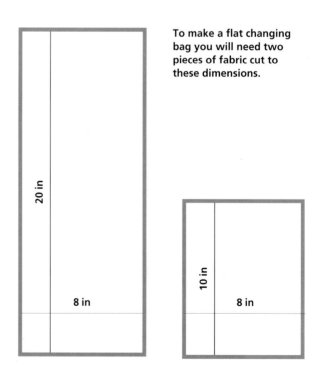

To make a flat changing bag you will need two pieces of fabric cut to these dimensions.

20 in

8 in

10 in

8 in

Fold the larger piece of fabric in two and insert the smaller piece between the fold. Stitch the sides and bottom seams together.

20 Tricks Using The Wonderful Changing Bag

There are literally hundreds of tricks that can be done with a changing bag, and if you have gone to the trouble of making one for yourself, you will be looking for ways to use it to full advantage. Here are 20 suggestions to get you started.

1 Several silk handkerchiefs are placed inside the empty bag, only to become knotted together.

2 Several silk handkerchiefs, together with a length of ribbon, are placed inside the bag. When they are withdrawn, the silks are seen to have tied themselves to the ribbon in a line.

3 Several silk handkerchiefs are placed inside the bag and are made to disappear.

4 The bag is shown empty, inside and out, yet when a spectator reaches inside, a quantity of silk handkerchiefs are pulled out.

5 A pocket handkerchief is torn into pieces and is magically restored to its original shape and size.

6 A length of rope is cut into pieces and placed inside the bag, only to become fully restored and the bag shown to be completely empty once again.

7 A pack of shuffled cards is placed inside the bag. The performer names three cards, and miraculously pulls them out and displays them to the audience.

8 Petals are plucked from a rose and placed into the empty bag. The flower petals magically come together to form a perfect rose bloom.

9 Several knotted loops of rope magically link together into a chain.

10 A red silk handkerchief placed inside the bag somehow changes into a yellow handkerchief.

11 A white handkerchief with dirty black stains on it become white and clean.

12 An item placed inside the bag replicates itself, so that another, exactly the same mysteriously appears.

13 A piece of white paper, of similar size to that of any paper currency, is dropped inside the bag, only to reappear later as a perfectly printed bank note or bill.

14 When an object is placed, first, in a small box and, second, inside the bag, the object disappears. To do this, place an empty, duplicate box into one of the compartments, and drop the full box into the other.

15 A spectator selects five letter cards from a Lexicon pack and drops them into the bag. Seconds later, you remove the cards to show that they spell M-A-G-I-C.

16 Two loops of colored ribbon are placed inside the bag and one further loop is placed inside the pocket. The pocket is shown empty (to achieve this effect, push the ribbon loop up to the top of the pocket, and bring out the lining to show the audience). When the loops of ribbon are taken out, the audience sees that they are joined by the other loop.

17 The bag contains coins that display different dates. The magician makes a prediction on a piece of paper, stating the date of the coin that will be selected. A spectator takes one coin from the bag. Of course, you have already made sure that the two coins in the other compartment bear the same date.

18 How would you like to change an egg into a chicken without waiting for nature to take its course? Here is the best way. Display an egg and drop it inside the bag. Strike a match and wave it below the bag. Then remove the toy chicken from the hidden compartment.

19 A blank piece of card magically turns into a photograph. This is especially successful if you can somehow manage to ensure that the photograph is of someone in your audience.

20 This last suggestion for using the wonderful changing bag is an alternative version of Capital Prediction (see page 138), and it is an effective mentalist experiment. It involves using a sheet of newspaper or a page torn from a magazine. The page is torn into pieces and these are dropped into the bag. The performer makes a prediction, and writes a few words on a slip of paper. You hand this slip to one member of your audience, and ask another spectator to reach inside the bag to bring out a slip of paper. When the prediction is unfolded and read aloud, the contents are the same as the words on the selected scrap from the bag. To prepare for this trick, tear the same sheets out of 10 or 12 copies of a newspaper or magazine. Make sure that the pages all bear the same information, hold the pages together and tear off a small section from each page. These pieces, which all show identical information, are dropped into the inside compartment. Save a full sheet from the same newspaper or magazine, and tear it up during your performance, in full view of your audience. Drop the pieces into the other side of the bag. When the selection is made, it is the opposite side that is offered to the spectator. This means that whichever piece is taken from the bag, the words are the same as on your prediction.

SUN AND MOON

HERE IS ONE IDEA FOR USING THE CHANGING BAG. THE CENTERS OF TWO SQUARES OF PAPER, ONE RED AND ONE YELLOW, ARE REMOVED. THE MAGICIAN RESTORES THEM, BUT THE RED CENTER IS NOW IN THE YELLOW SQUARE AND THE YELLOW CENTER IS IN THE RED SQUARE. THE MAGICIAN'S POWERS ARE ONCE AGAIN CONJURED UP, AND THIS TIME THE TWO SQUARES OF PAPER ARE RESTORED TO THEIR ORIGINAL FORM.

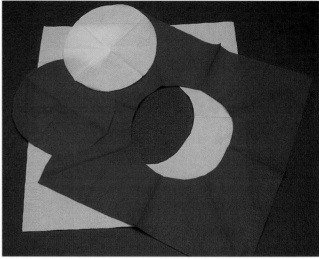

2 Use the same method to cut two slightly smaller circles from the centers of the two other squares. Discard the circles you have cut, and glue R1 to the hole in the yellow square and Y1 to the hole in the red square. You have a yellow square with a red circle in the center and a red square with a yellow circle in the center.

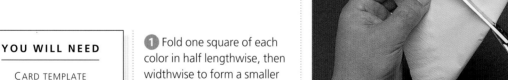

YOU WILL NEED

CARD TEMPLATE
(ONE-EIGHTH OF A CIRCLE)

4 SQUARES OF RED PAPER

4 SQUARES OF YELLOW
PAPER

SCISSORS

GLUE

PAPER CLIP

CHANGING BAG
(SEE PAGE 134)

1 Fold one square of each color in half lengthwise, then widthwise to form a smaller square. Fold this diagonally to give a triangle. Use the template to cut an arc from the triangle – this cuts a circle in the center of the square. For descriptive purposes, we will call the cut-out circles R1 (for red) and Y1 (for yellow). Keep the circles and discard the rest of each square.

3 When the glue has dried, fold the two prepared squares into four and put a paper clip over them. Now put them in the front compartment of your changing bag. Alongside them, place two ordinary squares (one red, one yellow), similarly folded. The two remaining squares are also folded into four and placed on your table. Before placing the squares on the table, draw part of a circle in pencil on their centers, using the same card template as before. You are now ready to perform the trick. Pick up the squares from the table and display them. Cut a circle from the center of each square, using your guides to get the cutting the right size.

6 Refold the squares – or tear them up, if you prefer – and put them into the rear compartment of the changing bag.

4 Show the two squares with the holes in them, and then show the two circles. Fold them all up and put them in the back pocket of the changing bag. Say a few magic words and then place your hand in the front compartment of the bag. Find the papers with the paper clip, pull off the clip, and bring them into view.

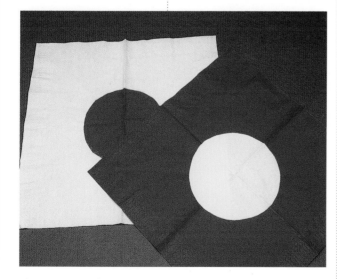

5 You claim to have restored the papers but when they are unfolded, it seems you have gone terribly wrong – the yellow square has a red circle in the center, and the red square has a yellow circle in the center.

7 This time, use some stronger magic words, before reaching into the front compartment of the bag to remove the squares. Open out the square, and they are seen to be fully restored – it is another miracle that has been accomplished!

137

A CAPITAL PREDICTION

IN THIS TRICK USING A CHANGING BAG, THE PERFORMER SHOWS A BAG CONTAINING NUMEROUS SLIPS OF PAPER ON WHICH ARE WRITTEN THE NAMES OF CAPITAL CITIES. SOME OF THE SLIPS ARE REMOVED FROM THE BAG AND THE NAMES ARE CALLED OUT TO GIVE SOME INDICATION OF THE RANGE AVAILABLE. FINALLY, ONE SLIP IS WITHDRAWN FROM THE BAG AND THE CHOSEN CITY IS NAMED. A LARGE ENVELOPE, WHICH HAS BEEN ON VIEW THROUGHOUT, IS THEN OPENED TO REVEAL A CARD BEARING THE NAME OF THE CHOSEN CAPITAL.

YOU WILL NEED

CHANGING BAG (SEE PAGE 134)

ABOUT 100 SLIPS OF PAPER, MEASURING APPROXIMATELY 3 × 1¼ IN.

BALL-POINT PEN OR TYPEWRITER

PIECE OF CARD

LARGE ENVELOPE

1 If you do not have a changing bag or if you need something to practice with, try gluing two paper bags together. Fabric is best, however, and a changing bag like this one is not very difficult to make.

2 On 50 slips of paper write the name of one capital city. Let's use Paris as an example. Fold these slips of paper in half and drop them into one side of your bag. Write the names of different capital cities on each of the remaining 50 slips. Fold these in half and place them in the other compartment of the bag. Write the name Paris on the card, place this in the large envelope, and you are ready to begin your act.

5 One slip is chosen and the name read out (it is, of course, Paris). Emphasize that the spectator had a perfectly free choice (another lie), and draw attention to the envelope that has been on view throughout.

3 Show the envelope to the audience and place it where it can be seen by them while you perform the trick. Pick up the changing bag, reach into the compartment with the different cities and pull out a handful of slips. Let them fall from your fingers and then let them fall back into the bag, as you say: "I have here over a hundred slips of paper [magic is all about lying] bearing the names of capital cities, and I would like someone to choose one of them." Invite someone from the audience onto the stage to help you, and ask that person to draw out a few slips from the bag, unfold them, and call out the names of the cities written on them.

4 You now explain that this time you want just one slip to be taken. While you are talking, alter the positions of your fingers on the bag so that the next time you open it, the spectator reaches into the other compartment (the one in which all the slips bear the same name).

6 When the envelope is opened, it is seen that you correctly predicted which capital city would be chosen.

IN BETWEEN SILK

THIS COLORFUL MAGICAL MYSTERY USES SILK HANDKERCHIEFS AND A CHANGING BAG, BUT A BAG
WITH A DIFFERENCE.

YOU WILL NEED

CHANGING BAG WITH A CUT IN
THE BASE (SEE STEP 1)

4 PURPLE SILK
HANDKERCHIEFS

2 YELLOW SILK
HANDKERCHIEFS

1 You will need a specially prepared changing bag for this effect. The basic bag is the same as that described on page 134, but rather than stitching all the way around the bag, leave a slit in the center of the base. Reinforce the edges of the slit and make sure it gives access to both compartments.

2 Before you begin your act, knot one of the yellow silk handkerchiefs between two purple ones. Carefully secrete the three knotted silks in one compartment, making sure that a corner of one of the purple silks is readily available to pull through the slit in the base of the bag. Leave the other compartment empty.

3 Display the bag to your audience, turning it inside out to prove that it is completely empty. Show the audience the two loose purple handkerchiefs, and place them in the empty compartment of the bag. As you are doing so, almost as an afterthought, pull the corner of a purple silk through the slit in the base of the bag. In fact, this is the corner of one of the handkerchiefs already in the other compartment. The same applies to the second purple silk in the secret compartment. This time, pull a corner out of the top of the bag so that it is hanging over the edge. It will appear to

your audience as if the two loose silks that you have just placed inside the bag are being displayed in this manner. In reality, of course, the two silk handkerchiefs that are already knotted are those that can be seen.

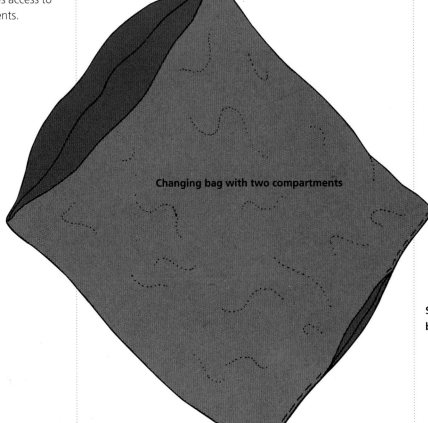

Changing bag with two compartments

Slit in base allows access to both compartments

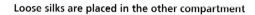

Loose silks are placed in the other compartment

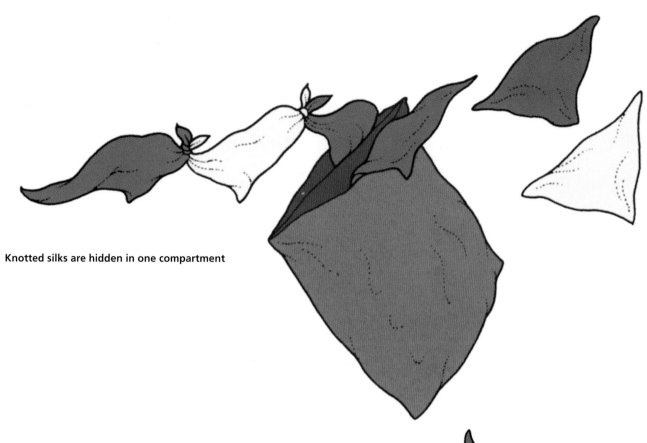

Knotted silks are hidden in one compartment

The second purple silk protrudes from the top of the bag

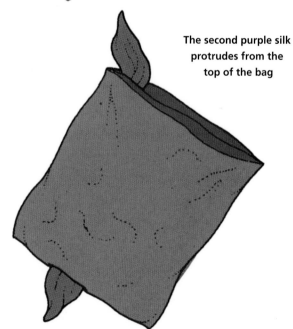

One purple silk protrudes from the slit in the bottom

4 Display the loose yellow handkerchief to the audience and then place it in the compartment that contains the two loose purple handkerchiefs.

5 Ask a member of the audience to pull the handkerchief out slightly at the top. Ask another spectator to pull gently at the handkerchief that is protruding from the base. As each spectator pulls, they quickly discover that the handkerchiefs become taut. When the handkerchief at the bottom of the bag is pulled out completely, the other two follow. To add to the audience's amazement, both purple handkerchiefs have been on view throughout the whole trick.

6 Once the set of knotted silks has been removed from the bag, you can show the audience that it is empty by turning it inside out again. Remember, to display the compartment that really is now empty.

RABBIT FROM A HAT

THE APPEARANCE OF A WHITE RABBIT FROM A TOP HAT HAS LONG BEEN THE SIGNATURE ACT OF THE MAGICIAN'S CRAFT, AND ALL MAGICIANS WORTHY OF THE NAME SHOULD BE ABLE TO PERFORM THIS CLASSIC FEAT OF CONJURING. THE EFFECT FOR WHICH YOU ARE STRIVING IS SIMPLE – BUT EFFECTIVE.

Rabbit loading bag

Black cloth

Curtain rings or similar

Top hat

Nail

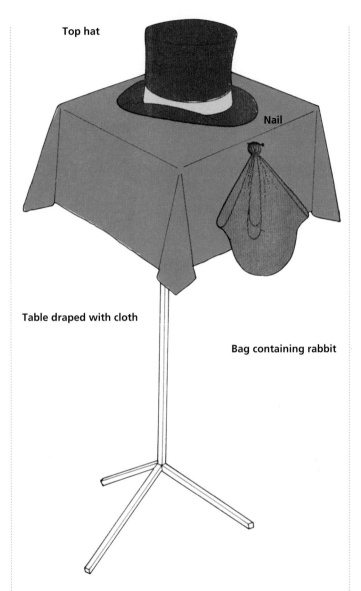

Table draped with cloth

Bag containing rabbit

YOU WILL NEED

A RABBIT (THESE COME IN ALL SHAPES AND SIZES, OF COURSE, BUT YOU MUST HAVE A SMALL VARIETY FOR THE TRICK TO WORK – THE NETHERLANDS DWARF IS IDEAL)

TOP HAT (EITHER AN OPERA HAT, WHICH FOLDS UP, OR A SOLID HAT, WHICH DOES NOT)

TABLE COVERED WITH A CLOTH DRAPE AND A HOOK OR NAIL HAMMERED INTO THE CENTER OF THE BACK EDGE

MAGIC WAND

"RABBIT-LOADER" BAG (SEE STEP 1)

1 The special "rabbit-loader" bag consists of a square of black cloth with a ring attached to each corner. The piece of cloth should be large enough to hold the rabbit safely and securely when the four corners are brought together, thus transforming the square into a bag.

2 Before your performance, place the rabbit in the bag and hook the four rings at the corners over the hook or nail in your table. Because the table is covered with a fabric drape, your audience will not be able to see the bag from the front. Place the top hat on the table, open mouth downward, positioning it approximately in the center but toward the back of the table, just in front of where the loader bag is concealed. Put the magic wand in your left jacket pocket.

3 Turn the hat upside down so that the mouth of the hat is uppermost. Now, remove the hat from the table. This not only allows the audience to see that the hat is empty but also that there is nothing else on top of the table. Display the hat to the whole audience, making a special point of showing that there is nothing inside it. If you are using a folding opera hat, gently collapse it as additional proof that it is, completely empty.

4 Replace the hat on the table, in the original position, mouth downward, and toward the center back of the table. With your left hand, take your magic wand out of your pocket and flourish it in the air. This movement is a deliberate misdirection so that your audience looks away from your right hand.

5 While the audience is looking at the wand in your left hand, lift the hat away from the table with your right hand, which executes the secret loading of the rabbit into the hat. This is done with one smooth, swift action. Lift the brim of the hat – the part of the brim lying toward the back of the table – and pivot it over from the back to the front. At the same time, disengage the rings from the hook at the rear of the table with your thumb, so that the loader bag containing the rabbit automatically swings inside the hat. The weight of the rabbit makes this action quite easy to perform.

6 Once the loader bag is inside the hat, tap the hat with your magic wand, release the rings, and the rabbit will free itself to make its appearance. The now flat piece of cloth will be hidden within the interior of the hat – and you have produced the proverbial rabbit from a hat.

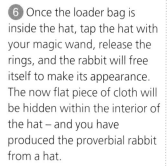

6 ♦

THE AMAZING THUMB TIP

IF THERE IS ONE SMALL PIECE OF A MAGICIAN'S EQUIPMENT THAT IS MORE VERSATILE THAN ALL THE OTHERS PUT TOGETHER, IT IS THE THUMB TIP. THESE LITTLE GADGETS ARE AVAILABLE IN ALL SHAPES and sizes, they are made in different materials, and they are designed for a whole series of tricks, which can be presented both in close-up and on stage.

USING THE THUMB TIP

The thumb tip fits over the magician's thumb and can be used on either hand. When you are selecting a thumb tip, choose one that matches the size and coloration of your own thumb. The tip should fit comfortably but should be loose enough to slide off easily and to accommodate an item such as a small silk handkerchief.

1 The thumb tip should fit comfortably on your thumb, but not so tightly that, say, a silk handkerchief cannot be hidden inside it.

2 Make sure that the thumb tip matches your own thumb in size and color as closely as possible. Make sure that it slips on and off smoothly. If it is too tight you will not be able to discard it easily.

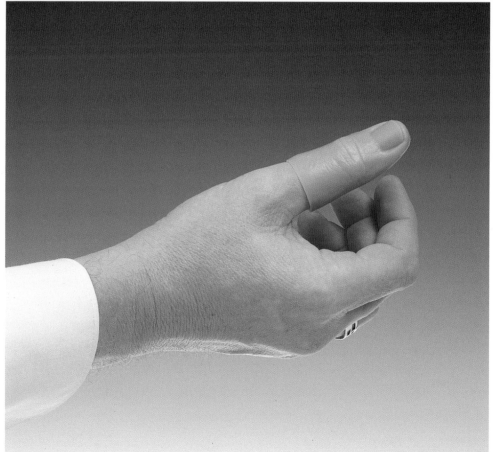

SHOWING THE HANDS EMPTY

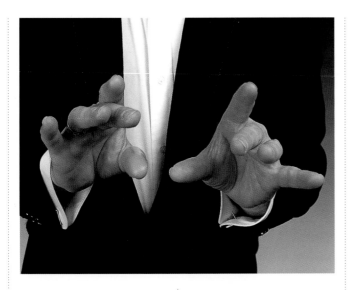

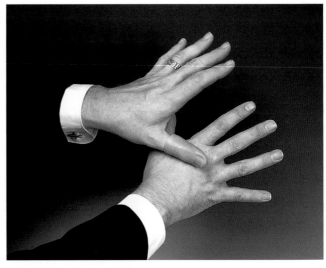

With the thumb tip on your right hand (assuming that you are right handed), you are ready to show the audience that your hands are empty. The full length of the thumb tip is actually never shown during the display.

1 Point all your fingers and both thumbs toward the audience. Make sure that only the tips of your fingers and thumbs are on view, including the tip of the thumb tip. This avoids the join between the end of the tip and rest of your own thumb being noticed.

2 If you are showing your hands in a static position, cross the thumb wearing the thumb tip behind your opposite hand.

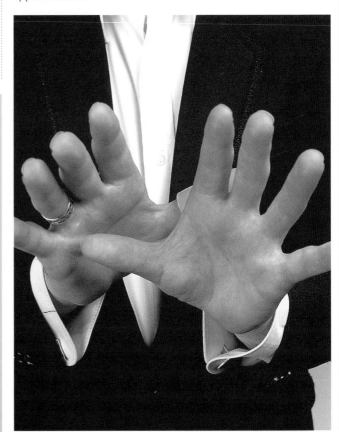

OBTAINING THE THUMB TIP DURING A PERFORMANCE

In many cases, you will not need the thumb tip until part way through your routine, and there is a correct procedure for placing it on your hand without the audience being aware of what you are doing. Depending on what particular effect you have planned, the thumb tip is normally secreted inside a jacket pocket. On other occasions, when you intend going to the back of your table to perform a trick with a container on the table, you can often secretly pick it up then. Of course, if your program begins with an effect that involves the thumb tip, you can wear it right from the start.

3 From the audience's point of view, the presence of the thumb tip cannot be detected.

PASSING THE SALT

FOR MANY YEARS, MAGICIANS HAVE BEEN MAKING SALT TRAVEL FROM ONE CLENCHED FIST TO THE OTHER, RELYING ON THE THUMB TIP AS THE PERFECT AID. THE SALT TRANSFORMATION EFFECT SEEMS IMPOSSIBLE, SINCE THE MAGICIAN IS DEALING WITH MINUTE GRAINS OF SALT, WHICH ARE QUITE UNLIKE PROPS SUCH AS HANDKERCHIEFS AND CIGARETTES.

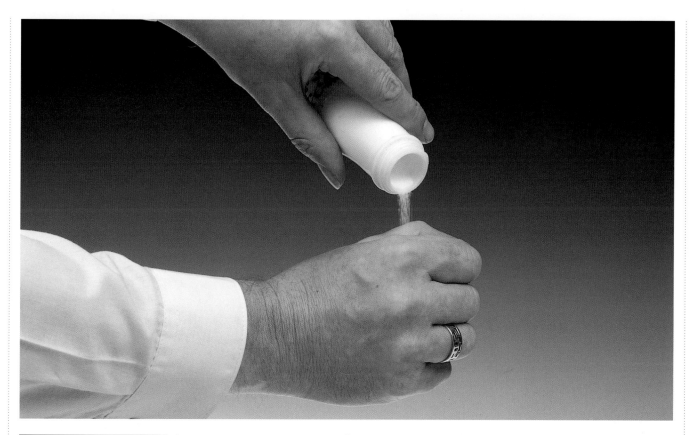

YOU WILL NEED

THUMB TIP

SALT SHAKER CONTAINING SALT (THE KIND WITH A SCREW-ON TOP IS BEST FOR THIS EFFECT)

GLASS BOWL OR ASHTRAY

1 Before you begin your performance, put the salt shaker, filled with salt, at the back of your table, behind your other props, together with the thumb tip, which should also be hidden from the audience's view.

2 Show the audience that both your hands are empty – you are not wearing the thumb tip at this stage. Pick up the salt shaker with your right hand and, at the same time, secretly insert your thumb into the thumb tip. Place the salt shaker on the front of the table. Use your right hand to bend the fingers of your left hand into a fist, and as you do so, insert the thumb tip into the closed left fist, with its open mouth facing upward.

3 Remove the lid of the salt shaker and pour the salt into your fist – into the thumb tip. It is important that you leave sufficient space for you to insert your thumb. Allow a few grains of salt to spill down your fingers, and push your right thumb down inside your clenched fist as if the salt is beginning to overflow at the top. As you do so, insert your thumb into the tip.

4 Extract both thumb and thumb tip from your left fist, quickly showing that your right hand is empty, form a fist with your right hand. With your fingers and palm gripped around the thumb tip, pull out your thumb.

5 Open your left hand, stretching out each finger to show that the salt has actually vanished.

6 Invert your right hand over the bowl or ashtray so that the salt within the concealed thumb tip can pour from the fist. Secretly transfer the thumb tip back to your thumb to end by showing your hands empty.

PRODUCING A HANDKERCHIEF

PRODUCING A HANDKERCHIEF FROM THIN AIR – THEN VANISHING IT AGAIN LATER – IS A SIMPLE MANEUVER WHEN YOU WEAR A THUMB TIP, BUT IS EFFECTIVE NONETHELESS. THE MAGICIAN SHOWS THE AUDIENCE HIS EMPTY HANDS BUT IS ABLE TO PRODUCE A BRIGHTLY COLORED HANDKERCHIEF FROM A CLOSED FIST.

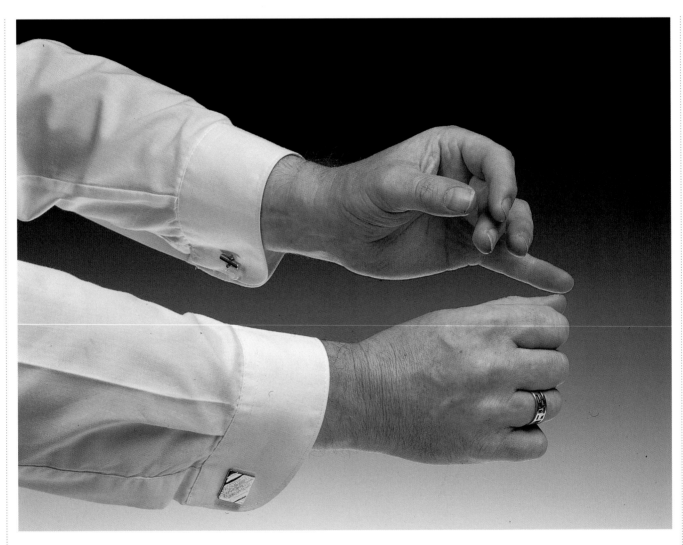

YOU WILL NEED

THUMB TIP

SMALL SILK HANDKERCHIEF

1 Before your performance, secrete inside the thumb tip the handkerchief, making sure that one corner is toward the open end of the thumb tip so that it can be quickly and easily extracted. Place the thumb tip on your right thumb (this assumes that you are right handed).

2 To some clever patter, show the audience that your hands are empty (see page 146). Wriggle your fingers and thumbs and keep your hands continually on the move. With your right hand, reach into the air, making a catching motion. As you do so, allow your thumb to bend inward so that it is in the palm of your hand, with your fingers also coming in to form a fist. Withdraw your thumb. The thumb tip is now firmly held within the fist, with its open mouth toward the top.

3 With the first finger and thumb of your left hand, begin to pull out the silk from the thumb tip.

4 It appears to the audience as if you are actually extracting the handkerchief from the fist itself.

VANISHING A SILK HANDKERCHIEF

This maneuver is as simple as producing a silk handkerchief. The empty thumb tip is already on your thumb as you begin, or it must be secretly obtained from your pocket.

1 Show both hands to be empty, and curl in the fingers and thumb of your right hand to make a fist.

2 With the thumb tip now removed from your thumb and held in your clenched fist, tuck the silk into the hidden thumb tip.

3 Once the silk is inside the tip, it is a very easy matter to insert your thumb back into the tip so that both hands can be opened to show that the handkerchief has, indeed, completely vanished.

DISCARDING THE THUMB TIP

There are two possible ways of discarding the thumb tip after use.

1 Allow your thumb to re-enter the tip when the handkerchief has just been pulled from it by your left hand. The tip is now back in its original position.

2 Alternatively, when the handkerchief has been displayed after its production, it can be quickly discarded or pocketed, and the thumb tip can secretly accompany it. This latter method is to be preferred to the first because it leaves your hands genuinely empty and ready for any other effects and tricks that you do not involve the use of the thumb tip.

VANISHING A LIGHTED CIGARETTE

THIS IS A POPULAR EFFECT AMONG PERFORMERS WHO LIKE CLOSE-UP MAGIC. THE DISAPPEARANCE OF A LIGHTED CIGARETTE INTO A BORROWED POCKET HANDKERCHIEF ALWAYS SEEMS TO AMAZE AND AMUSE THE AUDIENCE. IN CASE YOU CANNOT OBTAIN A CIGARETTE FROM A MEMBER OF YOUR AUDIENCE, MAKE SURE THAT YOU HAVE BOTH A HALF-SMOKED CIGARETTE AND BOX OF MATCHES ON YOUR TABLE. DURING THE EFFECT, YOUR HANDS ARE NEVER REALLY SHOWN TO BE EMPTY, BECAUSE YOU ARE NOT INTENDING TO PRODUCE SOMETHING FROM THEM. HOLD YOUR HANDS NATURALLY, AND BEND THE THUMB – WEARING THE THUMB TIP – INWARD, SO THAT IT IS NOT IN FULL VIEW.

YOU WILL NEED

THUMB TIP

HALF-SMOKED CIGARETTE

BOX OF MATCHES

1 Make sure that the thumb tip is already in place on your thumb before beginning the trick. Borrow a large pocket handkerchief from a member of the audience. This proves that it is genuine and is of value to that particular person. Display it on both sides to show that it is fully intact and that it is also good quality fabric.

2 Drape the handkerchief over your left fist. Use the thumb that is wearing the thumb tip to make a well in which the cigarette can be dropped. Dip in your thumb several times to make an indentation. Pull your thumb away, leaving the tip behind, concealed in the pocket handkerchief.

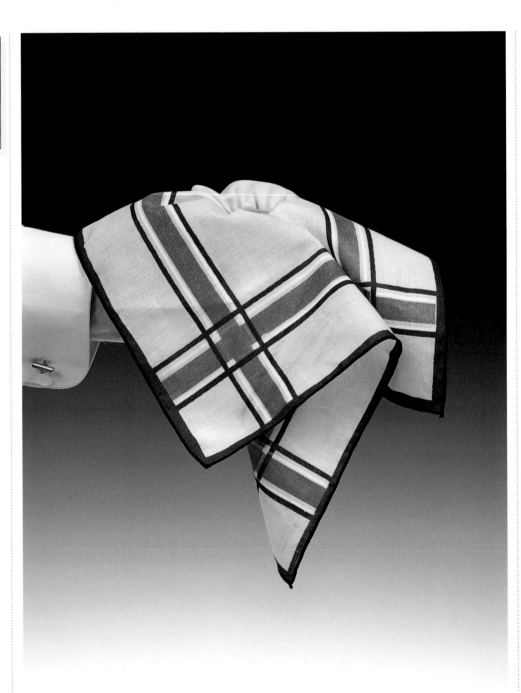

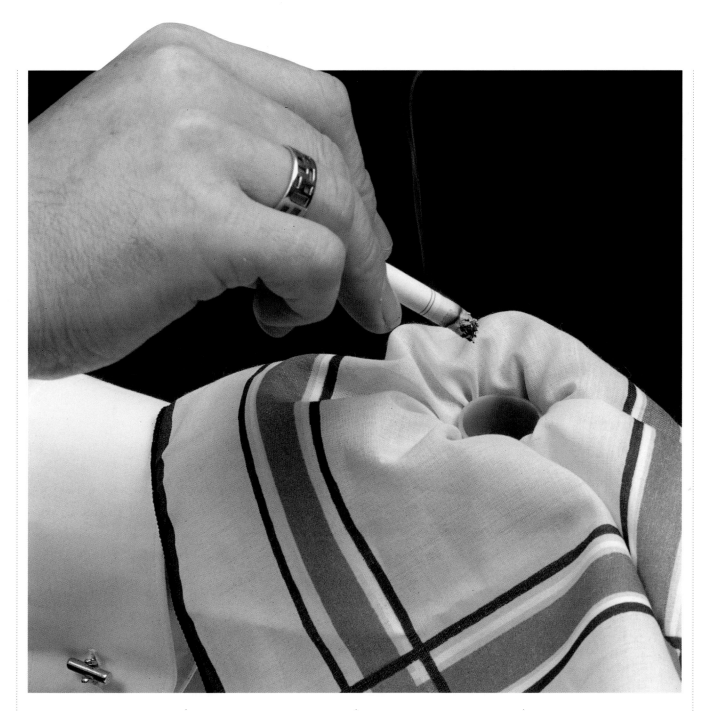

3 Simply drop the cigarette, lighted end downward, into the thumb tip so that a plume of smoke rises for the audience to see. You should have some patter ready at this stage, which you can deliver as you pretend to be unaware of the smoke that is rising from the handkerchief.

4 The audience's laughter draws your attention to the "burning" handkerchief. Repeatedly stub out the cigarette with your thumb, and, the final time, secretly withdraw the thumb tip.

5 Display the handkerchief face on to the audience, keeping both thumbs behind the top corners. Then, the handkerchief can be displayed for some time so that everyone in the audience can see that it is completely unharmed. Return it to the spectator. If you wish, discard the thumb tip at this stage, slipping it into your pocket when you replace the box of matches into a pocket.

Note: Children will need supervision for this trick.

BURNED AND RESTORED HANDKERCHIEF

THIS IS YET ANOTHER TRICK THAT EXPLOITS A BURNED AND RESTORED THEME, AS WELL AS MAKING
USE OF THE FAITHFUL THUMB TIP.

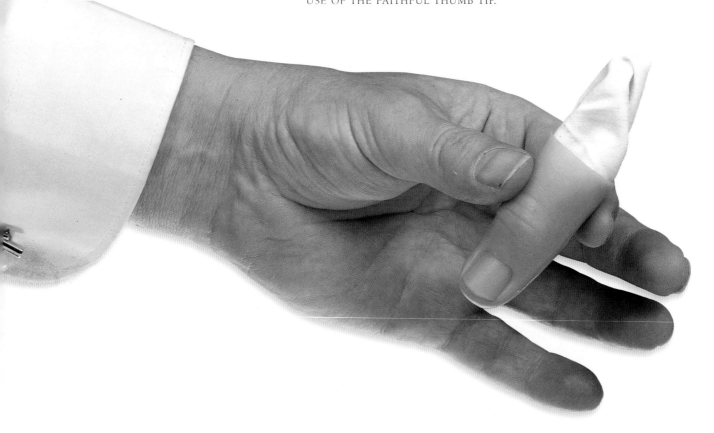

YOU WILL NEED

THUMB TIP

CIGARETTE LIGHTER OR BOX
OF MATCHES

SMALL PIECES OF WHITE
MATERIAL TAKEN FROM A
POCKET HANDKERCHIEF

Note: Children will need
supervision for this trick.

1 Gather up the four corners of the small piece of fabric and either stitch them together or bind them up with a small length of clear adhesive tape. Secrete the prepared piece of cloth, with the taped ends downward, inside the thumb tip and place the prepared thumb tip in your right-hand jacket pocket, next to the cigarette lighter or box of matches.

2 At the beginning of your presentation, ask to borrow a man's white pocket handkerchief from someone in your audience. It is important that at least the central section of the handkerchief is white and that it matches as closely as possible the section of fabric that you have previously secreted in the thumb tip.

3 Drape the pocket handkerchief over your left fist. Put your right hand in your pocket to remove the matches or cigarette lighter and, at the same time, push your thumb into the thumb tip. Remove the matches or lighter from your pocket with the thumb tip securely over your thumb. Distract your audience's attention with some patter, explaining to them that you are going to conduct an experiment to show that some fabrics burn and some do not.

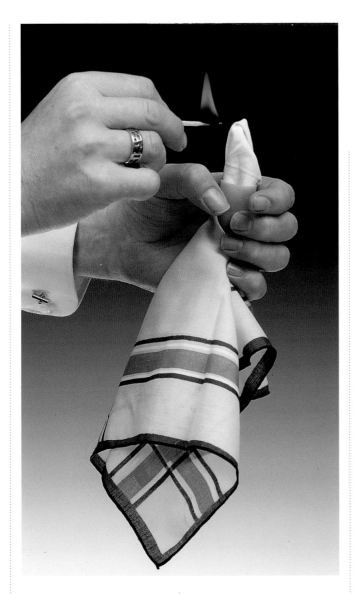

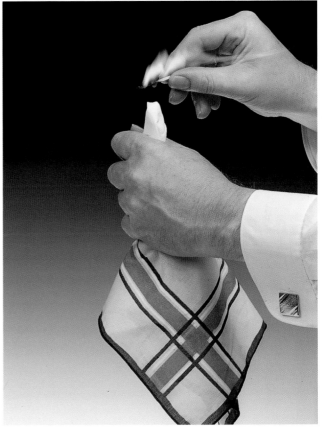

4 Put down the matches or the lighter on your table. Use your right thumb to push the handkerchief into your left fist, and on the last pass, leave the thumb tip behind. Casually show that your right hand is empty as you move to pull up the portion of cloth from the thumb tip so that it appears to be the central portion of the handkerchief. This is the portion that is going to be set alight.

5 Use the cigarette lighter or a lighted match to pass a flame quickly over the handkerchief. Then bring the flame carefully to the portion of cloth that is held within the thumb tip. Wave the flame quickly over the fabric until it catches light.

6 At first, pretend not to notice that the fabric is alight. From the audience's point of view it will look as if the center section of the handkerchief is burning. Then feign alarm and stub out the flames with your thumb. By this time, the cloth inside the thumb tip will be little more than ashes.

7 Before withdrawing your thumb for the last time, slip on the thumb tip. Collect the lighter or matchbox from the table and return them to your right-hand jacket pocket, leaving the thumb tip in your pocket at the same time. The right hand comes out of the pocket clean and empty.

8 Looking at what appears to be a burned handkerchief, make a magical pass over it. Then slowly open out the handkerchief to show that is is now fully restored. Return the borrowed handkerchief to the spectator.

Trick of the Trade

- When you are practicing this effect, it is always a good idea to have an ashtray nearby, because burning cloth can accidentally float away as it disintegrates.

THE PENETRATING THUMB

MATTER THROUGH MATTER – HERE IS A TRICK THAT WILL MAKE YOUR AUDIENCES GASP WITH
APPRECIATION AS YOU APPEAR TO PUSH YOUR THUMB THROUGH A BORROWED POCKET HANDKERCHIEF,
ONLY TO RETURN TO ITS OWNER IN ITS ORIGINAL STATE.

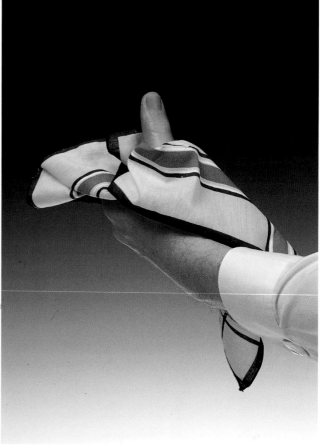

YOU WILL NEED

THUMB TIP

---

❶ Before you begin to do this trick, make sure you are wearing the thumb tip on your right hand.

❷ Borrow a handkerchief from a member of the audience. Explain what you are going to do: that you will drape the handkerchief over the clenched fist and that you will push your thumb right through the center of the handkerchief. As you talk, demonstrate the action by pushing the right thumb, which is wearing the thumb tip, into the well of the left fist. Withdraw your thumb, leaving the thumb tip concealed in your left fist.

❸ Now actually drape the handkerchief over the top of the left fist and use your right thumb to make a small well in the material, at the same time pushing your thumb and the fabric of the center of the handkerchief carefully into the thumb tip.

❹ Take the handkerchief n your right hand and show that your "thumb" really has penetrated the material of the handkerchief. Your real thumb and the fabric will fit comfortably within the molded shape of the tip.

❺ To reverse the procedure, grip the handkerchief and thumb tip in your left hand and pull them both away. Wave your right hand to draw your audience's attention away from your left hand, with which you slip the handkerchief and thumb tip into your left-hand pocket. Remove the handkerchief from your pocket, and display it to the audience to show that it is completely undamaged before handing it back to its owner.

MAGIC IN CLOSE-UP

ONE OF THE MOST POPULAR

BRANCHES OF MAGIC, CLOSE-UP MAGIC IS IDEAL

FOR AMATEUR AND SEMI PROFESSIONAL MAGICIANS WHO

LIKE TO ENTERTAIN IMPROMPTU PARTIES OR OTHER SOCIAL GATHERINGS.

Close-up magic makes use of almost every small household object you can

think of, from matches and coins, to keys and knives. The special qualities

needed to make a good close-up magician are the nerve to perform on the

spur of the moment combined with the ability to select the most suitable

members of the audience for the particular tricks. The close-up

performer should always pay especial attention to his or her personal hygiene.

A DATE WITH A MAGICIAN

THE FAMOUS OKITO BOX, WHICH IS MADE OF SOLID BRASS, SILVER, OR PLASTIC, IS STILL A VERY POPULAR PROP WITH CLOSE-UP PERFORMERS. HOWEVER, MOST SEEM TO USE THE BOX IN THE WAY IT WAS FIRST DEVISED, BRINGING NO INGENUITY OR FLAIR TO THE TRICK. THIS PARTICULAR VERSION AIMS TO BRING SOMETHING NEW TO THIS TRADITIONAL EFFECT.

YOU WILL NEED

PILL BOX OR CONTAINER WITH A PUSH-ON (NOT A SCREW-ON) LID; THE LID MUST ALSO FIT OVER THE BASE OF THE BOX

1 Begin your performance by displaying the small pill box to your audience. Then ask to borrow a coin, any coin, from anyone in the audience. The only proviso is that the coin must fit inside the box. Once a spectator has provided a coin, turn away. Still holding out the box to the audience, ask the spectator to drop the coin, date side up in the box. Ask the person who has provided the coin to remember the date on the coin. Throughout this, you should keep turned away so that you cannot watch the transaction. Then ask the spectator to place the cap or lid on the box.

2 Holding the box, sealed with its lid, in your right hand, rattle the box to prove that the coin is still inside.

3 Still holding the box in your cupped right hand, remove the lid with your left hand to show the audience the coin is still there. Now make a show of turning away to prove to your audience that you do not actually look at the coin at any time. In replacing the lid on the box, execute a simple yet clever move. Pivot over the box with your right hand so that the base is now upward. The coin is still inside but it is now actually resting on the palm of your right hand.

4 With your left hand, immediately place the lid of the box on top of the base. Shake the box, gripped with the right-hand fingers and the thumb, and even in this position, the coin can be heard to rattle inside. Tilting the box toward the audience, you can secretly glance at the date of the coin, which is now exposed. Now you divine the date of the borrowed coin, stating the date numeral by numeral. The spectator who loaned the coin will verify that the date is correct.

5 You are now ready to present the second part of the trick. With the box, containing the coin, resting on the palm of your right hand, remove the box with your left hand and, at the same time, turn over your right hand to palm the coin.

6 Place the box on top of the clenched fist of your right hand, which is now secretly concealing the coin. Simply but gently tap the box with your left hand and allow the coin to fall onto the table from within your hand. That is the penetration.

7 Pick up the box in your left hand and throw it on your table so that the lid and base separate. They can then be passed to members of the audience to inspect.

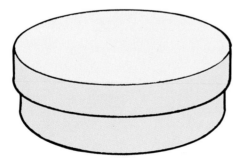

Pill box with flanged lid

The lid also fits over the base of the pill box

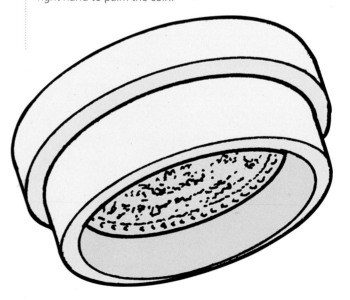

With the lid placed on the base of the pill box, you can tilt the box forward slightly so that you can glance at the coin

STIFF'N ROPE

THIS TOUCH OF MAGIC FROM INDIA IS A PLATFORM TRICK THAT OWES SOMETHING TO THAT GREAT CLASSIC, THE INDIAN ROPE TRICK. THE TRICK IS SIMPLICITY ITSELF. A LENGTH OF ROPE, BALANCED ON THE END OF YOUR INDEX FINGER, MAGICALLY BECOMES RIGID. WHEN YOU HAVE FINISHED YOUR TRICK, IT REVERTS TO ITS ORIGINAL LIMP FORM.

YOU WILL NEED

LENGTH OF SOFT WHITE ROPE

FLESH-COLORED COTTON THREAD

1 Before you attempt to perform this trick, stitch a small loop of flesh-colored cotton to one end of the rope.

2 With your right hand, hold the end of the rope, concealing the loop of thread.

3 To balance the end of the rope on the first finger of your left hand, slip this finger into the loop, and, with your right hand, hold the opposite end of the rope upward. The rope becomes stiff and rigid. Pull your hands against each other to make sure that the rope is kept taut.

4 To complete the trick, disengage the finger from the loop, and the length of rope resumes its original form.

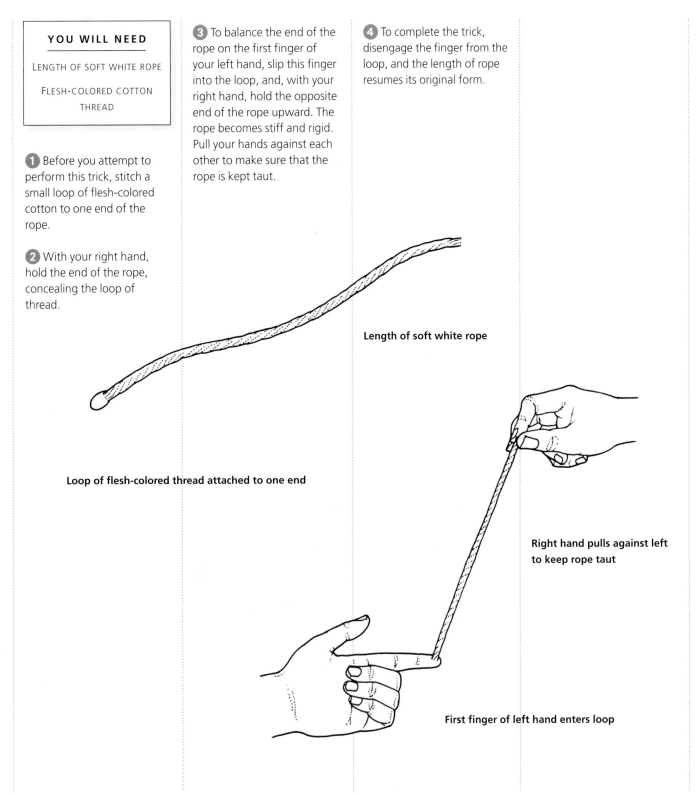

Length of soft white rope

Loop of flesh-colored thread attached to one end

Right hand pulls against left to keep rope taut

First finger of left hand enters loop

SPENT MATCHES

THIS QUICK TRICK NEEDS NO SPECIAL EQUIPMENT – JUST A MATCHBOX AND SOME MATCHES – BUT YOU WILL HAVE TO DO A LITTLE PREPARATION BEFOREHAND. YOU EMPTY THE CONTENTS FROM A MATCHBOX, THEN SHOW THAT THERE ARE FOUR MATCHES LEFT. YOU PUT THREE INSIDE AND CLOSE THE TRAY. YOU STRIKE THE FOURTH MATCH AND WAVE IT AROUND THE BOX. WHEN YOU OPEN THE BOX AGAIN, ALL THE MATCHES ARE SEEN TO BE SPENT.

YOU WILL NEED

EMPTY MATCHBOX

4 LIVE MATCHES

3 SPENT MATCHES

Note: Children will need supervision for this trick.

1 Prepare the matchbox by cutting away a section from one end of the inner tray. When you set the trick, wedge the three spent matches between the inner tray and the outer sleeve. Keep the box open at this position. Drop the four live matchsticks into the tray.

2 Display the opened box to the audience and tip out the four live matches onto the table. Show that the box is completely empty.

3 Drop three of the matches back inside the box and put the fourth one in a pocket. Hold the box in your left hand and tilt it so that the three live matchsticks slide out of the box into your waiting hand.

4 Close the box. This allows the spent matches, which are wedged at the top, to fall automatically into the tray.

5 With your left hand, go to your pocket as if to withdraw the fourth live match. In so doing, however, drop two of the three matchsticks you have already palmed, bringing out only one.

6 Strike the live match against the matchbox and wave it around the box. Open the box and empty the contents onto the table to reveal three spent matches.

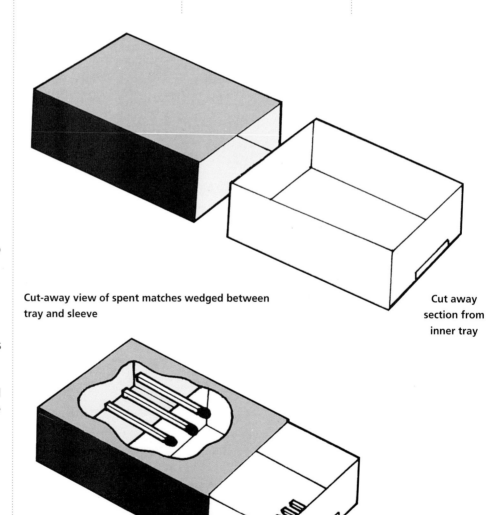

Cut-away view of spent matches wedged between tray and sleeve

Cut away section from inner tray

Live matches released through section cut out of inner tray

MATCH-IC

YOU WILL NEED A SIMPLE BOOK OF MATCHES FOR THIS EFFECT, WHICH CAN BE PERFORMED FOR A SMALL GROUP AS CLOSE-UP MAGIC. THE TRICK RELIES ON YOU SHOWING A BOOK OF LIVE MATCHES, THEN REMOVING ONE MATCH, WHICH YOU LIGHT AND WAVE AROUND THE BOOK. WHEN YOU SHOW THE BOOK OF MATCHES AGAIN, YOUR AUDIENCE SEES THAT AMONG THE LIVE MATCHES IS ONE SPENT MATCH.

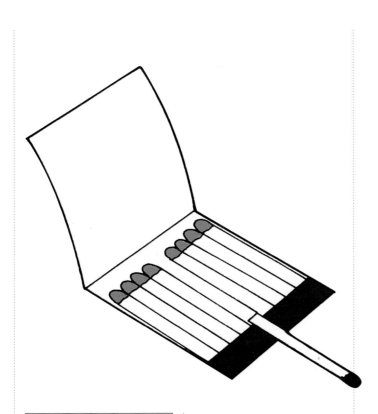

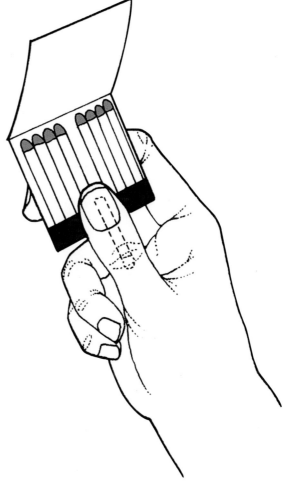

YOU WILL NEED

BOOK OF MATCHES

Note: Children will need supervision for this trick.

1 Before your performance, bend one match away from its original position – take care that you do not pull it away – strike its head and immediately blow out the flame. Have the book of matches, open, inside your right jacket pocket.

2 When you come to perform the trick, remove the book of matches from your pocket with your right hand, holding the base between your thumb and fingers so that your thumb hides the spent match, which is still attached to the book of matches but bent forward at an angle.

3 With your left hand, remove one of the live matches and light it against the edge of the book.

4 Close the packet from front to back, gently pivoting the bent match so that it is now inside the book. Secure the cover.

5 Wave the lighted match around the packet, and then open the cover to show that one match appears spent amid the other, live matches.

159

ODDS OR EVENS

THIS IS THE PERFECT TRICK FOR THE CLOSE-UP MAGICIAN. YOU WILL INVOLVE A MEMBER OF YOUR
AUDIENCE IN THE TRICK, BUT WHATEVER CHOICE THE SPECTATOR MAKES, YOU WILL NEVER FAIL TO
INTRIGUE BY ALWAYS GETTING THE CORRECT ANSWER.

YOU WILL NEED

ORDINARY MATCHBOX

19 MATCHSTICKS

1 To prepare the matchbox for your performance beforehand, place six matches inside the box, then place a seventh diagonally across the others, thus wedging the first six matches inside the box. If you invert the tray, all seven matches will remain in place and will not fall out. On top of these, place the remaining 12 matches. Slide the tray into the outer cover and you are ready to begin.

2 Place the prepared matchbox on your table so that it is in full view while you perform other tricks. The matchbox should also remain visible to your audience throughout this effect. Tell your audience that you can always prove them to be right or wrong, and that you will even place a bet on the teaser. Say that the matchbox contains either an odd or an even number of matches and that whichever choice a spectator makes – odd or even – will be proved, by you, to be wrong.

3 Invite a member of the audience to say whether he believes the matchbox contains an odd or even number of matches.

4 If the spectator selects odd, slide out the inner tray to show the matches inside and turn the tray upside down, allowing the matches to fall out. Only the 12 matches in top of the wedged ones actually fall from the tray onto the table. Close the box and count the matches to prove that the spectator is wrong.

5 If, on the other hand, the spectator chooses even, simply exert a little pressure on the sides of the tray to release the wedged match. When you turn the tray over, all 19 matches will fall onto the table, again proving the spectator wrong.

ONE IN THE MIDDLE

HERE IS AN EFFECT THAT REQUIRES ABSOLUTELY NO SKILL OR DEXTERITY ON THE PART OF THE PERFORMER. IT IS A BAFFLING CLOSE-UP TRICK THAT CAN BE PRESENTED, IMPROMPTU, ANYWHERE AND UNDER ANY CONDITIONS. IF YOU TRY IT FOR YOURSELF, YOU WILL DISCOVER THAT ALTHOUGH THE CENTRAL CARD VIEWED FROM THE PICTURE SIDE APPEARS TO BE THE ODD CARD, WHEN THE ROW IS REVERSED, IT IS NOT. NO MATTER HOW OFTEN THEY TRY, YOUR SPECTATORS NEVER MANAGE TO LOCATE THE ONE IN THE MIDDLE.

YOU WILL NEED

2 PAIRS OF IDENTICAL CARDS TAKEN FROM 2 PACKS AND AN ODD CARD FROM ONE OF THE PACKS

PAPER CLIP

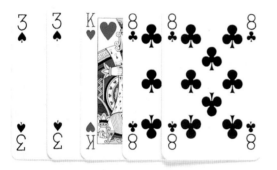

1 Arrange the cards in a row, from left to right, starting with the first pair and sticking each card on top of the one next to it. Cover about two-thirds of the face of each card. Place the odd card – we used the king of hearts – in the center of the row. Once it is stuck down, the unit can be handled as one, but actually refer to it as a row of cards.

2 Reverse the prepared row of cards and ask a spectator to place the paper clip on the king of hearts. The position of the paper clip indicates the obvious choice.

3 Turn over the row so that the cards are face-side up. Reveal the clipped card. The spectator has, in fact, attached the clip to the front card and not to the king of hearts at all.

SPOTLESS

THIS TRICK LENDS ITSELF PERFECTLY TO PERFORMANCE AT CLOSE QUARTERS. THE MAGICIAN SHOWS
THE AUDIENCE A SQUARE BLOCK, PAINTED BLACK, AND SAYS THAT IT IS A GIANT DIE THAT HAS LOST
ITS SPOTS. A SMALL STRIP OF WHITE PAPER IS INTRODUCED INTO THE PROCEEDINGS. IT IS FOLDED UP
NEATLY, CONCERTINA STYLE, AND PLACED ON TOP OF THE BLOCK. BOTH BLOCK AND FOLDED STRIP
ARE COVERED, AND THE MAGICIAN WAVES A PAIR OF SCISSORS OVER THE BLOCK, PRETENDING TO CUT
OUT SPOTS FROM THE PAPER STRIP BY OPENING AND CLOSING THE SCISSORS. WHEN THE COVER IS
REMOVED, THE STRIP IS UNFOLDED AND IS SHOWN TO HAVE HOLES CUT IN IT. THE BLOCK, MEANTIME,
BEARS WHITE SPOTS AND LOOKS LIKE A LARGE, SIX-SIDED DIE.

YOU WILL NEED

BLACK, SOLID INNER BLOCK
COMPLETE WITH SPOTS TO
RESEMBLE A LARGE DIE

BLACK OUTER SHELL

STRIP OF FOLDED PAPER WITH
HOLES CUT IN IT

STRIP OF PAPER (THE SAME
DIMENSIONS AS FOLDED
STRIP)

OUTER RED SHELL

1 The black outer shell
consists of an open-based
container that fits over the
spotted die. The outer surface
of the shell should be black to
match the die and the inside
should also be black. The
outer cover is similar in
structure to the black shell,
but is painted red. This outer
cover should fit neatly over
both the black outer shell and
the solid die.

2 Place the solid die on the table or on a plate or tray. Place the pleated strip of paper with the holes cut in it on top of the die and cover them both with the black shell so that it appears that you have a solid black block on display. Position the red outer cover and the whole paper strip nearby.

3 Display the black block to your audience. Show them the strip of paper before folding it up and carefully placing it on top of the black block. Cover both the block and the strip of paper with the red outer shell.

4 If you wish, make some snipping movements with a pair of scissors over the top of the red shell. Then remove the cover, together with the inner shell – the paper strip is wedged between them – to reveal the block covered with the white spots. The pleated paper sitting on top of the large die can be unfolded to reveal the circles cut out of it.

163

DOMINO CARD

ALTHOUGH THERE APPEARS TO BE A CERTAIN AMOUNT OF MENTALISM INVOLVED IN THIS NEXT EFFECT, IT IS REALLY A CLOSE-UP TRICK, AND ONE THAT NEVER FAILS TO BAFFLE THE AUDIENCE. IT WILL BE ESPECIALLY IMPRESSIVE IF YOU USE A BORROWED PACK OF CARDS, RATHER THAN RELYING ON YOUR OWN. YOU WILL NEED TO INVOLVE MEMBERS OF YOUR AUDIENCE IN THE TRICK.

YOU WILL NEED

PACK OF CARDS

SET OF DOMINOES

ENVELOPE

PIECE OF CARD OR PAPER

PEN OR PENCIL

---

1 Before you begin the trick, remove one of the dominoes from the set – the 3–2, for example. These are the numbers that will appear at the end of the chains when the domino game is completed. In this way you will know that the totaled number (in this case it is 5), and the position of the card to be divined.

2 When you begin your performance, display the pack of cards and shuffle them. Immediately hand them to a member of the audience and ask the spectator to select 12 cards from the pack and to display, face up, in a line. Take note of the card that is situated in position 5.

3 Produce the set of dominoes and scatter them over the table, with the spots uppermost. Ask a second spectator to help you by playing the game of dominoes, one at each end of the chain. Because you have removed the 3–2 from the set, the end numbers will be 3 and 2.

4 While the dominoes are being laid out, take a piece of card and write on it the two end numbers (2 and 3, in this instance) and also the name of the playing card that you have noted in position 5. Seal the card in the envelope and hand it to another spectator for safekeeping.

5 As soon as the second spectator has finished the domino game, ask him or her to add the two end numbers together and then announce the total – as you know, it will be 5.

6 Now ask the spectator who is in charge of the 12 playing cards to name aloud the card in the fifth position in the line of cards.

7 Finally, retrieve the envelope from the third spectator and open it. Remove the card from the envelope and read out the end-of-chain numbers and the name of the card, freely chosen by your from 12 cards, chosen by a spectator from a pack of 52.

KEY-RIFFIC

THIS CLOSE-UP EFFECT USES A KEY ON A SIMPLE KEY-RING. YOU DISPLAY TO YOUR AUDIENCE A KEY
THAT IS SECURELY ATTACHED TO A KEY-RING. THE KEY IS REMOVED AND HANDED TO A MEMBER OF
THE AUDIENCE, WHO HELPS IN MAKING IT VANISH FROM WITHIN A POCKET HANDKERCHIEF. THE KEY
MAGICALLY REAPPEARS ON THE KEY-RING AGAIN.

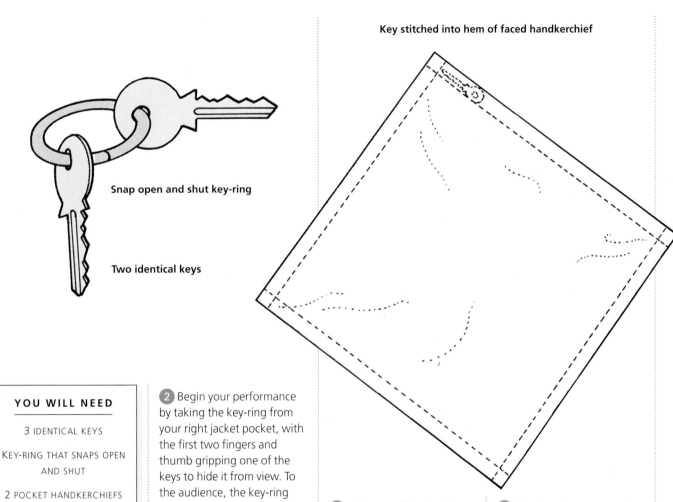

Key stitched into hem of faced handkerchief

Snap open and shut key-ring

Two identical keys

YOU WILL NEED

3 IDENTICAL KEYS

KEY-RING THAT SNAPS OPEN
AND SHUT

2 POCKET HANDKERCHIEFS
(SEE STEP 1)

1 Stitch one of the keys into the hem of one of the handkerchiefs. Secure the two remaining keys on the key-ring. Place the key-ring and two attached keys in your right jacket pocket together with the faked handkerchief. Place the real handkerchief in your left jacket pocket.

2 Begin your performance by taking the key-ring from your right jacket pocket, with the first two fingers and thumb gripping one of the keys to hide it from view. To the audience, the key-ring appears to have only one key on it.

3 Ask a member of the audience to open the key-ring and remove the visible key and hold it for you.

4 With your left hand, remove the real handkerchief from your left jacket pocket. Place the key-ring, with the second key still hidden, on the handkerchief and gather up the four corners to form a bag. Hand this to a second member of the audience to hold by the gathered corners.

5 With your right hand, remove the second – faked – handkerchief from your right jacket pocket. Take the key from the first spectator, and then pretend to place it underneath the handkerchief and up into the left hand. In reality, palm the key in your right hand and, at the same time, grip the key that is stitched into the faked handkerchief with your left hand. It is this key that you invite a spectator to feel through the fabric of the handkerchief. Secretly pocket the palmed loose key later.

6 Now for the transformation. Take hold of one corner of the handkerchief and suddenly reveal that the key has vanished. Show the handkerchief all round.

7 Ask the second member of the audience who is holding the handkerchief "bag" to unwrap it to reveal that the "vanished" key is now secured to the key-ring.

MISCELLANEOUS MAGIC

IN THIS SECTION ARE MAGIC

EFFECTS USING ALL TYPES OF ARTICLES. THESE

EFFECTS CANNOT NECESSARILY BE CATERGORIZED AS ANY

PARTICULAR BRANCH OF MAGIC. SOME ARE NEW AND ORIGINAL AND HAVE

been devised for this book. Miscellaneous magic covers, platform, close-up,

and impromptu work – look through the tricks on the following pages

and you are certain to find something that you can include in your program.

FAN-TASTIC

THIS CARD TRICK IS EFFECTIVE ON STAGE AS IT IS IN CLOSE-UP. THREE CARDS ARE SELECTED FROM A
PACK OF CARDS BY THREE DIFFERENT SPECTATORS. AN ELECTRIC FAN, STANDING ON A NEARBY TABLE,
HAS BEEN SWITCHED ON FULL POWER THROUGHOUT YOUR PERFORMANCE. IT LOOKS NORMAL, BUT
WHEN IT IS SWITCHED OFF, IT SLOWLY AND MYSTERIOUSLY REVEALS THE CARDS, ONE ON EACH OF THE
REVOLVING BLADES.

YOU WILL NEED

STRONG ELECTRIC FAN

3 MINIATURE CARDS FROM A
PATIENCE (SOLITAIRE) PACK

PACK OF CARDS

1 Before your performance,
stick the three patience
(solitaire) cards to the blades
of the fan – faces outward, of
course. You will find that
when the fan is on full power,
the cards will not be
recognizable. Only a splurge
of color will seem to whiz
around and around. That is
the secret of the effect.

2 Do not draw any
attention to the fan until you
have forced the three cards
on three different members
of the audience. (See pages
41–53 for forcing cards.)

3 Ask the three members of
the audience to announce
out loud the value and suit of
the cards they have selected,
then introduce the fan into
the performance. Unplug it,
and, as the blades slow
down, the cards will become
visible.

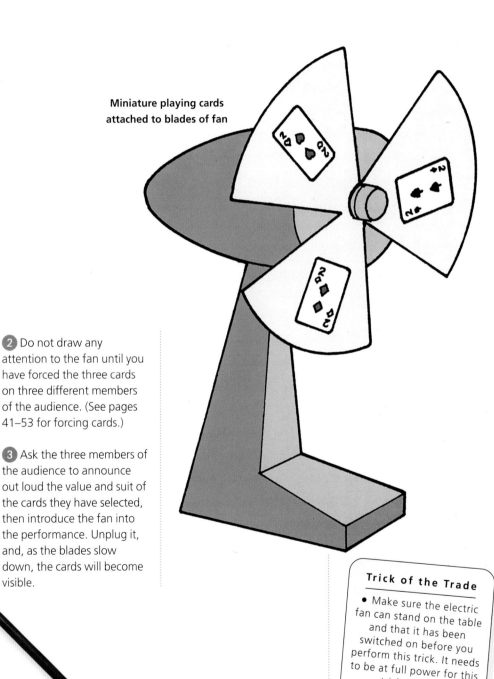

Miniature playing cards
attached to blades of fan

Trick of the Trade

• Make sure the electric
fan can stand on the table
and that it has been
switched on before you
perform this trick. It needs
to be at full power for this
trick to work.

167

★ ★ ★ ★

RING OFF ROPE

A FINGER RING IS THREADED ONTO A LENGTH OF ROPE OR CORD. EVEN THOUGH BOTH ENDS OF THE ROPE
ARE HELD BY MEMBERS OF YOUR AUDIENCE, THE MAGICIAN MANAGES TO TAKE THE RING OFF THE ROPE.

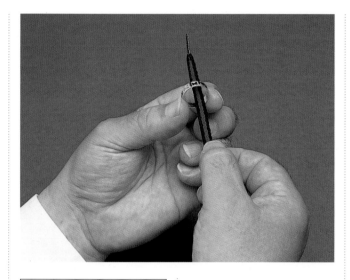

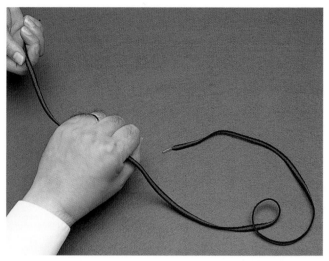

YOU WILL NEED
RING
LENGTH OF ROPE OR CORD (ABOUT 1 YARD)

1 Ask if you can borrow a finger ring from someone in the audience. Thread the rope through the ring and display the ring on the palm of your left hand.

3 As your left hand is turned over, your right hand comes in front of it and grasps the rope to the left. Your right hand continues to the left and gives the left end of the rope to a spectator to hold.

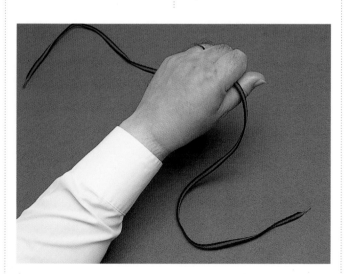

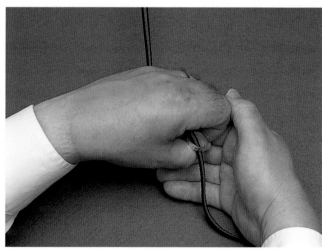

2 Close your left hand, and turn it over so that your fingers face the floor.

4 Now move your right hand back to the right so that you can give the right end of the rope to another spectator. It is now that the secret move that accomplishes the trick takes place. As your right hand passes beneath your left in order to get hold of the rope near to your left thumb, your left hand opens slightly to let the ring fall into your passing right hand.

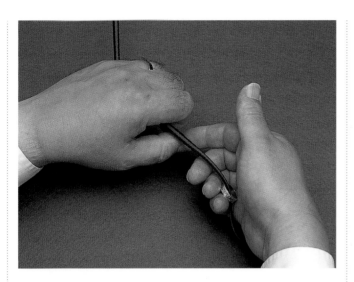

5 With the ring concealed by your fingers, your right hand continues toward the right end of the rope.

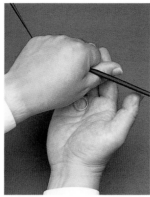

7 Keeping the ring hidden, pick up the right end of the rope with your right hand and give it to another member of the audience. Both ends of the rope are now held by spectators, and the ring is in your right hand.

8 Look at your left hand, which is still apparently holding the ring, and start a squeezing motion as if you are trying to maneuver the right through the solid rope. Bring your right hand under your left hand, and place them together, palm to palm.

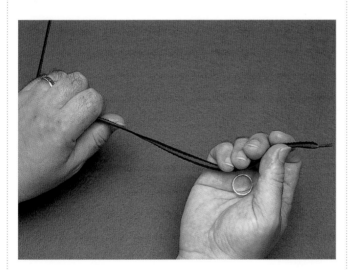

6 Just before your right hand reaches the end of the rope, look at the spectator holding the left end of the rope and ask for the rope to be held slightly higher. To emphasize this, raise your left hand. At this moment, your right hand moves farther to the right and takes the ring off the rope.

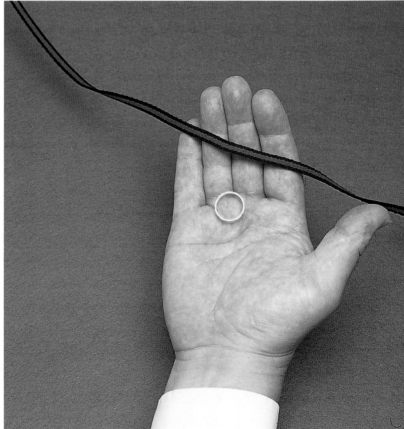

9 Roll your palms together for a moment, and then lift your left hand to reveal the ring on your right. It seems that the ring has penetrated the rope.

RING ON A PENCIL

A FINGER RING, BORROWED FROM A SPECTATOR, VANISHES AND REAPPEARS ON THE CENTER OF A
PENCIL. TO DO THIS TRICK YOU WILL NEED A SPECIAL HANDKERCHIEF WITH A RING STITCHED INTO A
POCKET IN ONE CORNER.

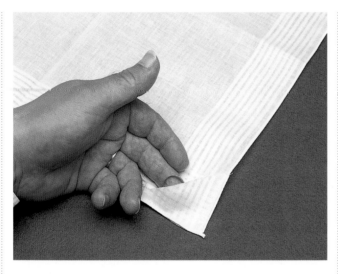

YOU WILL NEED

SPECIAL "VANISHING"
HANDKERCHIEF

PAPER BAG

LONG PENCIL

1 To make the handkerchief required for this trick, you will need, in addition to the handkerchief itself, a piece of matching fabric, a metal ring, and a needle and thread. Cut a small triangle from the spare fabric and stitch it to one corner of the handkerchief. Before you stitch the third side, place the ring in the pocket you have formed. Sew up the third side to enclose the ring.

2 When you come to perform the trick, borrow a finger ring from a member of the audience. Hold the ring between the thumb and first finger of your right hand, and then drape the handkerchief over it.

3 Now hand the handkerchief to a second volunteer from the audience with the request that he or she guard it safely. In fact, you now have the ring in your possession because, as you approach the second spectator, your right hand

takes the corner of the handkerchief containing the secret ring and puts it up into the fingers of your left hand. At the same time, the borrowed ring is allowed to drop into the palm of your right hand.

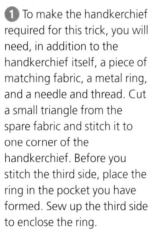

4 Hand the handkerchief to the second spectator, asking him or her to hold the ring securely. In fact, it is the secret ring that the spectator is holding, and it is a wise precaution not to ask the

owner of the borrowed ring with this part of the trick in case they recognize by touch that the ring they are holding through the handkerchief is not their own.

5 With your right hand concealing the ring, reach over to the paper bag that is lying on your table. Do this naturally and casually, and do not look at your right hand as you pick up the bag. If you look at your hand, you will draw attention to it, and this could arouse suspicions in the minds of the audience. Try to forget that you have a ring in your hand – if you start worrying about it, you could transmit your unease to the audience, and that would spoil the effect of the trick.

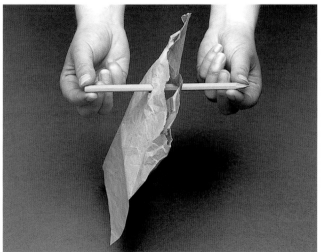

7 Hand the pencil to the spectator from whom you borrowed the ring and ask them to hold the pencil by its ends. Go back to the second spectator, who is still holding the handkerchief, and take hold of one corner of the handkerchief. Pull the handkerchief away – the ring has completely vanished.

6 Holding the bag in your right hand, reach inside it with your left to take out the pencil. This will subtly "prove" that the bag is otherwise empty. Do not mention the fact that the bag is empty, because by so doing you would only draw attention to it. Now push the pencil through one side of the bag and out the other. In so doing, you push the pencil through the hidden ring. Remove your right hand from the bag, and fold over the top of the bag.

8 Go back to the first person and pull the bag downward to reveal the ring suspended in the center of the pencil. Ask the owner to confirm that it is indeed the ring that you originally borrowed, then thank both your assistants for their help.

Trick of the Trade

- A similar handkerchief with a coin stitched into the corner pocket can be used to make a coin completely disappear.

BAD AIM

THE MAGICIAN'S ACCOMPLICE – WITH A LITTLE HELP – IS ABLE TO DIVINE A CARD SELECTED BY A
MEMBER OF THE AUDIENCE.

YOU WILL NEED

PACK OF CARDS

TWO ACCOMPLICES

---

1 Explain that with a friend, who just happens to be in the audience, you have been experimenting with telepathy, and you have found that you can pick up messages not only from each other but also, from other people – as you will now demonstrate. Introduce your friend to the audience, then send her to the back of the hall.

2 Ask a member of the audience to select a card, to note its value and to show it to one other member of the audience (who will be an umpire), but no one else. The card is returned to the pack.

3 Ask the volunteer to stand to one side of the hall and to concentrate very hard on the selected card, trying to beam its image to your friend at the back of the hall.

4 Stress that, whatever questions are asked, the spectator must only either nod or shake his head, then call back your accomplice from the back of the hall and spread out the cards, face up, on the table.

5 Pick out the appropriate card and say: "Was the chosen card the 3 of diamonds?" Your friend immediately claims that it was, but when you look at the volunteer, he just shakes his head. Your friend makes a similarly inaccurate positive identification of the next few cards that you choose from the spread-out pack.

6 You get angrier and angrier, until finally you turn to the audience and ask if anyone else has a clue. To everyone's surprise – especially the volunteer – a hesitant voice from the back of the hall suggests, say, the 8 of spades – which proves to be the chosen card. Berate the volunteer for having aimed his telepathic beam in the wrong direction.

7 The secret is, of course, that you forced a card – the 8 of spades, for instance, on the volunteer using one of the techniques described on pages 42–52.

Tricks of the Trade

• You can have the volunteer and the umpire choose the card between themselves. Either they must tell you the card they choose or you must find a means of glimpsing it.

• Beforehand, you will have arranged with the accomplices that there will be two "clue cards" – the queen of spades and 7 of hearts, for example. Both accomplices know that the second card you propose after the queen of spades will be the chosen card. The second "clue card" is a back up, in case the queen of spades is the chosen card.

• For the presentation of the trick you need two accomplices: the friend who guesses wrong and the diffident person at the back of the hall. The friend on-stage can clown as much as she wishes, but the other accomplice has a more difficult role to play, not only acting as just another member of the audience but also, after the trick, explaining to neighbors in the audience that the 8 of spades kept appearing in her mind, no matter what else she tried to think about . . .

CURRENCY CUT

THIS IS ANOTHER TRICK THAT INVOLVES BORROWING MONEY – THIS TIME A NOTE – FROM A MEMBER OF YOUR AUDIENCE. A BORROWED BANK NOTE IS SLID INSIDE A FLAT TUBE OF PAPER. THE AUDIENCE CLEARLY SEES THE PAPER CURRENCY THROUGH THE TWO WINDOWS CUT OUT AT EACH END OF THE TUBE. THE TUBE AND THE BANK NOTE ARE CUT IN HALF WITH A PAIR OF SCISSORS, YET MOMENTS LATER, THE NOTE IS PULLED FROM THE WRECKAGE, UNDAMAGED AND APPARENTLY AS GOOD AS NEW.

YOU WILL NEED

PAPER TUBE (SEE STEP 1)

SCISSORS

MONEY BILL

---

1 Make the paper tube from a long, narrow envelope. Seal the envelope, then cut a strip off each end to form a tube. Now cut two slits in the rear of the tube, about 2 in. apart, and deep enough to allow the money bill to slide through them. Carefully cut two square window shapes from the front of the tube.

2 Have the paper tube, slit side down, and the scissors on your table, ready to perform the effect.

3 Borrow a money bill and slide it through the paper tube so that it comes out the opposite end. Push it back inside again, this time forcing it through one slit and back into the tube through the other slit, so that the central portion of the money bill is outside the paper tube. The audience can clearly see the note through the windows cut in the front of the tube.

4 Cut through the center of the tube, but slide the scissors behind the bill so that you cut only the tube.

5 Hold together both cut sections as you quickly pull out the bill and show it to be restored. Crumple or cut up the paper tube to destroy the evidence.

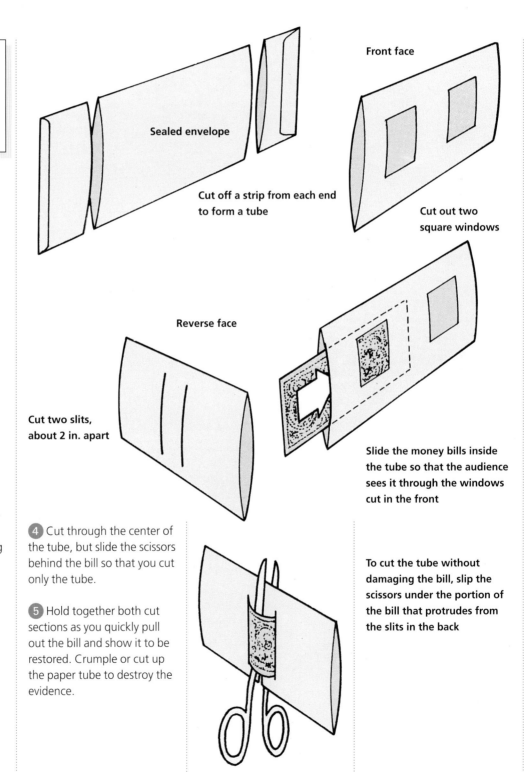

Sealed envelope

Cut off a strip from each end to form a tube

Front face

Cut out two square windows

Reverse face

Cut two slits, about 2 in. apart

Slide the money bills inside the tube so that the audience sees it through the windows cut in the front

To cut the tube without damaging the bill, slip the scissors under the portion of the bill that protrudes from the slits in the back

COIN IN A BALL OF YARN

THE MAGICIAN BORROWS A COIN AND MAKES IT DISAPPEAR. IT IS LATER RECOVERED IN THE CENTER OF A BALL OF YARN. YOU WILL NEED A SLIDE, WHICH IS SIMPLY A FLATTENED TIN TUBE THAT IS WIDE ENOUGH TO TAKE ANY COIN THAT YOU ARE LIKELY TO BE OFFERED.

YOU WILL NEED
BALL OF YARD
SPECIAL "SLIDE"
COIN
GLASS TUMBLER

1 Wind the yarn around the bottom portion of the slide. Place the ball of yarn in a coat pocket or behind a piece of equipment on your table so that it is in a position that you can "load" the coin into the slide with your left hand and then pull the slide from the yard without your actions being obvious.

3 Bring your right hand over the coin as if to take it from the left. As soon as your right hand covers the coin, let the coin drop from your fingertips into the palm of your hand.

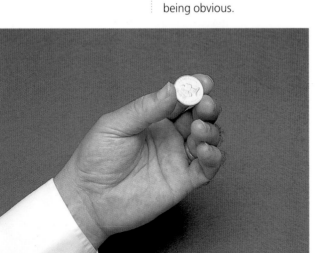

2 Borrow a coin from someone in the audience. Hold the coin between the tips of the thumb and forefinger of your left hand.

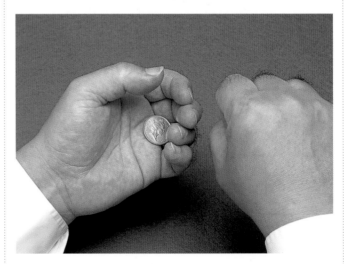

4 As the coin drops, close your right hand as if taking the coin, and move it away to the right. Look at your right hand as you do this, and let your left hand slowly fall away naturally.

5 Make some comment about the fact that money does not last very long. Then, with a squeezing motion, open the finger of your right hand. The coin has vanished! Try to forget that the coin is still hidden in your left hand. You must convince yourself that the coin really has vanished. If you do not convince yourself, you will not convince your audience.

7 Show the ball of yarn to your audience and place it in the glass tumbler. Take hold of the end of the yarn and pull it from the tumbler. When the yard is completely unraveled, the coin will tinkle into the glass tumbler.

6 While you are still gazing at your right hand in amazement, reach over with your left hand to recover the ball of yarn. Let the secreted coin enter the slide, and then pull the slide out of the ball of yarn. With practice, these movements should take only a few moments.

8 Hand the glass tumbler to the person from whom you borrowed the coin and ask if it is the very same coin.

Trick of the Trade

• To prove that the coin revealed in the yarn is the very same coin that vanished, it is a good idea to have a small gummed sticker available so that the spectator can stick this to the coin and even sign it if wished to prove that no substitution takes place. With an unusual coin, such as a piece of foreign currency, this is not usually necessary.

THE COIN FOLD

A COIN IS WRAPPED IN A PIECE OF PAPER FROM WHERE IT DISAPPEARS. THIS IS A SUPERB TRICK TO PERFORM ON THE SPUR OF THE MOMENT, FOR THE COIN CAN BE BORROWED AND THE PIECE OF PAPER CAN BE A SQUARE TORN FROM A NEWSPAPER OR WHATEVER ELSE IS AVAILABLE.

YOU WILL NEED

COIN

SQUARE OF PAPER

1 Take the square of paper and then place the coin in the center.

3 Fold the right edge of the paper back and then behind the coin.

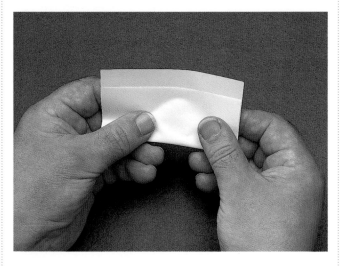

2 Fold the bottom edge of the paper up and over the coin. Do not bring the bottom edge right up to meet the top edge – it should be about ¼ in. below it.

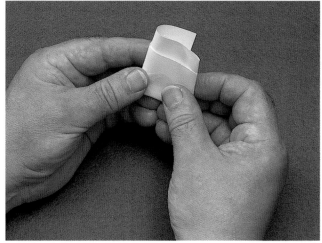

4 Fold the left edge back and behind the coin.

176

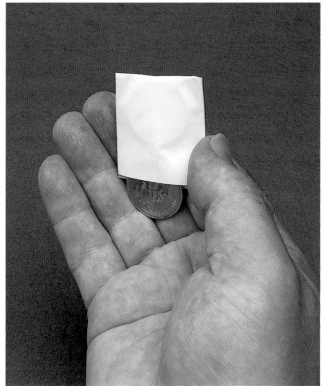

5 Make the final fold by bending the top flap of paper back behind the coin. It appears that the coin is secure in the paper, but in fact the top edge is open.

6 Turn the paper around so that the open edge is toward the bottom. The coin can now secretly slip from its paper prison into the palm of your right hand.

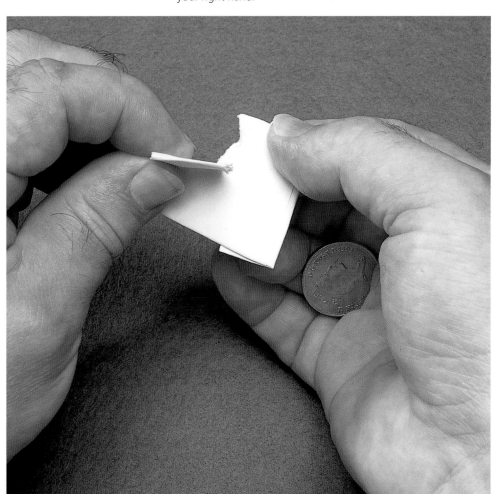

7 Tear up the paper and throw the pieces on the table. The coin has apparently vanished, but in reality it remains concealed in your right hand.

DYE-A-BOLICAL

Mᴀɢɪᴄɪᴀɴs ʜᴀᴠᴇ ʙᴇᴇɴ ᴜsɪɴɢ ᴛʜᴇ Oᴋɪᴛᴏ ᴛᴜᴍʙʟᴇʀ ғᴏʀ ᴍᴀɴʏ ʏᴇᴀʀs. Iᴛ ᴄᴏɴsɪsᴛs ᴏғ ᴀ ᴛʀᴀɴsᴘᴀʀᴇɴᴛ ᴘʟᴀsᴛɪᴄ ᴛᴜᴍʙʟᴇʀ ᴡɪᴛʜ ᴀ ᴄᴇɴᴛʀᴀʟ ʜᴏʟʟᴏᴡ ᴛᴜʙᴇ. Tʜᴇ ᴏᴜᴛsɪᴅᴇ sᴜʀғᴀᴄᴇ ᴏғ ᴛʜᴇ ᴛᴜᴍʙʟᴇʀ ɪs ғʟᴜᴛᴇᴅ ᴏʀ ᴍᴀʀᴋᴇᴅ sᴏ ᴛʜᴀᴛ ᴛʜᴇ ɪɴɴᴇʀ ᴛᴜʙᴇ ɪs ɪɴᴠɪsɪʙʟᴇ ғʀᴏᴍ ᴀ ᴅɪsᴛᴀɴᴄᴇ. Iᴛᴇᴍs sᴜᴄʜ ᴀs ᴀ sɪʟᴋ ʜᴀɴᴅᴋᴇʀᴄʜɪᴇғ ᴄᴀɴ ʙᴇ sᴇᴄʀᴇᴛᴇᴅ ᴡɪᴛʜɪɴ ᴛʜᴇ ᴄᴇɴᴛʀᴀʟ ʜᴏʟʟᴏᴡ ᴛᴜʙᴇ ᴀɴᴅ ᴘᴜʟʟᴇᴅ ᴏᴜᴛ ǫᴜɪᴛᴇ ᴅʀʏ, ᴇᴠᴇɴ ᴛʜᴏᴜɢʜ ᴛʜᴇ ᴛᴜᴍʙʟᴇʀ ʜᴀs ᴀᴘᴘᴀʀᴇɴᴛʟʏ ʙᴇᴇɴ ғɪʟʟᴇᴅ ᴡɪᴛʜ ʟɪǫᴜɪᴅ.

2 When you come to perform the effect, display the tumbler by picking it up with your left hand, your fingers cupped around it so that the handkerchief, tucked inside the hollow tube, is concealed from view.

3 With your right hand, lift up the jug of water and carefully pour the liquid into the main part of the tumbler. The water turns red as it mixes with the dye.

YOU WILL NEED

OKITO TUMBLER

12 IN. SQUARE RED SILK HANDKERCHIEF

RED DYE (COCHINEAL)

JUG OF WATER

PAIR OF TWEEZERS

1 Before the performance, pour some red dye into the main part of the Okito tumbler – not into the hollow tube. Place the red silk handkerchief in the hollow tube, tucking it down with a pencil so that it lies well down in the base of the unit. Make sure it is tucked so far down that when the tumbler is held in your cupped left hand the handkerchief is not visible to your audience.

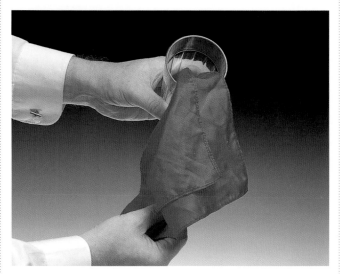

4 With the aid of a pair of tweezers, produce the red silk handkerchief from the center of the tumbler and flourish it to your audience, showing that it is completely dry.

CAN CAN

THE TRICK PASSE-PASSE BOTTLE AND GLASS HAS BEEN A FEATURE OF THE COMEDY ACTS OF MANY MAGICIANS OVER THE YEARS. THE VERSION DESCRIBED HERE IS JUST AS EFFECTIVE, ALTHOUGH IT USES ITEMS YOU WILL FIND AROUND THE HOME. TWO CARDBOARD TUBES ARE SEEN STANDING ON THE MAGICIAN'S TABLE. WHEN THESE ARE REMOVED, ONE REVEALS A CAN OF COCA-COLA AND THE OTHER A GLASS TUMBLER. THE PERFORMER CAUSES THE CAN TO CHANGE PLACES WITH THE TUMBLER AND BACK AGAIN.

YOU WILL NEED

2 IDENTICAL DRINKS CANS
(SEE STEP 1)

2 IDENTICAL TUMBLERS
SMALL ENOUGH TO FIT INSIDE
THE DRINKS CANS

2 CARDBOARD TUBES,
SLIGHTLY LARGER AND
TALLER THAN THE DRINKS
CANS

1 Cut away the base of each drinks can cleanly with a can opener and drain away the liquid. The top of each can should remain intact. Cut a thumb-hole toward the bottom of each of the cardboard tubes and paint them with metallic paint to make them look more impressive.

2 When you prepare to perform the trick, place both tumblers on the table, about 12 in. apart. Place the drinks cans over the tumblers. Finally, place the cardboard tubes over both units, making sure that the thumb holes are toward the rear.

3 To reveal a drink can, simply lift up the card tube. To reveal a tumbler, insert the thumb into the hole cut into the cardboard tube and lift both the tube and the can. The effect relies on the smooth operation of this delicate maneuver.

4 LIft both tubes at the same time, one with each hand, so that the one of your right reveals the drinks can and the one on your left reveals the tumbler. Reverse the procedure to effect the transposition and repeat as often as you wish.

BAFFLING BEAKER

THIS PIECE OF MAGICAL APPARATUS CAN BE USED FOR DOZENS OF DIFFERENT EFFECTS. THE BEAKER APPEARS TO BE GENUINE. IT IS OPAQUE AND CAN BE SHOWN, INSIDE AND OUT, TO YOUR AUDIENCE. IT CAN BE USED TO MAKE ARTICLES VANISH OR TO CHANGE INTO SOMETHING ELSE, AND IT CAN ALSO BE USED FOR EXCHANGING ONE ITEM FOR ANOTHER, WHICH APPEARS TO BE IDENTICAL BUT WHICH IS, IN FACT, DIFFERENT.

YOU WILL NEED

TWO IDENTICAL BEAKERS (SEE STEP 1)

SMALL HACKSAW

SCISSORS

ENVELOPES MEASURING ABOUT 9 × 6 IN. (SEE STEP 2)

Note: Children will need supervision for this trick.

1 Take the two identical beakers, which must be opaque, tall, and able to nest neatly one inside the other. Place one beaker inside the other and use a small hacksaw to carefully cut away the upper section of the top beaker so that the cut edge is flush with the top rim of the outer one. You now have an insert that sits within the main beaker and that can be removed easily whenever you want.

2 Cut away and discard the top and bottom sections of the envelopes. Fold the remaining sections in half, lengthwise, and then open them out to form four-sided paper tubes. Make sure that these tubes are taller than the actual beaker.

3 When you come to perform the trick, the beaker should stand in view on your table with the insert hidden inside a paper tube. If you want to make an article vanish – a handkerchief, for example – let the audience see you place it inside the beaker and then, with the empty insert hidden by the tube, make the handkerchief vanish when you place the tube over the beaker, only to remove it, leaving the insert inside the beaker. You can show the beaker, with insert in place, face on to the audience. It will appear as if the beaker is empty.

4 Alternatively, place an object in the insert, which is hidden by the tube, so that when you cover the beaker with the tube, you leave the insert behind when you remove the tube. The object can then be removed as if from the beaker itself and displayed to the audience.

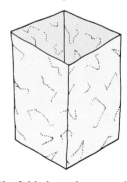

Make tubes from the envelopes from which the top and bottom section have been cut away

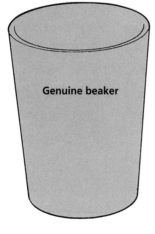

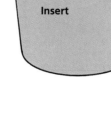

Genuine beaker

Insert

One beaker remains unchanged while the other, inserted within it is cut flush with the top rim of the outer one

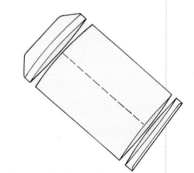

The folded envelopes can be made into four-sided tubes, which must be large enough to fit easily over the beaker to hide it completely

20 Tricks Using the Baffling Beaker

Here are just a few of the many effects that can be worked with this beaker.

1 To vanish colored silk handkerchiefs, pick up the beaker and display the interior. Place several handkerchiefs inside. Lift up the square tube of paper with the insert inside. Grip the insert so that it can be placed inside the beaker, covering the handkerchiefs. With your right hand, remove the paper tube as though it were taking something away. Make this into rather a suspicious-looking move to distract your audience. With your left hand, pick up both sections of the beakers as one and quickly show the audience the interior of the beaker (they actually see the insert) to reveal that the silk handkerchiefs have vanished. Place the beaker to one side and tear the tube into pieces to prove that it is empty.

2 Before you begin your performance, place a chain of linked paper clips inside and insert beaker and hide this in the paper tube. Display the beaker and inside it place some loose paper clips, dropping them in one by one. Cover the beaker with the paper tube and the insert. Remove the paper tube and show it to be empty. Finally, taking care that the loose clips are safely trapped between the insert and beaker, toss the linked clips into the air.

3 When you are preparing for the performance, drop some spent matches into the main beaker and place the insert on top. When you do the effect, drop several live matches into the beaker (in fact, into the insert), and cover the beaker and the insert with the paper tube. Light one further match, and wave it beneath the beaker for effect. Remove the tube and the insert and take out the spent matches.

4 A money bill can be placed inside the beaker. When the beaker is covered, the note changes into coins that add up to the denomination of the bill.

5 Pieces of colored tissue paper magically change into a Christmas decoration, which expands as it is pulled out of the beaker.

6 A safety pin and a piece of fabric are dropped inside the beaker. Seconds later it can be shown that the pin is now firmly attached to the piece of material.

7 Dates taken from a calendar magically change into dates to eat.

8 A length of ribbon and several loose buttons are dropped into the beaker. Later, the ribbon is shown to have the buttons stitched firmly to it.

9 A loose sewing needle and a length of thread are placed inside the beaker. Seconds later the needle is seen to have threaded itself.

10 Pieces of colored tissue paper change into a long paper streamer. After the beaker has been covered and the insert added, the beaker is inverted so that the center of the streamer uncoils and cascades onto the table. Use your fingers of the hand holding the beaker to keep the entire coil from dropping out while you produce it.

11 A skein of red silk thread magically changes into a square red silk handkerchief.

12 Two or three small colored silk handkerchiefs mysteriously change into a shower of confetti.

13 Water poured into the beaker instantly changes to ice cubes. You will, of course, have to perform this trick the moment you load the ice cubes into the insert.

14 A number of elastic bands are shown to have linked themselves together into a chain. To make the chain, use flat elastic bands and then make a cut in alternate bands, rejoining them with a rubber cement adhesive.

15 A ball of wool magically makes itself into a pompon.

16 Steel nails are placed inside the beaker and shaken up. When they are dropped onto the table, they are bent in half and a volunteer from the audience cannot bend them back to the original shape.

17 A small potato placed inside the beaker is sliced into French fries. The magician makes a pretense of slicing the potato by flicking a table knife in the air.

18 A quantity of sugar is poured into the beaker. When the magician looks again, the grains have turned into sugar cubes.

19 Water poured into the beaker turns into rice.

20 Water poured into the beaker changes color – to red. The paper tube covers the beaker, and when the liquid is poured again, it is green. For this last effect, place some red food coloring (cochineal) inside the beaker so that when water is poured into it, it changes the liquid to red. Green limeade or water colored with a green dye, already in the beaker, makes the switch possible.

DRINK FROM NOWHERE

A HANDKERCHIEF IS SHOWN ON BOTH SIDES AND THEN DRAPED OVER THE MAGICIAN'S HAND. SUDDENLY, A FORM APPEARS BENEATH THE FABRIC. WHEN THE HANDKERCHIEF IS REMOVED, THERE, STANDING ON THE MAGICIAN'S HAND, IS A WINE GLASS – FULL OF WINE! FOR REASONS THAT WILL BECOME OBVIOUS AS YOU READ THROUGH THE STEPS OF THIS TRICK, THIS HAS TO BE THE ONE YOU USE TO OPEN YOUR PERFORMANCE.

YOU WILL NEED

WINE, FRUIT JUICE, OR OTHER COLORED LIQUID

WINE GLASS

SHEET OF STRONG KITCHEN FILM (LARGE ENOUGH TO COVER THE MOUTH OF THE GLASS)

ELASTIC BAND

HANDKERCHIEF

---

1 Pour the liquid into the glass and cover the glass with kitchen film. Use the elastic band to hold the film in place. The elastic band must be tight enough to hold the film securely but with sufficient elasticity to enable you to remove it easily and without fumbling. You will have to experiment to find the right band for the glass you are using.

2 Place the wine glass in your left armpit, with the foot of the glass toward the audience. Adjust the material of your clothing to cover as much of the base of the glass as possible.

3 Walk onto the stage and begin your performance. Display the handkerchief between your hands.

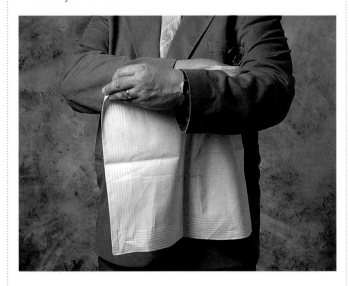

4 Now bring your left hand forward and to the right as your right hand moves to the left. This movement is to allow you to show the reverse side of the handkerchief to your audience, but it also brings your right hand into position to "steal" the glass from its hiding place.

182

7 Your left fingers now firmly grip the center of the handkerchief and lift it upward. As you do this, your right hand swivels the glass into an upright position.

8 Your left hand is now lowered and the fact that something has appeared beneath the handkerchief is immediately apparent to the members of the audience.

5 Grip the stem of the glass between the second and third fingers of your right hand, and then move your hands back to their opening position, together with the handkerchief stretched out between them. The wine glass is now hidden behind the top right corner of the handkerchief.

6 Carefully let go of the right corner as your right hand moves to the center of the handkerchief. At the same time, use your left hand to smooth the fabric out over your right palm. Because the glass is still hanging, upside down, from your fingers, there is no indication that anything has happened.

9 The fingers of your left hand, working through the fabric, pull the elastic band and cover from the glass. Then you quickly pull the handkerchief away. The glass is revealed, and while the audience is looking at it, you have the opportunity to put the handkerchief, with the cover and elastic band hidden inside, quickly to one side.

SOLID THROUGH SOLID

TWO COLORED HANDKERCHIEFS ARE WRAPPED AROUND ONE ANOTHER UNTIL IT IS QUITE IMPOSSIBLE FOR THEM TO BE PARTED. THE MAGICIAN BLOWS ON THEM, AND THE HANDKERCHIEFS APPEAR TO MELT THROUGH ONE ANOTHER. FOR THE PURPOSES OF THE DESCRIPTION, WE WILL ASSUME THAT ONE HANDKERCHIEF IS RED AND THE OTHER PURPLE, ALTHOUGH THE COLORS ARE, IN FACT, IMMATERIAL.

YOU WILL NEED

2 COLORED HANDKERCHIEFS

1 Take the diagonally opposite corners of each handkerchief and roll the fabric into a tube. Place the purple handkerchief on the table, and lay the red one across it to form a right-angled cross.

3 Your right hand now approaches from the right and goes beneath the purple handkerchief to take hold of the left-hand end of the red handkerchief.

2 Pick up the handkerchief at the point they cross between the thumb and fingers of your left hand.

4 This end is then taken to the right, below the purple handkerchief, and then back to the left, over the top of the purple handkerchief.

184

5 Take the nearer end of the purple handkerchief below the right-hand end of the red handkerchief and then back over the red handkerchief and away from you.

6 Carefully lay the handkerchiefs on the table, and take hold of the two ends of the red handkerchief in one hand and the ends of the purple handkerchief in the other. At this point it looks as if the handkerchiefs are firmly knotted together.

7 Gently blow on the handkerchiefs (to make the magic work) and then pull your hands apart. Amazingly, the handkerchiefs separate.

Trick of the Trade

• Although this trick works automatically, you must try to give the impression that both skill and your magical expertise are brought to play to achieve the result. And, even though it is automatic, you should practice it just as much as you would any of the difficult tricks.

HITTING THE HEADLINES

You will certainly make the headlines in more ways than one when you perform this unusual trick. The magician takes the front page of a newspaper and draws the audience's attention to its title and to the banner headline. The headline and title are ripped off and the newspaper is folded. The torn section is bundled up and made to vanish. When the newspaper is reopened, the title and headline are back in place again.

YOU WILL NEED

2 IDENTICAL NEWSPAPERS

SCISSORS

RULER

PVA ADHESIVE

1 Before the performance, take one of the newspapers and carefully cut the front page down the center fold line to just beyond the title and main banner headline. Fold this section down behind the rest of the front page, creasing it firmly.

2 Take the second newspaper and again cut the front page down the line of the center fold to just a little further down the first newspaper. Then, using a ruler as guide, carefully tear across the front page, separating the title and headline from the rest of the front page. Keep the torn-out section and discard the rest of the newspaper.

3 Take the torn-out title and headline and apply a little adhesive to the bottom reverse edge and carefully place it along the top, folded edge of the first newspaper, which now appears to be complete.

4 When you come to perform the effect, pick up the newspaper and display it to your audience, showing them the front and back. There is no need to open it out at this stage. Hold the newspaper in your right hand and with your left hand "rip" the top section off. Display this torn section and place it on the table. Show the newspaper with the missing section and then, with the back of the paper toward the audience, with the fingers of your right hand, secretly pivot up the section that is folded inside, bringing it into view and filling the space left by the missing section. Fold the newspaper in half, so that the front of the paper is inside the folds, and then place this on the table.

5 At this stage, you can vanish the torn section by crumpling it up into a ball and using any of the sleight-of-hand methods described on pages 14–40 for making balls vanish. It can also be vanished in a magic box, cabinet, changing bag, or any vanishing device you like to use.

6 When the section of newspaper has been vanished, pick up the folded newspaper and open it up, turning it toward the audience to show that the title and headline have magically returned to the front page.

BANK NIGHT

FOUR ENVELOPES, NUMBERED 1 TO 4, ARE SHOWN. THE MAGICIAN EXPLAINS THAT ONE OF THEM CONTAINS SOME MONEY AND THAT THREE LUCKY PEOPLE WILL BE GIVEN THE CHANCE TO WIN IT. THREE ENVELOPES ARE CHOSEN BY SPECTATORS, LEAVING THE MAGICIAN WITH JUST ONE. WHEN THE SPECTATORS OPEN THEIR ENVELOPES, THEY ARE SEEN TO BE UNLUCKY. THE MAGICIAN OPENS THE REMAINING, UNCHOSEN ENVELOPE, AND WINS THE CASH. BEFORE YOUR PERFORMANCE, PUT A PIECE OF PAPER IN EACH ENVELOPE. SEAL THE ENVELOPES AND NUMBER THEM, FROM 1 TO 4. THE NUMBERING CAN BE DONE WITH A PEN OR WITH THE NUMBERED STICKERS THAT ARE AVAILABLE IN MOST STATIONERY STORES – JUST AS LONG AS THE NUMBERS ARE VISIBLE TO THE AUDIENCE.

YOU WILL NEED

4 NUMBERED ENVELOPES

LARGE DENOMINATION MONEY BILL

4 PIECES OF PAPER THE SAME SIZE AS THE BILL

3 Now let each of three spectators select an envelope by calling out its number. Whichever number is chosen, you pull it from the fan and hand it to the spectator. It is important that you keep the bill concealed behind the fingers of your left hand as you do this.

1 Arrange the envelopes in a fan shape in numerical sequence on your table, with envelope number 1 to the left of the fan. Fold the bill into four and slip it against the edge of envelope number 2. Turn over all the envelopes so that the bill is now hidden beneath them.

2 In performance, pick up the envelopes between your left thumb and fingers, so that the numbers can be seen by the members of the audience. The concealed bill will be visible to you, but hidden from the audience's view.

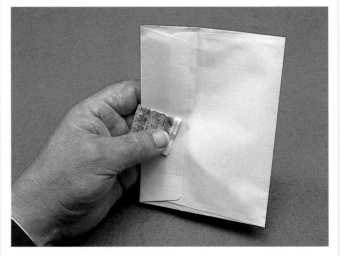

4 When you are left with just one envelope, hold it with the bill still hidden by your fingers.

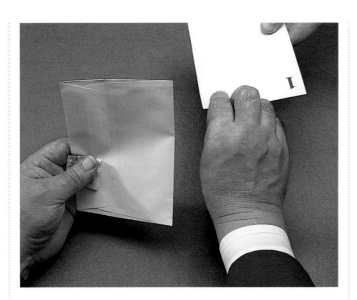

5 Ask the spectators if they wish to change their envelopes. They can exchange with one another or they can exchange with you. If they exchange with one another, you have nothing to worry about. If someone wants to exchange with you, take their envelope and place it in front of the envelope you are holding. Then remove your envelope and hand it to the spectator. In this way, the bill remains hidden at all times.

7 Place the fingers of your right hand into your envelope. Your thumb goes behind the envelope and onto the bill. Now move your hand to the right, pulling the bill to the right with your thumb.

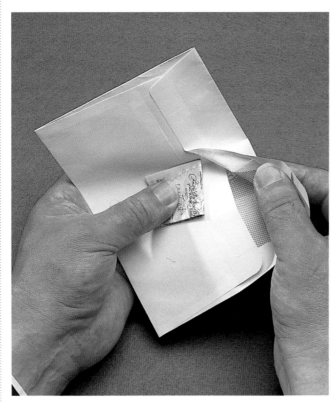

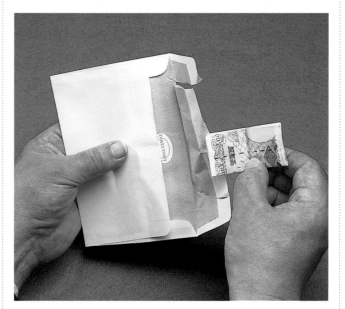

6 Ask all the spectators to open their envelopes to see if they have won the bill – unfortunately, they have not. Keeping the bill hidden, begin to open your envelope.

8 As your fingers clear the envelope, the bill, held between your fingers and thumb, becomes visible to the audience. The illusion that the bill has come from inside the envelope is absolutely perfect – and you appear to have won the money.

Trick of the Trade

• Instead of leaving the envelopes empty, each could contain a little message of consolation, which each spectator can be asked to read out. Suitable phrases include: "Money isn't everything," "You can't win them all," "Better luck next time," and so on. If you can come up with some amusing phrases, so much the better, because this will add a little light comedy to the proceedings.

189

BAFFLING BALLOONS

THIS IS AN UNUSUAL EFFECT USING EASILY OBTAINABLE ITEMS. TWO PAPER BAGS ARE SHOWN TO THE AUDIENCE, ONE WITH A RED SPOT ON THE FRONT, THE OTHER SPORTING A GREEN SPOT. THEY ARE EXAMINED BY MEMBERS OF THE AUDIENCE. TWO BALLOONS ARE THEN PRODUCED, ONE RED AND ONE GREEN, AND DROPPED INSIDE THE CORRESPONDING BAG. A SNAP OF THE FINGERS, AND THE RED BALLOON IS PULLED FROM THE BAG WITH THE GREEN SPOT, AND THE GREEN BALLOON IS PULLED FROM THE BAG WITH THE RED SPOT. A NEAT TRANSPOSITION.

YOU WILL NEED

2 GREEN BALLOONS

2 RED BALLOONS

2 PAPER BAGS

GREEN SPOT

RED SPOT

---

1 Prepare for the effect by sticking one of the colored spots to the front of each of the bags. Push a green balloon inside a red balloon, and push a red balloon inside a green one, using the blunt end of a pencil. Allow part of the neck of each of the inner balloons to protrude a little way.

2 Let a member of the audience examine the paper bags to prove that they are empty. Display the balloons and place them inside the bags so that the colors of the balloons match the spots on the bags. Hide the necks of the balloons with your fingers while you do this.

3 Wave your magic wand or snap your fingers to make the effect more magical. Remove the first bag from the table, and, holding it firmly by the base with your fingers gripping the balloon inside through the paper, reach with your right hand into the bag and pull out the inner balloon. Crush the bag, containing the original outer balloon, and cast it aside.

4 Repeat with the second bag and balloon to show that both balloons have been magically transposed.

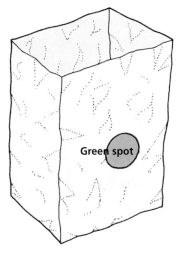

Two paper bags

Green spot

Green balloon

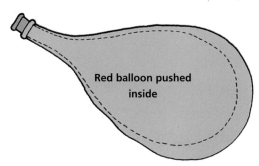

Red balloon pushed inside

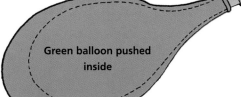

Green balloon pushed inside

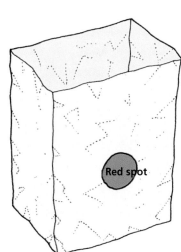
Red spot

Red balloon

MENTAL MYSTERIES

WHETHER OR NOT YOU BELIEVE IN MIND-READING, MANY AUDIENCES ARE FASCINATED BY MENTALIST EXPERIMENTS. THE FACT IS THAT THEY ARE ALL TRICKERY. PRACTITIONERS LIKE TO CALL THEIR TRICKS "experiments" because while tricks should never go wrong, some experiments can, and it is easy to blame a failure on the atmosphere or on the unsuitability of a member of the audience. Never mix mentalist experiments with other tricks or comedy routines.

SUITS ME

THE MAGICIAN PASSES THE FULL PACK OUT TO THE AUDIENCE ASKS FOUR VOLUNTEERS EACH TO
SELECT A CARD. THE ONLY PROVISO IS THAT THEY MUST CONSULT AMONG EACH OTHER SO THAT THEY
EACH SELECT ONE CARD FROM A DIFFERENT SUIT. WHEN THE PACK, WITHOUT THE FOUR CARDS, IS
RETURNED, THE MAGICIAN DEALS IT FACE UP ONTO THE TABLE, AND THEN QUICKLY ANNOUNCES THE
FOUR MISSING CARDS. THIS IS NOT A TRICK AND REQUIRES A LOT OF CONCENTRATION AND PRACTICE,
BECAUSE THE MAGICIAN NEEDS TO KEEP FOUR RUNNING TOTALS IN THEIR HEAD SIMULTANEOUSLY.

YOU WILL NEED

PACK OF CARDS

---

1 Imagine that you are keeping four ledger columns, one for each suit, running in the order of superiority used in contract bridge: spades, hearts, diamonds, clubs.

2 As you deal each card, add its value (jack = 11, queen = 12, king = 13) to the appropriate column. The total for a complete suit is 91, and you can count all the way up if you wish. A final tally line of 83, 79, 88, 85 means that the missing cards are the 8 of spades, the queen of hearts, the 3 of diamonds, and the 6 of clubs.

3 It is easier, however, to learn to count to the base 13, inventing easy names for the extra three digits: 1, 2, 3, 4, 5, 6, 7, 8, 9, x, y, z, 10, 11, and 12. Whenever a 10, 11, or 12 appears in a column, forget about the 1, so these become 0, 1, and 2. Once the count is complete, simply subtract your answer from 13 to get the value of the missing card.

Trick of the Trade

• This is not an easy act to perfect. When you are first learning it, try using only 26 cards – the spades and the hearts – leaving the others aside. Once you acquire more confidence, start using the diamonds as well, and then finally add the clubs. Don't be depressed if it takes you a long time to get the knack. In due course, you will be able to do it so quickly that you can deal out the cards without any perceptible pause for thought. The technique can be used as part of other tricks – you can always use it to identify a single missing card.

DOUBLEBACK

THE MAGICIAN OFFERS A FANNED-OUT PACK OF CARDS TO A MEMBER OF THE AUDIENCE, WHO IS ASKED TO SELECT ANY CARD. THE MAGICIAN SHOWS THAT THIS CARD HAS A DIFFERENT COLOR BACK FROM THE REST OF THE PACK. MYSTERIOUSLY, THE SAME CARD IN ANOTHER PACK ALSO MYSTERIOUSLY HAS A DIFFERENT COLOR BACK FROM THE OTHER CARDS IN THE DECK. HOW COULD THE MAGICIAN KNOW WHICH CARD WOULD BE SELECTED IN ORDER TO MAKE A SUBSTITUTION?

YOU WILL NEED

2 PACKS OF CARDS WITH DIFFERENT COLORED BACKS

1 Before the performance, take the blue-backed cards and remove any card – the 5 of spades, for example. Do not even bring this card on stage with you. Crimp all the other blue-backed cards so that, when held face up, they have a slight warp upward. Substitute the missing card with the same one – the 5 of spades – from the red-backed pack. Place the red-backed pack on your table, where it will be in full view of the audience.

2 Keep the red-backed 5 of spades at the bottom of the blue-backed pack as you shuffle the cards.

3 With the blue-backed pack face up, fan out the cards and ask a member of the audience to select any card at random and to name that card – the king of hearts, for instance. As the spectator removes that card, close up the fan.

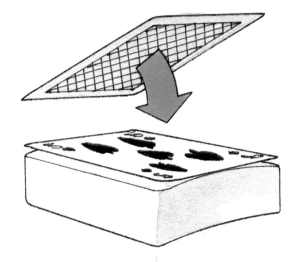

4 With the pack face up in your hand, put the king of hearts on top of the pack. It is on top of the uncrimped, red-backed 5 of spades.

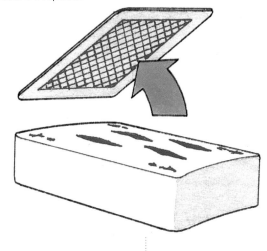

5 Because of the crimping, it is easy immediately to pick up the two top cards together and to show that the king of hearts has a red back.

6 Tell your audience that the card must somehow have got mixed up from your other pack, which is on your table. Pick up the red-backed pack and add the king of hearts to it. Shuffle briefly. At any time you can show that the king of hearts in this pack is the only one with a blue back.

Tricks of the Trade

• Although it does not really matter what the designs of the card backs are as long as they are sufficiently different to be easily distinguishable, traditional red and blue backs give the trick the greatest impact.

• You can make the effect more elaborate by writing a prediction at the beginning of the trick. Give the piece of paper to the spectator who is going to select the cards and ask him or her to keep it safe. The prediction should read: "You will pick the card with the wrong back – twice." Ask the spectator to read out the prediction after the selection of the first card and as you are preparing to pick up the second pack, which is lying out of reach of the audience. How was it possible for the magician to have known which card to substitute in the second pack?

PERPLEXING PENS

SIMPLE, EVERYDAY PROPS AND A DRAMATIC PRESENTATION SERVE TO PRODUCE A PUZZLING TEST OF YOUR MIND-READING ABILITIES. THE PERFORMER IS ABLE TO IDENTIFY THE COLOR OF THE INK IN ONE OF THREE APPARENTLY IDENTICAL PENS, SELECTED AT RANDOM BY A MEMBER OF THE AUDIENCE. NO MATTER HOW OFTEN THE TRICK IS REPEATED, THE PERFORMER CAN ALWAYS CORRECTLY FORETELL THE COLOR.

YOU WILL NEED

3 BALL-POINT PENS

---

1 The pens should be plastic ball-point pens, with opaque, not transparent, casings. Make sure that all the casings and caps are the same color, although the pens contain different colored inks – red, blue, and green.

2 Display the three pens and ask a member of the audience to test them, scribbling on a note pad. Make sure that the audience can see that, although the pens look identical, the inks are of different colors.

3 Ask the spectator to replace the caps and to mix up the pens before replacing them on your table. You can be blindfolded at this point or just simply turn away from the audience.

4 Ask the spectator to choose one of the pens and to hand it to you. Now, turn to face the audience and, at this point, execute the important move. Using both hands, and behind your back, quickly uncap the pen, then stroke the ball-point end across your thumbnail in order to leave a trace of the color behind. Swiftly replace the cap and bring the pen out toward the front. Hold it up for all to see.

5 Recap the points of the effect for the audience, then hand the chosen pen to the spectator. If you are wearing one, remove the blindfold and glance at your thumbnail to spot the chosen color. Divine the color, and ask the spectator to confirm that it is the correct color.

DOUBLECROSS

THIS EXPERIMENT IN "TELEPATHY" IS, IN FACT, ALMOST EMBARRASSINGLY SIMPLE. YOU WILL NEED LITTLE MORE THAN APLOMB AND ABSOLUTELY NO SHAME TO CARRY IT OFF CONVINCINGLY, AND TO EXPLAIN HOW THE SUBLIMAL TELEPATHY OPERATING BETWEEN TWO VOLUNTEERS ENABLED THEM TO SELECT THE SAME CARD.

YOU WILL NEED

PACK OF CARDS

2 BLINDFOLDS

2 MARKER PENS

---

1 Before the performance, mark both the front and back of the 2 of diamonds with a large red cross. As you fan the deck at the beginning of the trick, make sure that this card is next to your hand – you can shuffle it toward the center later. Also before the performance, dry out two marker pens so that they do not work.

2 Explain to your audience that you are going to conduct an experiment in "sublimal telepathy" and ask for two volunteers, one to stand on each side of the stage. Blindfold each of the volunteers in turn.

3 Picking up the deck of cards, shuffle it (keeping the 2 of diamonds near your hand) and fan it briefly both face out and back out to the audience to show that it is a perfectly normal pack.

4 Give each of the blindfolded volunteers a marker pen. Shuffling the cards as you walk (and bringing the 2 of diamonds to the center), cross to the first volunteer, fan out the cards face up, and ask him or her to select one card, draw it out, and mark the front of the card with a large cross. Ask the volunteer to replace the card in the pack by "feel."

5 Walk across to the other volunteer and repeat the procedure, but this time asking the volunteer to mark the back of the card.

6 Giving the cards a final shuffle, move back to center stage and ask the volunteers to remove their blindfolds. Fan out the cards, face up, and ask the first volunteer to identify the card he or she marked with a cross. The card will be, the 2 of diamonds for example.

7 Leaving the card in the pack, shuffle the cards again and turn to the other volunteer, this time offering the fanned pack face down. When the volunteer identifies the marked card, it is, amazingly, also the 2 of diamonds.

Trick of the Trade

• As the blindfolded spectators replace their cards into the deck by "feel," they will want to use two hands. Obligingly take the marker pens so that both their hands are free, and pop them absent-mindedly into your jacket pocket. That way, you don't run the risk of either volunteer thinking afterward to check the pen.

DUPLICATED DIVINATION

THIS MENTAL EFFECT CAN BE PRESENTED IMPROMPTU OR AS PART OF THE MENTALIST'S PROGRAM. THE PERFORMER IS ABLE TO DIVINE WHICH OF SIX ESP SYMBOLS HAS BEEN CHOSEN BY A MEMBER OF THE AUDIENCE, EVEN THOUGH THE BLOCK BEARING THE SYMBOLS IS CONTAINED WITHIN A CLOSED CARDBOARD BOX. THE SECRET OF THE TRICK LIES NOT IN THE PERFORMER'S ABILITY TO READ MINDS BUT IN THE ABILITY TO HANDLE THE PROPS.

YOU WILL NEED

2 SMALL CARDBOARD BOXES, EACH ABOUT 2 IN. SQUARE, WITH REMOVABLE FLANGED LIDS

2 IDENTICAL BLOCKS THAT WILL FIT SNUGLY INSIDE THE CARDBOARD BOXES WITH THE ESP SYMBOLS (STAR, WAVY LINES, SQUARE, CIRCLE, CROSS, AND TRIANGLE) ON THE SIDES

1 Before your performance, place a block inside each box and put the lids on top.

2 Explain to your audience that it is sometimes possible to have duplicate thoughts – two people may think the same thing at the same time.

3 Display both boxes and ask a member of the audience to examine them. Draw attention to the fact that each contains a similar block with identical ESP symbols on them. Emphasize that both the outer boxes and the inner blocks are identical in every way – size, shape, and color.

4 Ask the spectator to choose one of the boxes, to remove the block, look at one of the symbols and to then concentrate on it, changing their mind if they wish. While the spectator is making up his or her mind, you should turn your back so that you cannot see what the spectator is doing. Once the spectator has made a definite choice, ask him or her to place the block inside the box so that the chosen design is uppermost. The lid is replaced, and the box is placed on the table. Ask the spectator to then concentrate on the chosen symbol.

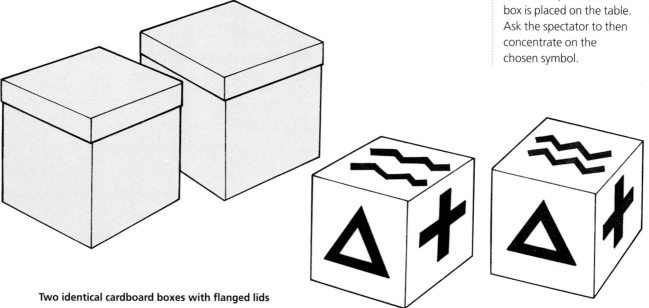

Two identical cardboard boxes with flanged lids

Two identical blocks bearing ESP symbols

Performer's view

Lid placed on side of box

Box rotated to reveal chosen symbol

5 Turn to face the audience and recap on what has happened so far. In doing so, pick up the spectator's box and hold it behind your back. It is at this point that the vital move is made. Out of view of the audience, rotate the lid and slide it down one side of the box. Then rotate the whole box so that it appears to the audience as if the lid is still on top. Bring the box to the front. The chosen face of the block inside the box is now visible to you, but not to the audience. Glance at the symbol that is showing, and put the box on the table.

6 Now go to the second box and make a show of reading the thoughts of the spectator, turning the block this way and that, finally placing it inside its box with the correct pattern uppermost.

7 This being done, all that remains is to reopen both boxes and prove the divination is correct. Pick up the spectator's box and, in one swift but casual movement, cup your right hand over the lid and pull it away, allowing your left hand to rotate the box upward so that the base of it now rests on the palm of your left hand. This rotation should not be detectable by the audience.

8 Remove the lid so that the audience can see the chosen design on top. Ask the spectator to open the lid of your box to reveal the identical design.

9 If you wish, invite someone else in the audience to examine both the blocks and the boxes.

197

HOW MANY?

IF YOU HAD SIX MATCHBOXES, EACH CONTAINING A DIFFERENT NUMBER OF MATCHES, AND THESE
WERE MIXED UP WHILE YOU WERE OUT OF THE ROOM, WOULD YOU BE ABLE TO TELL YOUR AUDIENCE
JUST HOW MANY MATCHES WERE INSIDE THE BOX FREELY CHOSEN BY A SPECTATOR?

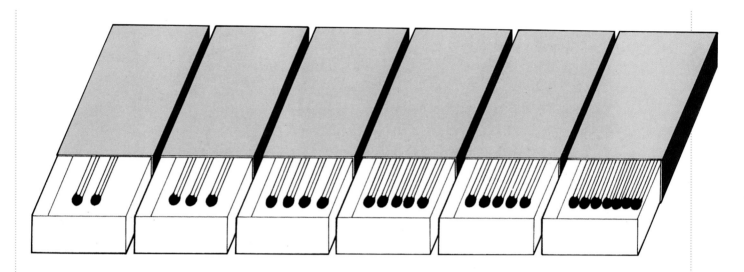

YOU WILL NEED

6 IDENTICAL MATCHBOXES

MATCHES

PAPER BAG

---

1 Before the performance, place matches in each of the boxes. Although the number can be of your own choice, it is a good idea not to have too many. At first, at least, insert two, three, four, five, six, and seven matches in the boxes. Place the paper bag near the filled matchboxes.

2 Display all six matchboxes and allow the audience to open them. Bring to the attention of your audience that no two matchboxes contain the same number of matches.

3 Turn your back on the audience or leave the room, leaving the following instructions. Ask a spectator to close the matchboxes, to mix them up well, and to hand a box to each of six different members of the audience. The first spectator chooses one member of the audience, who opens his or her box, counts the matches inside, and closes it again.

4 Turn around or come back onto the stage, and ask which spectator is holding the selected matchbox. Pick up the paper bag in your left hand and then take each matchbox in turn with the right hand, dropping it into the paper bag. When you come to the selected box, open it slightly as you drop it into the bag. When all six boxes have been placed inside the bag, crumple up the top and ask a spectator to give it a good shake.

5 Now begin the divination. Pick the first box out of the bag and place it against your forehead, appearing to concentrate hard. Announce that this is not the box in question. Do the same with the next couple of boxes. When you remove the box that is partly opened, glance at the opened end and quickly count the matches that are showing. Close the box before it comes into view of the audience. Put it to one side of the others and extract the remaining boxes.

6 Pronounce the number of matches inside the chosen box you have put to one side of the others, and then prove that your divination has, indeed, been accurate as you count out the matches.

COUNTING CARDS

This is, in effect, a self-working trick, but your audience will not know that. The magician counts out a number of cards from the top of the pack, then, asking for a number between 10 and 20, is able, by simple arithmetic, to find the selected card.

YOU WILL NEED

PACK OF CARDS

1 Count out 10 cards at the outset. Do not draw attention to the fact that you actually count 10 cards, either saying the numbers *sotto voce* or, if you are counting aloud, say 11, but stop just before you drop that particular card on the heap. Distract your audience's attention by saying that the power of magic is always present in everyone's mind, but that in most cases it is unrealized.

2 As you return the heap of cards to the rest of the pack, secretly glance at the bottom card – in this instance, the 10 of hearts. As you do this, say that everyone in the audience has the subconscious knowledge of where in the pack every card is – for example, the 10 of hearts.

3 Ask for someone to give you a number between 10 and 20. If that number is, say, 17 count out the cards as before, this time actually counting out 17.

4 Put the remainder of the pack to one side, pick up the packet of 17 cards and add the digits of the chosen number, 1 and 7, together, to give 8.

5 Deal out eight cards from the packet. The eighth card wil be the 10 of hearts.

Trick of the Trade

● The trick obviously does not work if the number selected is 20, but it would seem contrived to request a number between 10 and 19, and, in fact, it is very unlikely that a spectator will select 20. If someone does select that number you can stress that you asked for a number *between* 10 and 20. Alternatively, ask the audience as a whole for a number and simply do "not hear" any call for 20.

COUNTING CARDS –
A VARIATION

THIS TRICK REALLY DOES INVOLVE A LITTLE MENTAL AGILITY. THE MAGICIAN GIVES A MEMBER OF THE AUDIENCE A SET OF NINE CARDS, RUNNING FROM THE ACE TO THE 9, IN MIXED SUITS. THE CARDS ARE LAID OUT IN THREE ROWS OF THREE. THE MAGICIAN TURNS AWAY FROM THE TABLE AND CORRECTLY IDENTIFIES THE CARD THAT THE SPECTATOR HAS REMOVED FROM THE ARRAY.

YOU WILL NEED

PACK OF CARDS

PEN OR PENCIL

PAPER

1 Although the cards appear to run at random from the ace to the 9, they are in fact chosen by you. You can use whatever mnemonic you find works for you to remember what they are. An easy one is to think of the order of precedence of the suits in games like contract bridge – spades, hearts, diamonds, clubs. The first two suits represent odd numbers; the second suits represent even numbers. Because spades are superior to hearts, they represent more numbers – that is, 1 (ace), 5, and 9 are spades, while 3 and 7 are hearts. Following a similar line, 2 and 6 are diamonds, and 4 and 8 are clubs.

2 Count out the nine cards you have previously placed at the top of the pack and hand them to a member of the audience, asking him or her to arrange them in three rows of three cards. Before the cards are arranged on the table, turn away so that you cannot see how they are being laid out.

3 Still with your back to the cards, ask the spectator to remove any one of the cards from the array.

4 Ask the spectator to think of the cards in each row as digits making up a three-figure number – for example, a row with the 4 of clubs, the 8 of clubs and the 6 of diamonds would be regarded as 486. The gap where the card was removed should be regarded as 0. The spectator is asked to add up the three rows, then to tot up the digits of the total. Your volunteer may find it helpful to jot these down on a piece of paper.

5 Ask the spectator to tell you the total of the digits, and you will then be able to identify the card that has been removed. Determining the numerical value of the chosen card is easy. You simply subtract the spectator's final total from 9 (if it is less than 9), from 18 (if it is between 9 and 17), or from 27 (if it is 18 or greater). A simple mathematical principle determines that the result of your subtraction is the correct numerical value.

Trick of the Trade

• This trick can be repeated three or four times, with your back still turned and with different members of the audience laying out the cards in any ordering of three rows of three. Do not use too simple a mnemonic – for example, someone might notice if all the black cards were odd and the red cards were even.

COUNTING CARDS –
A FURTHER VARIATION

THE MAGICIAN DEALS OFF THE PACKETS OF CARDS, APPARENTLY AT RANDOM, AND IS ABLE TO DIVINE
THE VALUE OF A PACKET OF CARDS COUNTED OUT BY A MEMBER OF THE AUDIENCE.

YOU WILL NEED

PACK OF CARDS

PEN OR PENCIL

PAPER

1 Before you begin this trick, you must stack the deck of cards. Separate the 2s, 7s, and the queens from the rest of the pack.

2 Take one numerical set from the remainder, in mixed suits, and lay it out in a shuffled row – for example, 3, 5, jack, king, 9, ace, 4, 6, 8, and 10.

3 From the remaining 30 cards, choose another numerical set in mixed suits and lay it out in a row below the first one, following the same random order.

4 Do this twice more, and then collect the rows as four packets to make a deck of 40 cards.

5 Thoroughly shuffle the 12 cards you earlier put to one side (the 2, the 7s, and the queens) and put them on top of the pack.

6 When you do the trick, count out the first 10 cards, face up, and ask a spectator to count the numerical value of the cards (with jack = 11, queen = 12, and king = 13). Gather the cards up and return them to the pack. However, while the audience's attention is focused on the spectator who is announcing the total, return about half the cards to the top of the pack and about half to bottom.

7 Repeat the next process by counting out the first 10 cards from the top of the pack. This time, while your volunteer is adding up the figures and announcing the total, you should write "70" on a piece of paper. Fold up the paper and hand it to someone else to look after.

8 Take back the second group of 10 from the spectator, this time putting it back at the top of the pack, and announce that you have written down the total number of the 10 cards that he or she will now deal.

9 Cut the pack at random and hand the spectator the bottom half. The spectator will count out the first 10 cards from the packet, totaling their value – which will be 70.

Tricks of the Trade

• Between different performances you can vary the total by excluding a different trio of numbers – for example, if you discarded the 2s, 8s and the queens, rather than the 2s, 7s and the queens, the total of the spectator's cards would always be 69.

• You can add to the effect by allowing the volunteer to make the cut for him or herself, relying on the fact that the cut will always be made somewhere near the middle. If, against expectations, your volunteer looks as if the cut is going to be made near the top or bottom of the pack, grab the cards back on some pretext or other ("It's a new pack and the cards seem to be sticking together – no, everything seems to be all right"), then return the pack. It's unlikely that your volunteer will be so perverse the next time.

BAFFLING BOOK TEST

Mɴɢɪᴄɪᴀɴꜱ ᴀɴᴅ ᴍᴇɴᴛᴀʟɪꜱᴛꜱ ᴀʟɪᴋᴇ ʜᴀᴠᴇ ʙᴇᴇɴ ᴜꜱɪɴɢ ʙᴏᴏᴋ ᴛᴇꜱᴛꜱ ꜰᴏʀ ɢᴇɴᴇʀᴀᴛɪᴏɴꜱ. Mᴇᴛʜᴏᴅꜱ ᴠᴀʀʏ, ʙᴜᴛ ᴛʜᴇ ᴇꜰꜰᴇᴄᴛ ᴀʟᴡᴀʏꜱ ꜱᴇᴇᴍꜱ ᴛᴏ ʙᴇ ᴛʜᴇ ꜱᴀᴍᴇ. Yᴏᴜ ᴄᴀɴ ᴅᴏ ᴛʜᴇ ᴛʀɪᴄᴋ ᴜꜱɪɴɢ ᴀ ʙᴏᴏᴋ ʏᴏᴜ ʜᴀᴠᴇ ʙᴏʀʀᴏᴡᴇᴅ ꜰʀᴏᴍ ᴀ ᴍᴇᴍʙᴇʀ ᴏꜰ ᴛʜᴇ ᴀᴜᴅɪᴇɴᴄᴇ, ᴡʜɪᴄʜ ʜᴇʟᴘꜱ ᴛᴏ ᴀᴅᴅ ᴛᴏ ᴛʜᴇ ᴀɪʀ ᴏꜰ ᴀᴜᴛʜᴇɴᴛɪᴄɪᴛʏ ʏᴏᴜ ᴀʀᴇ ꜱᴛʀɪᴠɪɴɢ ᴛᴏ ɪᴍᴘᴀʀᴛ ᴛᴏ ʏᴏᴜʀ ᴍᴇɴᴛᴀʟɪꜱᴛ ᴇxᴘᴇʀɪᴍᴇɴᴛꜱ ʙʏ ᴘʀᴏᴠɪɴɢ ᴛʜᴀᴛ ᴛʜᴇ ʙᴏᴏᴋ ɪꜱ ᴄᴏᴍᴘʟᴇᴛᴇʟʏ ɢᴇɴᴜɪɴᴇ.

YOU WILL NEED

PAPERBACK BOOK OF ABOUT 180 PAGES

PLAYING CARD OR BUSINESS CARD

1 Hand the book to a spectator, asking him or her to flick through the pages to check that each page is different. Also ask the spectator to verify that the book has not been prepared in any way.

2 Give the playing card or business card to the spectator and ask him or her to turn to any page in the book and to look at the page number and the last word on that page. Next, ask the spectator to concentrate on that page, especially on the last word, and to insert the business card in the book as a marker.

3 Reclaim the book from the spectator. The card is inserted as a marker, but it is also there to help you obtain the information you require – that is, the page number and the last word on that page.

4 Recap to your audience what has happened so far, and as you do so, riffle through the pages of the book, saying that it must contain thousands of words. As you do this, you will find that your thumb stops briefly at the position where the card is inserted. Your thumb will jump, landing on the page next to it. In that brief second, note both the page number at the bottom and the last word on the page, then continue to flick through the remaining pages. The whole procedure should be presented as if you are simply establishing the fact that the book has 180 pages and contains thousands of words.

5 The rest of the experiment is easy. Ask the spectator to concentrate on the page number and the last work, and then divine both.

CLEMENTINE'S CARD TRICK

THIS IS A TRICK THAT WILL, BASICALLY, WORK ITSELF, BUT THE MAGICIAN HAS TO DO A LITTLE MATHS. IT IS ONE OF THOSE EFFECTS THAT WORKS BETTER IF THE MAGICIAN CAN KEEP UP AN ENTERTAINING PATTER WHILE GETTING A MEMBER OF THE AUDIENCE TO DO ALL THE WORK.

YOU WILL NEED

PACK OF CARDS

---

1 Tell the audience that this trick was invented in 1849 by none other than the father of Darling Clementine, who later taught it to his daughter, who in turn taught it to her Little Sister, who finally passed it on to Stephen Foster as the only way she knew to get his hands off her. The authenticity of this tale, which the audience may not immediately believe, can be gauged from the fact that it uses only 49 cards, rather than the complete pack of 52. This is because Clementine's father lost three cards from his pack during the hurly-burly of the Gold Rush – hence, of course, the expression "49er" – as the more historically minded members of your audience are sure to know.

2 Discard three cards from the pack and give the remainder of the pack to a member of the audience. Ask the volunteer to select one card and memorize it, to shuffle the pack thoroughly, then, with the cards face down, to deal the cards into seven face-up heaps.

3 Stand well away from your table as the spectator does this. Ask the spectator to search through the piles of cards until he or she finds the selected card. Counting from left to right, ask for the number of that packet. Then ask the spectator to pile up the heaps by putting the second on top of the first, the third on top of both of them, the fourth on top of that and so on.

4 When all seven packets are assembled together, ask the spectator to deal out the face-down cards into face-up piles of seven and again to state which pile contains the selected card. At this point, tell the audience that the Little Sister used to make Stephen Foster repeat this part of the trick and over and over again, but that twice is enough for the purposes of this demonstration.

5 Ask the spectator to pile up the cards as before and then to start dealing them out again, one by one. After a while, stop him and say that the next card will be the one originally chosen. And, of course, it is.

6 In fact, the simple mathematics is that you deduct 1 from the second reported heap number, and then multiply this new number by 7. Add the first reported heap number and the total gives the position of the card in the deck when it is ready for the final deal. For example, imagine that at the outset the volunteer's card is the third one down when the pack is dealt. The chosen card will, therefore, be in heap 3. On the second deal, it shows as third from the rear of heap 1. Now, $1 - 1 = 0$; $7 \times 0 = 0$; $0 + 3 = 3$. The chosen card will be the third one dealt off the next time.

Trick of the Trade

• More usually, the result of your calculations will be a number somewhere in the 20s or 30s, which is a lot of cards to count. In this event (or even not), don't make anything special of the final deal, but, while the volunteer is laying out the cards as before, start looking impatient and remark to the audience that by this time even the Little Sister was getting bored. At the right moment, stalk across to the table and then pull the correct card from its place.

RECITING THE DECK

THE ABILITY APPARENTLY TO DIVINE THE IDENTITY OF ALL 52 CARDS IN A PACK IS THE MARK OF A TRUE MENTALIST. THIS TRICK, AND THE TWO THAT FOLLOW, ARE IMPRESSIVE WAYS OF DOING JUST THAT. IN THIS FIRST VERSION, A PACK OF CARDS IS SHUFFLED BY A MEMBER OF THE AUDIENCE, BUT EVEN SO, THE MAGICIAN IS ABLE TO DIVINE THE SUIT AND VALUE OF THE CARDS IN THE PACK AS THEY ARE TURNED UP.

YOU WILL NEED

2 IDENTICAL PACKS OF CARDS

1 Before the performance, arrange one pack of cards in the following order: ace of clubs, 8 of diamonds, 5 of hearts, 4 of spades, jack of clubs . . . .This order will seem random to the audience, but in fact you have used two alphabetical sequences at once: clubs, diamonds, hearts, and spades; and ace, 8, 5, 4, jack, king, 9, queen, 7, 6, 10, 3, 2.

2 Hand the other pack to a member of the audience to shuffle as thoroughly as possible. As the spectator hands the shuffled cards back to you, pretend to notice someone else in the audience who is looking disgruntled, and then ask this second person to shuffle the cards as well.

3 Take the double-shuffled pack back to your table, muttering about cynics and people who have no confidence in "real" magic. As you distract the audience's attention with this patter, switch the shuffled pack with the prepared stack from your jacket pocket.

4 To general amazement, proceed to turn up the cards one by one, calling out each one before you turn it up and display it to the audience.

Trick of the Trade

• It is very unlikely that the audience will notice the regularity of the ordering. However, if you are worried about it, run the order of suits backward and forward: clubs, diamonds, hearts, spades, spades, hearts, diamonds clubs, clubs diamonds . . . and so on. You can also vary the arrangement by having two clubs in a row, followed by a diamond, a heart, and a spade, then a club, two diamonds, a heart, and a spade, then a club, a diamond, two hearts, and a spade, and so on.

RECITING THE DECK – A VARIATION

As in the previous trick, the magician invites one or more members of the audience to shuffle the pack of cards, but is, nevertheless, still able to divine the value and suit of each card before it is turned up.

YOU WILL NEED

PACK OF CARDS

PREPARED CARD (SEE STEP 1)

1 Before the performance take a spare, but matching card (the joker will do), and remove the top left-hand corner so that you can see the suit and value of any card beneath it.

2 Ask a volunteer to shuffle the pack. If you wish, find a cynical-looking or sceptical member of the audience to give the pack of cards a second shuffle.

3 Return to the stage and put the deck behind your back and announce that you are giving it a final shuffle. In fact, that is only to account for the movement of your arms as you do two things. First, reverse the card at the top of the pack so that it is face up. At this point, remove from a pocket or other place of concealment the prepared card and place it face down on the bottom of the pack. As you bring the pack back into view, make sure that your thumb is over the torn-away corner.

4 With the dummy card face up and toward the audience, you can see the top corner of each card facing you and can read it out its value and suit to the audience.

5 Make a point of throwing each card to the audience to be checked (see pages 25–7 for throwing cards). This distracts the spectators' attention from the fact that the cards are facing the wrong way as you pull them one by one from the pack.

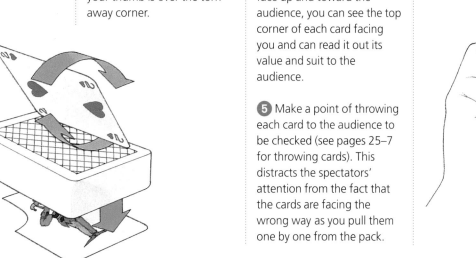

MUTUS NOMEN COCIS DEDIT

THE MAGICIAN ASKS A MEMBER OF THE AUDIENCE TO SHUFFLE THE PACK AND THEN TO DEAL FROM IT THE TOP 20 CARDS IN THE FORM OF 10 PAIRS. THE MAGICIAN IS ABLE TO DIVINE THE SUIT AND VALUE OF THE TWO CARDS THAT A VOLUNTEER HAS SELECTED, EVEN THOUGH THE CARDS ARE RE-DEALT. THE TRICK DEPENDS ON THE MAGICIAN'S REMEMBERING A PIECE OF LATIN: *MUTUS NOMEN COCIS DEDIT*.

YOU WILL NEED

PACK OF CARDS

1 Ask a volunteer to shuffle the cards and then to deal the top 20 cards in the form of 10 pairs. Put the rest of the pack to one side.

2 Ask the volunteer to decide on one of the pairs, but not to tell you what it is.

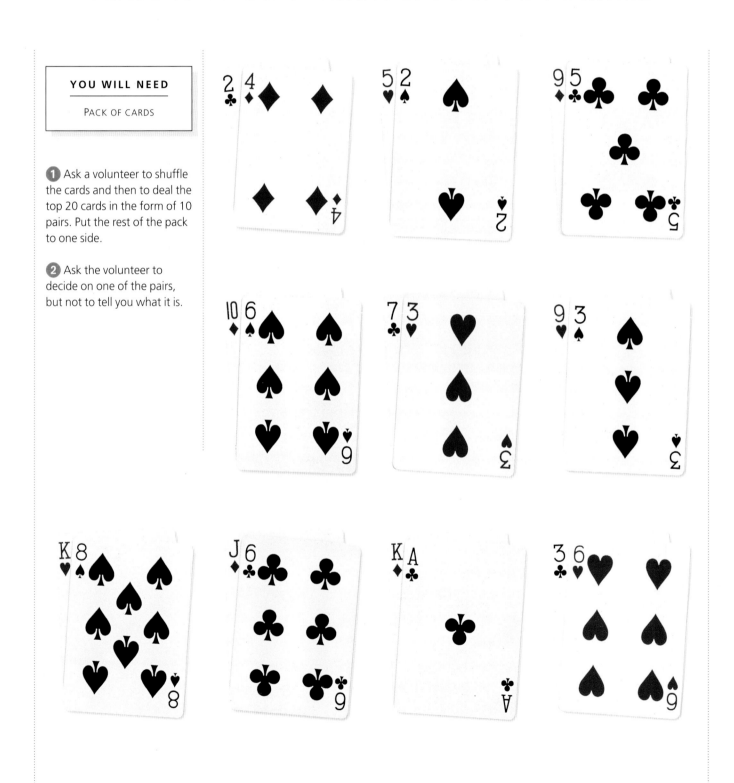

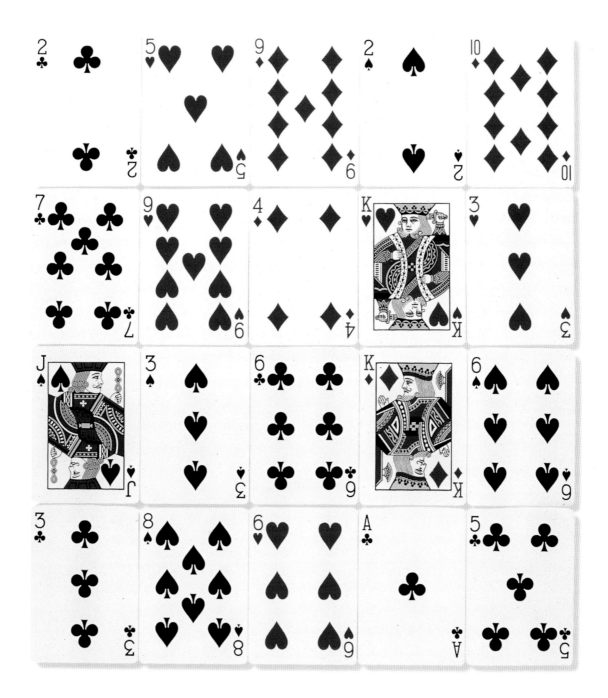

3 You gather together the 20 cards and set them out on the table in apparently random order in four rows of five, then ask the volunteer to locate the now-separated cards of the selected pair but, again, not to say what they are only the row or rows in which the cards appear. You are immediately able to identify the cards.

4 In fact, when you are laying out the cards in four rows of five, you should imagine that the letters of the Latin phrase are laid out in front of you:

```
M  U  T  U  S
N  O  M  E  N
C  O  C  I  S
D  E  D  I  T
```

Place the first card at the top-left corner of the imaginary grid, in the position denoted by the M; second card goes in the center of the second row, in the other position denoted by M. The next two cards go in the two positions denoted U, etc. until the grid is complete.

5 The information as the row or rows in which the two cards appear is, as you can see, sufficient for you to identify the volunteer's pair.

Trick of the Trade

• For the best effect, ask several volunteers mentally to select pairs of cards – as many volunteers as you wish. The face that you can determine a single pair of cards from the given information is only moderately impressive. That you can do it several times, at speed, is what really gives the impression of magic.

FIFTY-TWO THOUGHTS

As a clever card worker or simply as the possessor of an amazing memory, you will win a lot of admiration when you perform this trick, which is another variation on Reciting the Deck (see page 204). In it, a pack of cards is shuffled by a member of the audience and returned to the magicians who, one by one, reveals the names of all 52 cards. Although this version is more cumbersome than the two methods suggested under Reciting the Deck, it does have the advantage that you could perform it blindfolded – provided, of course, that the blindfold had been put in place by an accomplice so that you were able to squint down your nose at the revealed card each time.

YOU WILL NEED

PACK OF CARDS –
A BORROWED ONE IF YOU
WISH

1 Ask a member of the audience to shuffle the cards for you. As you take back the pack, memorize the top facing card.

2 Place the cards behind your back, using both hands and secretly cut the pack, approximately in the center. Again without allowing the audience to know what you are doing, place the two sections back to back so that one stock of cards is facing one way and one stock is facing the other.

3 Bring out the pack to the front, making sure it is face on to the audience. The card that your audience can see is the one you have already memorized. Announce its name. At the same time, glance at the card that is now facing you.

4 Place the cards behind your back again, remove and discard the top card, and then secretly reverse the pack once more.

5 Bring the pack out to the front again. The card that is now facing the audience – apparently the one that was beneath the card that has just been divined and discarded – is the second card you memorized (in step 3). Announce its name.

6 Follow the same procedure until all the cards have been named and discarded. You must reverse the pack each time you hold it behind your back so that you have an opportunity to glimpse the next card. Your audience will never know that half the pack is facing toward you during the presentation if you cleverly square up the cards each time.

MATCH THAT

Wᴴᴼ ᴡᴏᴜʟᴅ ʟɪᴋᴇ ᴛᴏ ᴘʟᴀʏ ᴀ ɢᴀᴍᴇ ᴏꜰ Mᴀᴛᴄʜ Tʜᴀᴛ? Tʜɪꜱ ɪꜱ ɴᴏᴛ ᴀ ᴄʜɪʟᴅ'ꜱ ɢᴀᴍᴇ, ʜᴏᴡᴇᴠᴇʀ, ʙᴜᴛ ᴀɴ ᴇxᴘᴇʀɪᴍᴇɴᴛ ᴛʜᴀᴛ ᴇʟɪᴄɪᴛꜱ ᴛʜᴇ ᴀᴛᴛᴇɴᴛɪᴏɴ ᴏꜰ ᴛʜᴏꜱᴇ ᴍᴇᴍʙᴇʀꜱ ᴏꜰ ʏᴏᴜʀ ᴀᴜᴅɪᴇɴᴄᴇ ᴡʜᴏ ᴀʀᴇ ʟᴏᴏᴋɪɴɢ ꜰᴏʀ ꜱᴏᴍᴇᴛʜɪɴɢ ᴀ ʙɪᴛ ᴅɪꜰꜰᴇʀᴇɴᴛ.

YOU WILL NEED

PACK CONSISTING OF 27 PAIRS OF CARDS

ENVELOPES

1 Explain to the audience that you are holding a pack of cards made up of matching pairs. Hand the pack of cards to a member of the audience to shuffle. Take the cards back and select, or ask a spectator to select one card at random. Glance at it secretly and seal it in the envelope without letting the audience see its face.

2 Fan the cards, face up, to the audience so that they can inspect the pack, but as you do so, note the position of the card matching the one in the envelope.

3 As you close up the pack, secretly cut it so that the duplicate card is the top card of the pack (all the cards are now face down). Casually rest the envelope on top of the pack, and ask a spectator to sign it to prove that it is actually genuine.

4 As you remove the envelope and place it to one side of your table, secretly remove the top card as well. Ask a second spectator to cut the pack, then mark the cut by sandwiching the envelope (and the hidden card) between the stacks. The duplicate card is now at the cut-at position.

5 Announce that it would be a very strange coincidence indeed if the card that had been randomly selected and placed in the sealed envelope and the card that the spectator had freely chosen by cutting were, in fact, a matching pair, then ask the first spectator to part the pack, take the envelope, identifying it as the one previously signed, and remove the card.

6 Turn to the second spectator and ask him or her to remove the cut-at card on top of the bottom stack and to place it face down beside the first. Reverse both cards to show that they are, amazingly, a matching pair.

X-RAY FINGERS

A ᴍᴇᴍʙᴇʀ ᴏꜰ ᴛʜᴇ ᴀᴜᴅɪᴇɴᴄᴇ ᴄᴜᴛꜱ ᴀɴᴅ ᴅᴇᴀʟꜱ ᴛʜᴇ ᴄᴀʀᴅꜱ, ʙᴜᴛ ᴛʜᴇ ᴍᴀɢɪᴄɪᴀɴ ɪꜱ ᴀʙʟᴇ, ᴛʜʀᴏᴜɢʜ ᴛʜᴇ ᴘᴏᴡᴇʀꜱ ᴏꜰ ᴄᴏɴᴄᴇɴᴛʀᴀᴛɪᴏɴ, ᴛᴏ ɪᴅᴇɴᴛɪꜰʏ ꜰɪᴠᴇ ᴄᴀʀᴅꜱ ꜰʀᴏᴍ ᴛʜᴇ ʙᴀᴄᴋꜱ.

YOU WILL NEED

PACK OF CARDS

1 Before the performance, stack the bottom of the pack with five cards whose values and order you have just memorized, plus, at the very bottom, the queen of spades.

2 Announce to your audience that you need to get rid of two cards because you want to deal out five equal packets. Ask a spectator to remove two cards, which are always regarded as unlucky – the queen of spades and the ace of spades.

3 Shuffle the pack, keeping the five memorized cards and the queen of spades together at the bottom of the pack. Ask the spectator to find the ace first, and then to cut the pack. This cut does not affect the order of the cards.

4 Then ask the spectator to remove the queen of spades and to cut the cards again. This second cut, when the queen of spades is removed, has the effect of bringing the five memorized cards once more to the bottom of the pack of cards.

5 Ask the spectator to deal the remaining cards into five equal piles, working one, one, one, one, one, then two, two, two, and so forth, rather than completing each packet of 20 cards in complete deals.

6 Press your fingertips to the top of the first heap and screw up your eyes in concentration. Announce that the top card is, say for example, the 8 of spades – which, sure enough, it proves to be. Repeat the process four more times.

FILL THE GAP

THIS BASICALLY SIMPLE MENTALIST EXPERIMENT, REVEALS THE MAGICIAN'S ABILITY TO DIVINE THE SUIT AND VALUE OF A CARD SELECTED BY A MEMBER OF THE AUDIENCE. WHAT MAKES IT ESPECIALLY EFFECTIVE IS THAT IT INVOLVES NO FEWER THAN FOUR MEMBERS OF THE AUDIENCE, AND THE MAGICIAN IS TURNED AWAY FROM THE AUDIENCE AND THE CARDS THROUGHOUT. TOTALLY MYSTIFYING.

YOU WILL NEED

PACK OF CARDS

1 Before your performance, have three random cards from the pack in your top jacket pocket.

2 Place the pack of cards on your table and turn your back. Ask a member of the audience to draw four cards from the pack and lay them out, face down and left to right, in a row.

3 Still with your back to the table, ask the spectator to return to his or her place and ask another volunteer to come forward and select one card from the face-down row. This card – the 5 of hearts, say – should be shown to the audience as a whole and then returned to its place.

4 You then call for a third member of the audience to gather up the four cards in order and bring them to you. Send the volunteer back to his or her seat, study the cards, put one of them in your top pocket, and ask for a fourth volunteer to collect the remaining three cards and to lay them out in a row, as before, but with a gap in place of the missing card.

5 For the first time, turn around to face the audience. Glance at the depleted row of cards on the table, and pull the fourth card from your pocket, placing it face up in the gap that has been left. Sure enough, of course, it is the 5 of hearts.

6 Every time you have turned your back to the table, you can use the distraction of the volunteers coming and going from the stage to bring out these three cards. While you are telling the audience that you are putting a single card into your pocket, you are putting away all four cards from the table. When you turn, the position of the gap tells you the position of the selected card. Reach into your pocket and find the right card. Draw it forth as if it were the only card there.

THE SHEEP FROM THE GOATS

THE MAGICIAN SUCCESSFULLY PREDICTS THE DIFFERENCE IN NUMBERS BETWEEN HEAPS OF RED CARDS AND BLACK CARDS, DEALT BY A VOLUNTEER. THIS IS, IN FACT, A VERY EASY DECEPTION, BUT THE MAGICIAN'S PATTER AND A LITTLE UNNECESSARY COMPLICATION MAKE IT AN ENTERTAINING LITTLE TRICK.

YOU WILL NEED

PACK OF CARDS

PEN OR PENCIL

PAPER

1 Before your performance, remove any two of the black cards from the pack.

2 When you come to perform, shuffle the pack and ask a volunteer to do the same. For good measure, ask another member of the audience to shuffle the pack as well.

3 While the shuffling is being done, write a prediction on a sheet of paper, fold it a couple of times, and then pass it to someone in the front row, with strict instructions that it is not to be opened.

4 Ask the volunteer to deal out the shuffled pack in pairs. If two red cards are turned up, they should go in one heap; if two black cards are turned up, they should go in another heap; mismatched pairs should be discarded.

5 When the volunteer has finished dealing out the cards, ask him or her to total the number of cards in the red pile and then the number of cards in the black pile.

6 Finally, call on the person with the piece of paper to stand up and read aloud your prediction: "You will have two more red cards than you have black." The volunteer confirms that this is true.

10 ♦

ILLUSIONS

THE CREATION OF ILLUSIONS

REQUIRES LARGE-SCALE APPARATUS, A MORE

SPACIOUS PERFORMING AREA AND THE HELP OF AN ASSISTANT.

THE EQUIPMENT REQUIRED FOR A PROFESSIONAL ILLUSION SHOW

can be expensive, but in this chapter we look at a number of illusions that can

be performed effectively with the minimum of outlay. The illusionist's

assistant is a very important person. It is often the case that the assistant

performs the illusion, while the performer simply makes the presentation.

SENSATIONAL SACK ESCAPE

MASTER ESCAPOLOGIST HARRY HOUDINI FREED HIMSELF FROM CHAINS, PADLOCKS, AND SACKS AS NO OTHER ESCAPE ARTIST COULD. HOUDINI BECAME A HOUSEHOLD NAME DURING HIS LIFETIME, AND EVEN TO THIS DAY, HIS NAME IS STILL FAMILIAR TO THE PUBLIC. ALTHOUGH THE PROPS FOR THIS TRICK ARE EASY TO MAKE AND THE TRICK IS SIMPLE TO PUT INTO PRACTICE, IT IS JUST AS BAFFLING AS THOSE ENACTED BY HOUDINI HIMSELF.

YOU WILL NEED

CANVAS SACK THAT IS LARGE ENOUGH TO CONTAIN A HUMAN (SEE STEP 1)

PLENTY OF ROPE

PORTABLE SCREEN OR CURTAIN

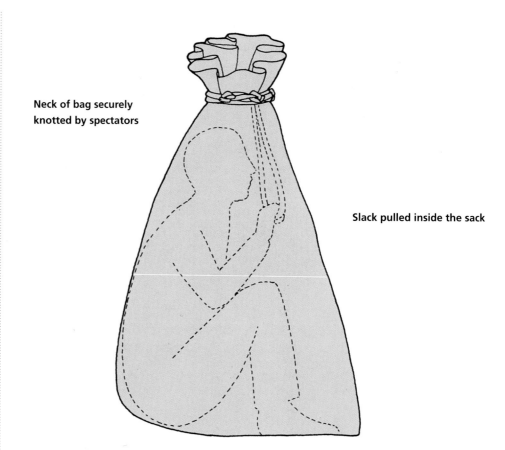

Neck of bag securely knotted by spectators

Slack pulled inside the sack

Note: Children will need supervision with this trick

1 A bag of black canvas is made. Several holes are cut along the top hem of the bag (you can add grommets for better wear if you intend to do this trick on a regular basis) so that a length of rope can be threaded through. Make sure that there is plenty of rope left at each end of the threaded length. The folding screen should be upright with the sack hanging over the top when you begin your performance.

2 Although it is possible to do the trick with just one spectator, if you have two members of the audience, the illusion looks all the more difficult to accomplish, because the tying and checking of the sack should appear to be the most important part. Ask the spectators to examine the sack closely, to place it on the floor, and to fold back the sides so that the inside base can be seen.

3 Stand on the base and ask the spectators to bring up the sides of the sack. At the same time, lower one hand slightly and duck inside. It is at this stage that you execute the one important move that makes the illusion work. Because plenty of rope was threaded around the neck of the sack, as you duck down, pull in some slack, holding this down firmly. As the spectators pull the length of rope tightly to close the sack, you must retain a firm grip on the slack inside.

4 When the spectators have tied as many knots as they wish around the top of the bag, they can erect the folding screen in front of the sack and return to their seats.

5 To accomplish your escape, release tension on the slack rope, push open the top, peel the sack down, and step out. You could prolong the presentation by making noises as if you were struggling to free yourself. Once free, throw the sack over the screen and then make your appearance.

Trick of the Trade

• It takes only a matter of seconds to escape from the sack, but asking a member of the audience to time you with a stop watch makes for good showmanship and a better presentation.

ROD THROUGH BODY

P ENETRATING SWORDS, RODS, AND CANES THROUGH ASSISTANTS ENCASED IN A CABINET IS ONE
THING, BUT PUSHING A SOLID METAL ROD THROUGH A SPECTATOR'S BODY WITHOUT THE AID OF
CABINETS OR CONCEALMENT OF ANY KIND IS ANOTHER.

YOU WILL NEED

SOLID ROD OF STEEL, ABOUT
15 IN. LONG AND TAPERING
AT ONE END TO MAKE IT
LOOK MORE DANGEROUS

2 IDENTICAL SOLID WOODEN
BALLS (SEE STEP 1)

CONTACT ADHESIVE

POCKET HANDKERCHIEF

Note: Children will need
supervision with this trick

1 Bore a hole halfway into
one of the solid wooden balls
and force the blunt end of the
steel rod into it. If you wish,
add a spot of contact
adhesive to make sure that
the ball and rod are securely
attached to each other and
can be used as a single unit.
The second ball should also
be drilled, but this time all the
way through and so that the
hole is slightly larger than the
diameter of the rod at its
widest point. An added touch
is to doctor a white pocket
handkerchief with red paint
representing blood stains so
that when the handkerchief is
folded up the stains cannot
be seen.

2 You must wear a jacket to
perform this trick. Place the
duplicate loose red ball
handle, together with the
pocket handkerchief, inside
the right jacket pocket. Place
the rod on your table.

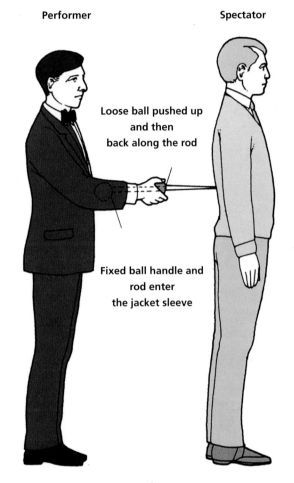

Performer   **Spectator**

**Loose ball pushed up
and then
back along the rod**

**Fixed ball handle and
rod enter
the jacket sleeve**

3 Select a member of the
audience to help you with
this illusion – call him or her
the "victim" – but assure the
audience that at no time is
any danger involved.

4 Hand the steel rod to the
spectator to examine, and,
for dramatic effect, whack it
down on top of the table to
demonstrate that it is solid.

5 Remove the handkerchief
from the right jacket pocket,
saying that you may need it if
there is a "slight accident."
Then at the same time,
secrete the loose ball within
your right palm.

6 Place the handkerchief,
which has now served its
purpose, on the table and, at
the same time, secretly slip
the palmed ball onto the
tapered end of the rod.

7 Ask the spectator to take
up their position, standing
sideways on in front of the
rest of the audience. While he
or she does this, secretly push
the duplicate ball down the
rod toward the opposite end
so that it rests against the
fixed one.

8 Holding the loose ball
handle and working with the
right-hand side of your body
toward the audience, prod
the tapered end of the rod
into the center of the
spectator's back.

9 The loose ball handle is
the only one one view – the
fixed one is concealed behind
the right arm. Push the loose
handle along the rod, thus
allowing the fixed handle and
the rod to enter inside your
right jacket sleeve. It appears
to the audience that the rod is
actually penetrating the
spectator's body.

10 Now pick up the
handkerchief, cover the loose
ball and rub the handkerchief
along the length of the rod.
As the handkerchief comes to
the end of the rod, so, too,
does the loose ball. Secretly
drop the loose ball into your
waiting left hand – this side
of your body is actually away
from the audience.

11 Place the rod on the table
and then open out the
handkerchief to reveal the
artificial blood stains. Discard
the handkerchief, together
with the palmed ball, in your
left jacket pocket, and then
allow the rod to be examined
once more.

TWO-TUBES ILLUSION

MOST ILLUSIONS ARE BASED ON OLD METHODS. THIS PARTICULAR EFFECT RELIES ON A PRINCIPLE THAT IS STILL WIDELY USED TO THIS DAY – BLACK ART. THE PRINCIPLE IS THAT BLACK OBJECTS ARE INVISIBLE AGAINST A BLACK BACKGROUND. TWO LARGE TUBES ARE SHOWN TO BE EMPTY. THEY ARE NESTED TOGETHER, AND, AT THE SOUND OF A PISTOL SHOT, AN ASSISTANT IS PRODUCED FROM INSIDE THE TUBES.

YOU WILL NEED

3 LARGE CARDBOARD TUBES
(SEE STEP 1)

RED, YELLOW, AND BLACK
MATTE PAINT

PIECE OF BLACK VELVETEEN
FABRIC

CRAFT KNIFE

STAPLES OR CONTACT
ADHESIVE

BLANK CARTRIDGE GUN OR
STARTING PISTOL (OPTIONAL)

1 Try to obtain three cardboard boxes of the kind that are used for packaging large electrical appliances like washing machines, ovens, and refrigerators. These come in all shapes and sizes, but it is important that you find three that will nest together – you may need to cut and trim sections of the boxes to achieve this. Remove the tops and bottoms of the boxes to create tubes.

2 Use a sharp craft knife to cut out a decorative section from the largest of the three boxes. This will be the outer box, and you should paint it red. The middle box can be left whole, but paint it yellow. Paint the third and smallest box, the inner box, matte black inside and out. Paint the insides of the outer and middle boxes matte black. Use staples or contact adhesive to attach the black velvet to the black box, leaving a flap of fabric at the top long enough to cover the open top of the box.

3 Prepare for the effect by nesting the three boxes together, with your assistant crouched down inside the inner black box with the black fabric draped over the top of the box to cover your assistant's head.

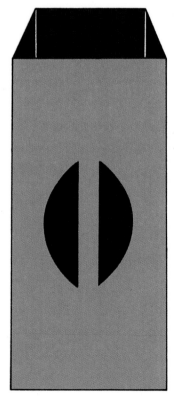

Outer box

Middle box

Inner box

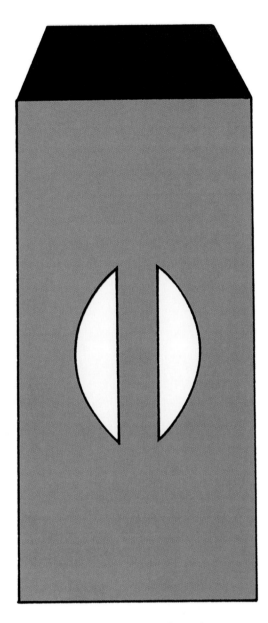

The three boxes nested together

4 Throughout the illusion it is essential that the audience believes that only two tubes are being used. The third, inner tube is hidden by the black art principle. To create the illusion, first pull up the outer, red tube and display the open top end to the audience so that they can see the black interior.

5 Replace the red tube over the yellow tube, then remove the inner yellow tube from the nest – it is visible through the cut-out pattern in the front of the red, outer tube. Pull the yellow tube up and clear of the red tube, to display the interior to the audience. The cut-out segments in the red tube appear to show through to the matte black interior of the red tube. In fact, the matte black velveteen fabric is visible. Both boxes appear empty, but a certain amount of misdirection should be introduced when you are displaying the second tube. All eyes should be on your movements. Replace the yellow tube.

6 Your assistant now peels back the loose section of fabric that was draped over his or her head and tucks it down inside the front of the box. Fire a blank pistol or make some other dramatic sound, and your assistant can leap out of the boxes into view of the audience. If you wish, complete the illusion by folding the boxes flat.

SEE-THROUGH PRODUCTION

THIS IS A VARIATION – ALBEIT ON A SMALLER SCALE – OF THE PRECEDING ILLUSION, AND IT WORKS ON EXACTLY THE SAME PRINCIPLE. A BOX IS SHOWN COMPLETELY EMPTY. THEN THE MAGICIAN PROCEEDS TO PRODUCE A VARIETY OF HANDKERCHIEFS AND COLORED STREAMERS FROM IT.

YOU WILL NEED

SQUARE BOX WITH AN OPEN FRONT

TUBE GLUED INSIDE THE BOX

SQUARE TUBE (SMALL ENOUGH TO FIT INTO THE BOX BUT LARGE ENOUGH TO GO OVER THE FIXED TUBE)

SILK SCARVES, RIBBONS, PAPER STREAMERS, AND SO FORTH

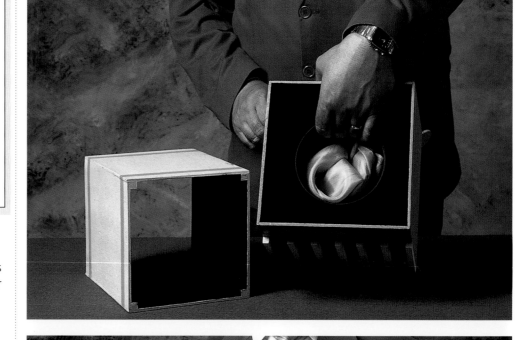

1 Put the ribbons, streamers, or whatever else is to be produced into the inner tube. Place the square tube into the box.

2 In performance, you just lift out the square tube and show it to be empty. At this point, although you must not draw attention to the fact, the audience can see through the cut-out in the front of the box. Because the interior is black and the inner tube is also black, it seems that the box is empty.

3 Place the square tube back in position.

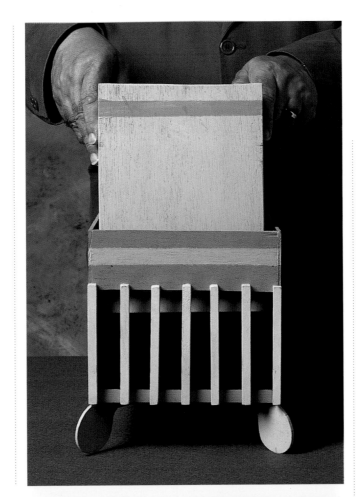

Tricks of the Trade

• If you are using this apparatus to produce large silk handkerchiefs (known to magicians as "silks"), do not simply put them on top of each other in the inner box. It is a good idea to interleave them so that as you pull one "silk" out, it brings up the next one, making it easier and smoother to produce.

• The dimensions of the apparatus required for this trick depend on the purpose for which you wish to use it. If it is for a small production of ribbons and so on, the box – which can be made from wood, plastic, metal, or cardboard – should be about 8 in. high and about 6 in. wide. If you want to use the apparatus to produce an animal or even a person, the dimensions will have to be increased accordingly. The interior of the box and the tube should be painted matte black. The exterior of the inner, fixed tube must also be black.

• A colored streamer can easily be made by gluing together lengths of crepe paper, but you can also buy them from magic suppliers or novelty stores. When the streamer is pulled from the box, the effect can be magical.

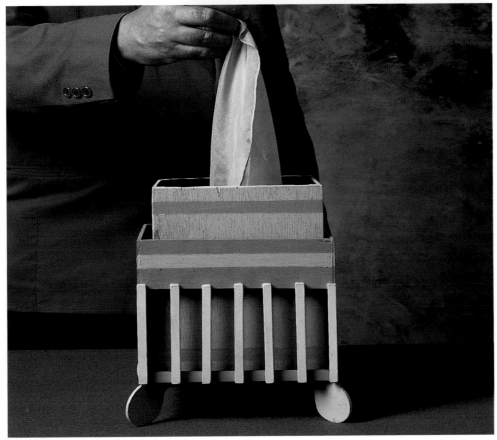

4 Wave your hands over the boxes in a very mysterious manner, and then reach in to produce the ribbons, scarves, handkerchiefs, streamers, and so on.

217

FOLDING SCREEN PRODUCTION

THE ILLUSIONIST DISPLAYS TWO FOLDING SCREENS, FOLDING EACH FLAT BEFORE ERECTING THEM UPRIGHT TO FORM A CABINET. THE PERFORMER PLACES A SMALL STOOL NEXT TO THE SCREENS AND STANDS ON IT, REACHING INSIDE TO PRODUCE ALL KINDS OF THINGS BEFORE STEPPING DOWN TO REMOVE THE SCREENS TO REVEAL AN ASSISTANT. ALTHOUGH THE METHOD EMPLOYED IS A SIMPLE ONE, THE SECRET IS TO TIME ALL THE MOVEMENTS CAREFULLY SO THAT THE DISPLAYING AND ERECTION OF THE SCREENS APPEARS NATURAL AND SMOOTH. IT IS, THEREFORE, VITAL THAT BOTH PERFORMER AND ASSISTANT REHEARSE ALL THE SEQUENCES THOROUGHLY BEFORE PRESENTING THE ILLUSION IN FRONT OF AN AUDIENCE.

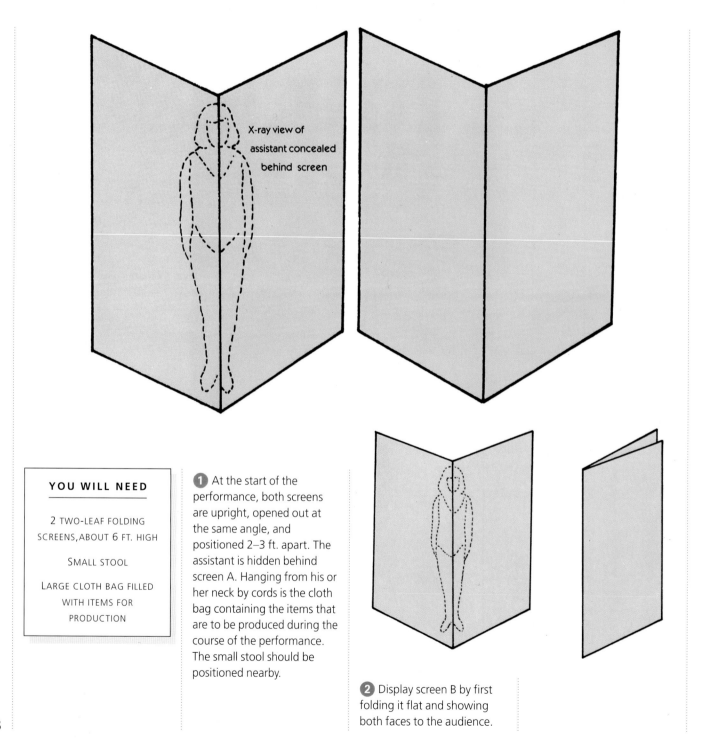

X-ray view of assistant concealed behind screen

YOU WILL NEED

2 TWO-LEAF FOLDING SCREENS, ABOUT 6 FT. HIGH

SMALL STOOL

LARGE CLOTH BAG FILLED WITH ITEMS FOR PRODUCTION

1 At the start of the performance, both screens are upright, opened out at the same angle, and positioned 2–3 ft. apart. The assistant is hidden behind screen A. Hanging from his or her neck by cords is the cloth bag containing the items that are to be produced during the course of the performance. The small stool should be positioned nearby.

2 Display screen B by first folding it flat and showing both faces to the audience.

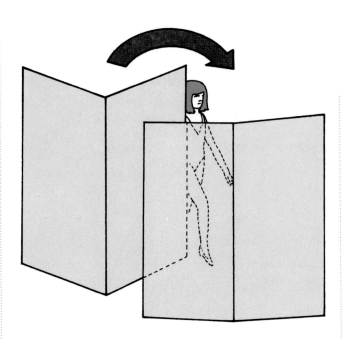

3 Open out screen B so that both panels are then fully extended, allowing one leaf to overlap the edge of screen A. At this point, the assistant behind screen A secretly moves out and in behind screen B.

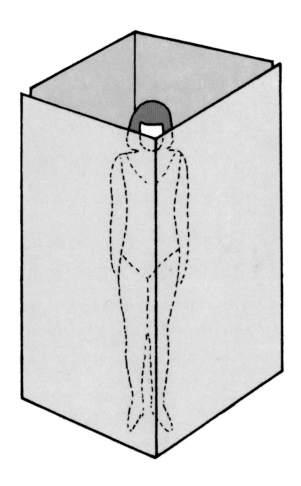

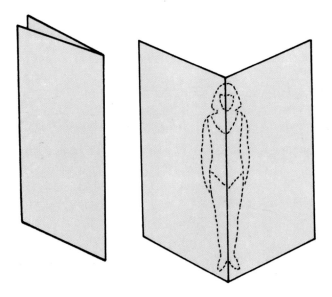

4 Now, set screen B at an angle so that it stands upright, with your assistant hidden behind it. Display screen A to the audience.

5 Place screen A on the opposite side of screen B to form an enclosed cabinet, with the assistant enclosed within the four-sided structure.

6 Stand on the small stool to reach inside the cabinet and, with the help of your assistant, produce the items from the cloth bag. To ensure that the performance is smooth, your assistant should hand up the items in quick succession.

7 Finally, produce the cloth, so that the assistant is left absolutely clean before his or her appearance. With a flourish, part the screens to reveal your assistant.

GLOSSARY

back-palm To conceal an object at the back of the hand.

black art The principle that black on black shows no join or that black on black is invisible.

book test In mentalism, a demonstration in which the performer divines or predicts a freely chosen passage in a book or magazine handled by a member of the audience.

bottom card The card whose face can be seen when the pack is assembled; also called the face card.

bottom deal This is the secret dealing of the bottom card of the pack, instead of the top card.

bottom stock The portion of a pack of cards that is at the bottom when the pack is cut.

break A small gap held at the edge of a pack of cards and maintained by, usually, the tip of a finger.

bridge A gap in a pack of cards caused by bending some cards.

c and r Abbreviation for cut and restored, usually applied to tricks in which a rope, thread, string, tape, etc., is cut and then mended.

changing bag This is a cloth bag with two (or more) compartments, used for exchanging one article for another.

conjurer's choice No choice at all. *See also* FORCE.

crimp Secretly to bend one corner of a card.

cut To divide a pack of cards into two or more sections. A complete cut is made when the sections are reassembled.

drop To drop the balance of cards held in the hand during the shuffle so that they fall on the shuffled cards.

effect Description of a trick of what is seen by the audience.

end grip The manner of holding a pack of cards with the thumb at one end and fingers at the other.

escapology The art and craft of the magician who specializes in escaping from handcuffs, ropes, and other restraints.

ESP Abbreviation for extra-sensory perception, which includes mind-reading, clairvoyance, and kindred phenomena achieved by unrecognized physical means.

ESP cards Specially designed cards, used for ESP experiments. There are five designs – circle, cross, wavy lines, square, and star – and a pack of 25 cards contains five of each design. In addition to their use in genuine ESP experiments, they are now widely used by conjurers.

face card *See* BOTTOM CARD.

fair shuffle This is a genuine shuffle of the cards. *See also* FALSE SHUFFLE.

fake This is a piece of apparatus that has been secretly prepared for trickery.

false count A method of counting cards, coins, etc., to show that there are more or fewer than the real number.

false shuffle A method of apparently shuffling a pack of cards without changing the order of some or all of the cards.

first card This is the top card of the pack when the cards are held face down. The first card to be dealt, whether face up or face down.

force To restrict a spectator's choice to a single item when he or she believes that there is a choice of more than one.

key card A card that is some way distinctive so that it can be recognized by the magician.

knife force A method of forcing a card on a spectator by having him or her thrust a table knife into the pack. Manipulation then brings the forced card into position above or below the blade.

load An article or collection of articles prepared so that it can be secretly inserted into a container for production later.

mentalism The branch of conjuring involving alleged mind-reading, clairvoyance, divination, etc., but using practical and physical means to achieve what appear to be psychic results.

misdirection The art of diverting the spectator's attention at the critical moment of a trick.

move The manipulation required to perform a trick.

overhand shuffle The normal way of shuffling cards in the UK, in which the cards held edgeways in the left hand are picked up and replaced in batches by the right hand (or vice versa if left handed).

palm To conceal an object secretly in the hand, not necessarily by a convulsive clutch in the actual palm.

production This is the production of articles from a supposedly empty container or from thin air.

reversed card A card that is returned to the pack either back to front or upside down.

riffle shuffle To shuffle a pack, divided into two equal stacks, by interlacing the cards. A number of modern card tricks depend on this being done with total accuracy. It requires considerable skill.

rope cement An adhesive that is sometimes used for joining two pieces of rope.

set-up This is the pre-arrangement of apparatus.

side-grip The practice of holding a pack of cards by its long edges.

sleeve Secretly to insert an article in the sleeve.

sleight This is the secret manipulation required to perform a trick.

square To adjust the edges of a pack of cards by pressing them into alignment with fingers and thumb after, for example, the cards have been shuffled.

stage money Imitation money bills and treasury bills that are used for stage purposes, including conjuring.

stock The main portion of a pack of cards, as opposed to those being immediately dealt or otherwise used for playing or magical purposes.

switch Imperceptibly to exchange one article for another that appears to be identical.

throw To deposit the balance of the playing cards on the rest after a shuffle.

top card The card lying face down on the top of the pack or the card lying face up on the top if the pack is presented with all the cards face up.

transposition The exchange of position between one object and another.

FURTHER READING

BOOKS

It is not usually possible to find books on magic on the shelves of general book stores or in public libraries. There are, however, a number of specialist publishing houses that only publish books about magic and conjuring, and they sell by mail order or at magicians' conventions.

Adair, Ian, *Encyclopedia of Dove Magic*, vols. 1–5, Supreme Magic Company Ltd., Bideford, Devon, 1987 (rev. ed.). Over a period of two decades the author has gathered together the ultimate material in dove magic with the very best effects of the leading magicians working with doves throughout the world.

Adair, Ian, *Know-how Book of Jokes and Tricks*, Usborne Publishing Ltd., London, 1977. A paperback book designed for children. Cartoon illustrations and easy-to-follow text describe simple yet effective magical tricks and joke items.

Adair, Ian, *Magic Step-by-Step,* Arco Publishing Company Inc., New York, 1972. Aimed at the beginner, with tips and advice on all aspects of conjuring, plus a wide selection of magical effects.

Adair, Ian, *Television Card Manipulations*, Supreme Magic Company Ltd., Bideford, Devon, 1962. A small book outlining the correct techniques used to produce, vanish, change, and manipulate playing cards.

Bobo, J.B., *The New Modern Coin Magic Book*, Magic Inc., Chicago, 1966. A complete work on the manipulation and techniques used in coin magic.

Booth, John, *The John Booth Classic*, Supreme Magic Company Ltd., Bideford, Devon, 1975. The author's three major books have been amalgamated into one publication.

Braue, Fred, and Jugard, Jean, *Royal Road to Card Magic*, Dover Publications, New York, 1980. Accepted as the card-workers' "bible," here is a step-by-step course in card conjuring.

Clark, Keith, *Encyclopedia of Cigarette Magic,* Tannens, New York, 1952. The methods, the gadgets, and the sleight-of-hand movements that make possible the production of cigarettes from the fingertips.

Corinda, Tony, *Thirteen Steps to Mentalism*, Supreme Magic Company Ltd., Bideford, Devon, 1978. Acclaimed as one of the finest books to cover mental magic. In 13 steps, the author discusses predictions, divinations, ESP mysteries, and telepathic experiments.

Fox, Karrell, *Clever Like a Fox*, Supreme Magic Company Ltd., Bideford, Devon, 1976. Clever and original magical effects from one of the USA's leading magic performers.

Fox, Karrell, *My Latest Book*, Supreme Magic Company Ltd., Bideford, Devon, 1987. The latest in the author's series. (Fox has written at least ten books.) This book offers readers yet another selection of the kinds of magical notion for which he is famous.

Ganson, Lewis, *Art of Close-up Magic*, vols. 1 and 2, Supreme Magic Company Ltd., Bideford, Devon, 1970. Brilliant close-up magic, designed for impromptu work.

Ganson, Lewis, *Card Magic by Manipulation*, Supreme Magic Company Ltd., Bideford, Devon, 1971. A small book dealing with the production and vanishing of playing cards when manipulated by the hands.

Gibson, Walter, *The Complete Illustrated Book of Card Magic*, Kaye & Ward, London, 1970. A large illustrated book that provides the reader with countless card tricks.

Hooper, Edwin, *Edwin's Magic*, vols. 1 and 2, Edwin's Magic Art, Bideford, Devon, 1989. Two great volumes by the founder of the largest magic dealing company.

McComb, Billy, *McComb's Magic – 25 Years Wiser*, Supreme Magic Company Ltd., Bideford, Devon, 1972. A professional magician working in the USA, McComb shares his best magic secrets.

Pavel, *The Magic of Pavel*, Supreme Magic Company Ltd., Bideford, Devon, 1970. Original conceptions from one of magic's most prolific magical inventors.

Rice, Harold, *Rice's Encyclopedia of Silk Magic*, vols. 1–3, Silk King Studios, Cincinnati, 1962. Magic using silk handkerchiefs of all different sizes and colors.

Stickland, William G., *Introducing Bill's Magic*, Supreme Magic Company Ltd., Bideford, Devon, 1970. A book on unusual originations using new principles.

Tarbell, Harlan, *Tarbell Course in Magic,* D. Robbins & Co. Inc., New York, 1980. Possibly the greatest course in magic ever published.

MAGAZINES

Perhaps because they are not available from news-stands and supermarkets, most newcomers to magic do not realize that there are such things as magic magazines, which are produced especially for the student of magic. These periodicals are available on subscription only.

At present there are more than 20 journals and magazines internationally available. Some appear quarterly, some monthly, but there is only one weekly magazine of magic, *Abracadabra*. Goodliffe the Magician, who was well known in his day and is still a name to conjure with, first published this magazine nearly 50 years ago. Today, Donald Bevan, who has been responsible for 30 years of continued production, has released the magazine on a weekly basis without fail.

Monthly magazines include *The Magigram*, a 72-page magazine of magic, which is distributed in 80 different countries, including Russia. Printed in Britain on the premises of the Supreme Magic Company. The same organization also produces a sister periodical, *The Trixigram*, which brings subscribers news, views, and reviews of the world of magic. *Alakazam*, a magazine for children's entertainers, has been published.

Abracadabra, ed. Donald Bevan, Goodliffe Publications Ltd., Bromsgrove, Worcestershire. A well-established weekly that covers all aspects of magic, including tricks, patter, presentations, book reviews, society reports, news, views, and topics on the magic scene.

Alakazam, ed. Maurice Day, Supreme Magic Company Ltd., Bideford, Devon. A bi-monthly magazine of magic primarily designed for the children's entertainer.

Info, ed. Dennis Patten, International Magic Studio, London. A glossy bi-monthly magazine, which includes a general assortment of magical effects, from close-up to illusions.

The Genii, ed. Bill Larsen, Los Angeles. A glossy, monthly magazine, which is well established in its field.

The Magigram, ed. Ken de Courcy, Supreme Magic Company Ltd., Bideford, Devon. The contents are varied with effects and routines for all types of magic performers including close-up workers, children's entertainers, mentalists, escapologists, balloon modelers, and even illusionists.

The Tops, ed. Gordon Miller, Abbott's Manufacturing Co., Colon. A monthly house magazine created by the founder of the company, Percy Abbott. The contents include reports, gossip, trick cartoons, illusion plans, and a wide selection of magical effects and routines.

Trixigram, ed. Ian Adair, Supreme Magic Company Ltd., Bideford, Devon. This monthly periodical contains news and views on what is happening on the magic scene throughout the world.

CLUBS AND SOCIETIES

Magic is no different from any other hobby or profession in that there are many clubs, societies, and organizations to join.

The famous Magic Circle, formed in 1905, started with just a few magicians, but over the years it has attracted more and more members, so that there are now almost 2,000 members across the world. Membership in the Magic Circle depends on merit, and there is a strict hierarchy of membership. Associate members progress to full membership, eventually becoming associates, then full members of the Inner Magic Circle. The Magic Circle has its own meeting place in London, and magicians meet regularly to share different ideas, discuss new tricks, and hear visiting speakers.

A similar organization is the International Brotherhood of Magicians, with headquarters in the United States. Although it is larger than the Magic Circle, the International Brotherhood of Magicians has no regular meeting place. Members keep in touch with each other through the pages of the official magazine, *The Budget,* a monthly publication distributed only to members. The major event of the year is the Annual Convention, which often attracts 2,000 or more magicians. Lectures, dealers' demonstrations, gala shows, teach-ins, close-up sessions, and many other interesting aspects of magic are planned each year to keep magicians informed.

The majority of small magic societies draw perhaps 20 or 30 members from the local area, but they are all dedicated to learning and practicing the art of magic.

Annual subscription fees differ from one club to another. It is often the case that members of a small society are members of both the Magic Circle in London and the International Brotherhood of Magicians. Some magicians become members of several organizations connected with magic so that they enjoy a well-balanced and varied outlook on what is happening in the whole world of magic.

Joining a magic club or society can be an enjoyable experience, and one that is shared by all the members, each of whom endeavours to elevate their craft to the highest possible standard.

INDEX